THE

HUGE

LITTLE

BOOK

OF

TRUMP

The ENCYCLOPEDIA OF TRUMP

First Edition

Copyright 2016

Don Fass

A CELEBRATE RADIO NEWS BOOK

CONTENTS

Part 1

Part 2

Part 3

INTRODUCTION

By Don Fass

In June 2015, when he first announced his Presidential campaign, I thought it would be fairly easy to write and compile this book...after all, just the 'facts' and if he was your 'normal' candidate, there would be his positions to get together, his background and his comments in debates. Also, I had observed Trump as a New Yorker myself in the 70s and 80s when he first became well known and always highly controversial with his deals and his affairs and marriages and so I had that background for starters.

And like you, I watched his birther stuff and the attention he loved getting with it throughout President Obama's first term.

Trump has always been controversial, since he entered the Manhattan real estate market decades ago and in New York, was constantly accused of bigotry, greed, repeated adultery and sometimes shady business deals...and politically since he became the voice of the birther movement, claiming that President Obama was not born in the U.S.

Back in June, 2015 when he declared his candidacy for the Presidency with remarks deemed racist about Mexican immigrants and later about Muslims and many others, as well as all the names he has called his fellow republican candidates, Trump has pretty much been known as a flame-thrower, putting out one inciting remark after another.

(In Trump's The Art of the Deal, actually ghostwritten by Tony Schwartz, Trump pretty much says he will do and say anything to get attention.)

Often he cites sources like the National Enquirer, like when he said Ted Cruz' father was with Lee Harvey Oswald at the Kennedy

4

assassination or simply saying he *'read it somewhere,'* or that he "gets (his) news from the shows."

Clearly, Trump is also a magnet for white supremacists, including former KKK Grand Wizard David Duke, who he almost never disassociates himself from and major conspiracy theorists. His newest campaign manager has a career of favoring them journalistically.

Not surprisingly, there's been quite a backlash, with detractors calling him a bigot, demagogue, clueless, racist, a misogynist, a sociopath, king of the narcissists, dangerous, unhinged and a pathological liar with a serious narcissistic personality disorder and more. Numerous therapists and commentators are now openly making these descriptions gain even more traction.

Trump, who says he has 'a very good brain' has been asked where he gets the policy information he puts out. Finally, he has some actual advisors but still, he often continues to say *'I listen to myself'* or *'I get it from the shows'* in response.

Nothing probably prepared any voter or both party's leaders for the more than a year between the Donald's announcement at Trump Tower in June 2015 and the Republican National Convention in Cleveland in July, 2016 and the weeks after.

The Primary campaign

Trump was up against 17 candidates for his party's nomination and went through 17 or 18 debates (one he refused to show up for!). He was constantly on every news channel many times a day, calling in to them if they hadn't scheduled an interview that day. Or tweeting late at night if he needed still more attention. Anything to get the constant attention he craved, get $2.5 billion of free air time and not have to do the 'self funding' he promised but has done very little of.

But the broadcast media, particularly the news channels, were addicted to Trump giving him every minute of air time he wanted because they knew he pumped up the ratings. The President of CBS Television summed that up when he said 'Trump is bad for the country, but good for CBS!" Only after a year did TV commentators and interviewers really start questioning Trump on what he said, one saying 'that's what a 5-year-old would say,' or another 'you know that's not true.'

He reveled in attacking everyone he encountered or encountered him and many who didn't. He changed his positions constantly. He turned domestic and world crisis always into something about him. Frequently, he seemed not to know what he had said hours before on a subject or unable to make up his mind. Fact checkers all concluded that 70-85% of the time he just made stuff up, including greatly inflating his net worth. He repeatedly re-tweeted the tweets of white supremacists and then said he didn't understand why so many hate groups including the Ku Klux Klan support him. He thrived on insulting all kinds of people and all kinds of groups. Going into the convention, 70 per cent of Americans viewed him unfavorably. Many big-name and status conservative Republicans distanced themselves from him.

After he picked controversial Conservative Republican Indiana Governor Mike Pence as his running mate and was about to introduce him the next morning, Trump was struggling to get out of that pick. The opening song of his rollout of his running mate was the Rolling Stones 'You Can't Always Get What You Want!" The first logo for the new Trump-Pence ticket was so ridiculed for its sexual suggestiveness that it lasted less than 24 hours.

Trump wasn't just debated on his positions, many of which were a complete reverse of where he had been months or years before, he aroused deep emotions as he attacked women, Muslims, immigrants, Mexicans, the disabled, gays and others, asked his audiences to physically attack and 'punch in the face' some who disagreed with him and called for the censorship of journalists, many of whom he wouldn't allow into speeches and rallies. He thrived on insulting all kinds of people and all kinds of groups. Going into the convention, 70 per cent of Americans already viewed him unfavorably. It would get worse!

His actual pronouncements of issues, when he made them, often were just shocking statements about nuclear bombing parts of Europe, destroying ISIS, leaving NATO or repealing the First Amendment, with rarely any substance behind them.

After more terrorist tragedy had happened, Trump often spoke more about himself. The day after Britain voted the Brexit to leave the European Union, he stood on a Trump golf course in Scotland doing a commercial pitch for it and saying that the UK leaving the E.U. and the devaluing of the British pound it cost would be good for his golf course business.

At his candidacy announcement rally in New York, he hired paid actors to fill the room.

Beyond obvious opponents, even many Republicans supporting Trump or not, called him a racist or someone who constantly uses racist rhetoric, a narcissist, a sociopath, a fascist, con man, faker, thief, bigot and philanderer. Even Senator Marco Rubio, while continuing to support his nomination called Trump 'a con man' as late as August of this year. Many questioned his 'Christianity' when he seemed not to know much of anything in the Bible and said he never asks God for forgiveness, yet the latest July, 2016 polls showed that 70 per cent or more of evangelicals supported Trump *(see our Trump A-Z under religion)*.

Trump praised 'uneducated voters' among his supporters and said that *"I could shoot someone on Fifth Avenue in front of my supporters and I wouldn't lose their votes."* He trotted out his Trump steaks, wine, magazines and more like a TV pitchman, even though most of the items were failures or no longer existed.

The media loved Trump for over a year as their ratings went up. The President of CBS even openly said that *"Trump is bad for America but good for CBS."*

Fact-checkers found that 70-85% of what he said couldn't be found to be true, while 70 per cent of the country viewed him unfavorably.

Endorsements

Four former Presidents (including the two former Republican Presidents) said they wouldn't vote for him and weren't going to be attending the GOP convention. Bush family matriarch Barbara Bush asked '*how can any woman vote for him*' and Laura Bush, wife of Republican President George W. Bush, said she would be likely be voting for Hillary Clinton.

Long-time conservative Republicans Mary Matalin, Republican spokeswoman Nicole Wallace, conservative commentator and icon George Will and others said they were leaving the Republican Party because of Trump as was the head of the Young Republicans. Bill Kristol repeatedly wrote how much he disliked Trump. Other GOP Presidential candidates including John Kasich and Jeb Bush made it clear that, as of the convention, they still could not endorse or even vote for Trump and didn't appear at their party's convention.

The last 2 Republican Presidential nominees, Mitt Romney and John McCain didn't attend the convention and Romney said he absolutely could not vote for Trump. The two Bush former Presidents would not support him or appear at the convention either. Neither would Republican Governor John Kasich, in whose state, Ohio, the convention took place.

Senator Ted Cruz did show up and speak but gave no endorsement, telling delegates instead to '*vote your conscience*' (which a day later, Trump greeted with reviving his quoting of the National

Enquirer that Cruz' father may have been involved with Lee Harvey Oswald and the assassination of President Kennedy). Numerous major corporate sponsors pulled out of supporting the Republican Convention early on.

Republican Senate Majority Leader Mitch McConnell and Speaker of the House Paul Ryan did appear at the convention but gave lukewarm endorsements with Ryan having publically called many of Trump's statements 'racist.' (Both would also later denounce Trump for statements he made about a Gold Star family.)

Well over 100 Republican security and foreign affairs experts signed a letter stating that Trump must not become President. Politifact and others issued a new analysis that Trump statements were only true 9-14% of the time.

From a few days before the GOP Convention, when Trump announced Indiana Governor Mike Pence, a hard right winger, would be his VP pick to days the opening night with his wife Melania's address, all the media talked about was Melania. There had been the discovery that whole chunks of her speech, which she said she wrote most of, had been plagiarized from Michelle Obama. It was denied and denied by the Trump team until a Trump staffer suddenly fell on her sword and said it was her mistake.) By day 4 of the convention, reporting shifted to Trump's 1 hr. 15 min. acceptance speech that was called by many 'Mad Max' or 'Mourning in America," "The Apocalypse" or *worse*. The speech by Trump was the darkest acceptance speech by a nominee that any one of us can remember and basically said that America was finished and only Trump could rescue it.

It was pretty much panned, even by many major Republicans.

The Democratic Convention

Trump also, of course, took a walloping from Democrats at their convention. Well-received speeches included those from Michelle

Obama, Bernie Sanders, Elizabeth Warren, President Obama, Vice-President Biden, the moving Goldstar Muslim-American Khizr and Ghazala Khan, former CIA director and Secretary of Defense Leon Panetta and numerous others. It was a much more encouraging and positive outlook on America while pointing to problems to be solved.

Trump has a really bad, long month, rebounds, then falls again.

Not surprisingly, after the conventions and at the start of the general election season,(after a year of endless primaries and debates), things got even worse for Trump, leading to Time Magazine's mid-August 'Meltdown of Trump' cover story.

Much of what made things even worse for Trump were things he said after both conventions.

There was his much denounced put down of Mr and Mrs. Khan, a Muslim-American Gold Star family whose son was killed in Iraq and who had delivered a moving and much talked about speech at the Democratic convention. Trump had responded with speculation that Mrs. Khan hadn't been allowed to speak because she is Muslim and that, like the Khan's son, Trump had himself 'made a lot of sacrifices.'

Then Trump had called for 'second amendment' remedies to Hillary Clinton 'taking away your guns,' if she was elected. Most commentators, writers, pundits and others from both parties said that it sounded like a call for violence or assassination. It produced another firestorm for days.

There was Trump's continued refusal to release any of his tax returns even for all the years *not* under audit. That produced much more speculation on what he must be hiding.

10

There was Trump's probably personal Russian business connections and his praising of Putin as a 'great' leader. He had said he knew Putin, then that he didn't know Putin and there was his campaign manager Paul Manafort's clear lobbying ties to the Russian government. Trump made all that still worse by saying that he would keep Putin from going into Ukraine and the Crimea though that had already taken place 2 years earlier. Trump had also called for the Russians to hack the Democratic campaign (which it appears they did before and after his call for them to do so).

There were public rebukes from Trump's own allies Newt Gingrich and Chris Christie.

There were letters from dozens of stalwart Republican security and international affairs experts warning that a Trump presidency would be dangerous and another letter from numerous Republicans to the RNC to stop funding Trump's campaign altogether and instead donate only to Congressional races. *(both letters are in this book, in full).*

More Republican senators and congressmen jumped ship saying they would not endorse Trump. Republican newspaper the Houston Chronicle came out with an 'early endorsement' of Trump's rival and The Dallas Morning News, instead of traditionally backing a Republican candidate, denounced Trump.

Trump disputed the dates set for three Fall Presidential debates, saying that the NFL agreed that the debates should be moved to other dates and that he had received a letter from them. The NFL said there was no letter. He tried to stop Anderson Cooper from being one of the debate moderators.

There was Trump's pronouncement (going completely against facts—see Iraq in our A-Z section) that President Obama and Hillary Clinton were 'the founders of ISIS.'

Much of broadcast media, for the first time since Trump announced his campaign in June, 2015 started to fact check his speeches and interviews as they were happening.

As we were finishing editing this book, The Donald was back up in the polls, then started having really bad weeks again despite Hillary Clinton's bout with pneumonia and a very weird health letter of his own. Then, on September 16, Trump suddenly, in a few sentences and with no apology or explanation, announced, after 5 years of his birther stance that really launched his political career, that 'Barack Obama *was* born in the U.S.A."

Trump was criticized for saying the election was 'fixed' and later that the only way Clinton could win Pennsylvania was by 'cheating.'

Several major Republican operatives announced they were either leaving the GOP or voting for Hillary because of Trump. That included HP executive and GOP fundraiser Meg Whitman who announced she'll vote for and support Hillary Clinton, get other important GOP donors on board her campaign and donate millions to it. A Republican congressman from New York says he will support Hillary. Top Republican surrogates and strategists for people like Governor Christie announced they are leaving the party. Former Republican Governor of New Jersey Christie Todd Whitman says she's voting for Hillary. Another GOP billionaire donor, Seth Klarman, announced that his allegiance has switched from Trump to Clinton.

Several other billionaires, including Warren Buffet, Mark Cuban and Michael Bloomberg, each much wealthier than Trump, questioned his business record, the amount of his claimed wealth and competence.

The federal judge, presiding over one of many huge lawsuits from those harmed and defrauded by Trump University, a judge who Trump had made seeming racist statements against for his Mexican-American heritage, made several preliminary rulings against Trump's case. The New York State case against Trump also advanced and that state's Attorney General announced he was investigating Trump's dubious family foundation dealings.

Numerous psychologists and commentators alike are openly speculating that The Donald had serious mental issues ranging from narcissistic personality or character disorder to being bipolar. Pulitzer Prize winning columnist Eugene Robinson asks, "is Trump really crazy?"

It also didn't help that major Trump media supporter, Roger Ailes, the long-time head of Fox News Channel, had been driven out of Fox after major allegations of sexual harassment from 30 or more Fox employees and female anchors including Megan Kelly. But that wasn't the end of Ailes. It was reported that Trump had asked the accused harasser to prep him for the debates.

The polls dramatically turn.

Hillary Clinton, depending on which polls one looked at, had received a 7-12 point bump from the Democratic Convention. Polls indicated that Trump's speech at the GOP Convention, criticized as dark and fear-mongering, had shown him losing more voters rather than gaining them, but by mid-September, during Hillary's bout with pneumonia, her lead was eroding again down to, still ahead, 5-7 points .

The New York Post, staunchly pro-Trump and Republican, had released two days of front-page nude photos of Trump's wife, following on his wife Melania's speech plagiarism at the Republican Convention. There were reports that Melania never graduated from college as her web site said she did. Her website suddenly disappeared. There were stories that she first illegally worked in the U.S. before she became a citizen.

Because of Trump's continued refusal to release any tax returns at all, there was increased speculation that Trump wasn't worth $10 billion as he said or anywhere near it and that he underpaid his taxes or paid no taxes at all.

Tony Schwartz, the *real* writer of Trump's best-selling 1987 "The Art of the Deal," which Trump always talks up, gave interviews about how he spent 18 months 'living with Trump' and by writing the book ' made America see Trump with an unfailing knack for business. Tony Schwartz helped create that myth—and now regrets it. In a New Yorker article, Schwartz says, "I put lipstick on a pig," and that he feels "deep remorse." *(See our separate article on Schwartz and the contents of that book elsewhere here).*

All this and Trump's refusal to pivot to the general election in terms of what he says and his temperament continued to fuel a dramatic drop in the polls for Trump nationally with similar poor results in most swing states, except for Iowa. Some non-swing Republican states also began to look like they were in play including very red Georgia. Mitch McConnell was openly pessimistic about keeping the Senate in GOP hands and retaining his leadership of it.

Trump also talked about how against him CNN was, despite the news channel having 7 paid Trump surrogates / spokespeople on the payroll.

Mr. and Mrs. Khizr Khan replied for days on MSNBC, CNN and elsewhere about Trump's putdown of them and Trump saying that he too 'had sacrificed' like their hero son.

After all that, President Obama, meeting with the President of Singapore on August 1 and after all the latest controversies, talked passionately about how Trump was 'unfit' to be President.

Trump withheld endorsing Speaker Paul Ryan in his primary and Senator John McCain for days while his running mate endorsed them.

Several times in a major interview, Trump said, on various topics, 'why can't we use nukes.'

In another Washington Post interview, Trump stopped the interview 5 times to watch TV.

NEW CAMPAIGN MANAGERS--AGAIN

Not surprisingly, mid-August, Trump and his campaign announced their third major campaign shakeup. This time, the head of far-right/ alt-right conspiracy website Breitbart, Steve Bannon, was being put in charge over Paul Manafort, who himself replaced Cory Lewandowski. A few days after the announcement, Manafort resigned from the Trump campaign amidst continued allegations about his unregistered lobbying for Russia and failure to pay taxes on it.

Trump, at various times, has said he may not debate, though now he says that he will and appeared in a forum on NBC and MSNBC with Hillary Clinton on national security in early September.

A few months ago, Trump declared that even if he wins the election, he might then resign the presidency. His behavior and statements have often been so out of bounds that some have said that it seems like he wants to throw the election and lose. Some conspiracy minded folks have taken it a step further and continued to speculate that Trump may be a Democratic 'plant' ...or now even a Russian one.

More and more rumors are swirling that Trump may yet pull out as the GOP nominee (Trump himself said that if the poll numbers looked bad, he might quit)---and weeks after the conventions, they are better for him but possibly turning still again. Word is that the GOP is now preparing for that possibility or simply to stop funding his campaign any longer as more than 50 influential GOPers have requested.

There is new speculation that with Breitbart's Bannon and Fox' Roger Ailes on board, Trump is looking to start a future Trump TV News network, way to the right of Fox.

Many Republicans had asked for Trump to 'act more Presidential' for the general election campaign than he had during the primaries. But Trump kept his behavior and words pretty much the same instead of changing and it was said that the new Trump campaign CEO from

Breitbart definitely wanted Trump to continue his flame-throwing as he had done since his candidacy's first day back in 2015.

In September, Trump's shocker was his announcement, with no explanations, that President Obama *was* born in the U.S. But that didn't last long as a few days later, Trump let it be known he 'only said that to get back to the campaign' and didn't believe what he said!

In this book, you will find the enormity of everything on Donald Trump; truly an Encyclopedia of Trump, unlike any other…his full bio and that of his family and his running mate, his full candidacy and acceptance speeches, by-far-the-most complete compilation of Trump quotes anywhere in our **Trump A-Z section** that's a real eye-roller and puts much in perspective, Trump's views on religion and his own religious outlook, Trump University and other Trump business ventures and dealings (many of them failed), editorials for and against Trump, how Trump is viewed overseas, what dozens of others whose names you likely know in both parties and beyond them view Trump.…

Newsweek and Washington Post revelations that Trump's overseas entanglements, financially, would not enable him to properly do his job if he was elected, that he was profiting by charging his campaign for millions for the use of Trump properties and that his charitable foundation was being used to pay his business debts, buy him a painting of himself and more (for which it was being investigated).

Then, as we were about to send this book for final formatting.….

THE FIRST PRESIDENTIAL DEBATE September 26.

You could call the first presidential debate at Hofstra the Long Island smack down! It was judged by all networks including Fox and most everyone else a big take down of Trump by Hillary Clinton.

Trump interrupted 51 times. He snorted and grimaced throughout and did a Marco impersonation with water. He dodged questions and moderator Holt's fact-checking on being for the Iraq war, on why he birthered for 5 years, on stiffing thousands of employees, on not releasing tax returns and paying no taxes, on being happy to profit from the housing meltdown and being sued for anti African-American housing discrimination, on insulting one of his Miss Universe winners. Trump said his very best quality was his great temperament, which drew laughter from the well-behaved audience at Hofstra.

TV show host and former Mayor Jerry Springer quipped that Trump belonged on his show rather than in the White House. Surgeon General Murthy warned of acute alcohol syndrome if people drank every time Trump lied.

The purpose of this book is to report on and objectively chronicle Trump's campaign and his positions for you, so you can decide… and share with friends and family…and so you can have a keepsake of the strangest, most unforgettable and most upheaval-filled campaign of all time….

For us, we've worked hard on compiling a *neutral and complete* look at candidate Trump, a little less than 3 months before the national election.

Most of all, we have spent tens of hours compiling the Trump A-Z section and Everyone on Trump sections….unlike anything else available anywhere and very eye-popping.

It's our own highly researched compilation of hundreds and hundreds of Trump quotes on over 75 subjects and people. You can draw your own conclusions as with The Huge Little Book of Trump, to borrow a phrase from his campaign backers, we are truly just *'letting Trump be Trump!'* as thoroughly as we can.

Whether you keep this book as a memento of a very unusual and certainly memorable 16-month campaign so far, use it to educate others on the other side of where you are at (friend or foe) or just have your own amazing look at Donald J. Trump, we hope you'll enjoy this very unique, fact-filled look at the most tumultuous Presidential campaign in memory!

And, whatever you do, VOTE!

DONALD J. TRUMP BIOGRAPHY

Compiled from Wikipedia, WWE, books on Trump, quotes by Trump and other reliable media and internet resources.

Donald J. Trump is a real-estate developer, former TV show host (The Apprentice), author of several ghost-written best-selling books, entrepreneur (several clothing lines all manufactured overseas), the Miss Universe pageant, golf courses, the failed Trump Airlines, Trump steaks, Trump casinos, Trump University, Trump Network and Trump vitamins), and is a very controversial "outsider" who won the 2016 Republican Presidential candidacy. He was once a Democrat.

"The Donald", as he's frequently referred to now, was born in 1946, in Jamaica Estates, Queens, New York City, one of five children of Mary Anne, a Scottish homemaker and Fred Trump, who she met in the U.S. when she was 18. Fred was a major real estate developer leaving Donald Trump with $1 million dollars inheritance (equal to at least $15 million now) and then investing mega-millions more into his son's real estate endeavors.

Trump has a brother, Robert and two sisters: Maryanne, a federal judge and Elizabeth. Another brother, Fred Jr. died in 1981 from alcoholism. Trump has three adult children, from 2 wives, in business with him and a young son from his current third wife, Melania.

Trump's father was born in Queens, the son of immigrants from Germany . Frederick worked as a Klondike Gold Rush restaurateur and is believed to have also been a brothel keeper. In a 1976 *New York Times* biographical profile and his ghost-written 1987 book, *The Art of the Deal*, Trump stated that his father was Swedish, because "he had a lot of Jewish tenants and it wasn't a good thing to be German", according to a nephew identified as a family historian. Donald Trump later acknowledged his German ancestry.

Donald Trump attended a Queens school where his father was a trustee. Because of his behavior problems, Trump left that school when he was 13, enrolling in New York Military Academy. In 1983, Fred told an interviewer that Donald "was a pretty rough fellow when he was small." Trump finished eighth grade and high school at the Academy, attaining the rank of captain. In 2015, he told a biographer that NYMA gave him "more training militarily than a lot of the guys that go into the military." Trump attended Fordham University for two years and then the Wharton School of Business at the University of Pennsylvania and its real estate studies departments. He graduated with a B.A. in economics in 1968.

Trump has never served in the military. During Vietnam, he had four college deferments and then a medical deferment for 'heel spurs' (1-Y, later converted to 4-F) obtained prior to the lottery being initiated. Trump was deemed fit for service after a military medical examination in 1966 and was briefly classified as 1-A by a local draft board shortly before his 1968 medical disqualification according to a 2015 biographer, but told an Iowa campaign audience he suffered from a spur in one foot, although he could not remember which one. "I actually got lucky because I had a very high draft number", he told WNYW in 2011. Selective Service records website from the National Archives show that Trump did eventually receive a high selective service lottery number in 1969.

His career

Trump claimed in 2015 that in 1968, he was worth about $200,000. At age 23, he unsuccessfully invested $70,000 to become co-producer of the 1970 Broadway comedy "Paris Is Out!," which flopped. Trump began his real estate career at his father's company, Elizabeth Trump and Son, which focused on middle-class rental housing in the New York City boroughs. During his undergraduate study, one of Trump's first projects had been the revitalization of the foreclosed Swifton Village apartment complex in Cincinnati, Ohio, which his father had purchased for $5.7 million in 1962. Fred and Donald Trump became involved in the project and with a $500,000 investment, tripled the 1,200-unit complex's occupancy rate. Trump oversaw the company's 14,000 apartments across Brooklyn, Queens, and Staten Island. In 1972, The Trump Organization sold Swifton Village for $6.75 million. In 1971, Trump became involved in larger construction projects in Manhattan with the continued financial help of his father.

Trump became quite known in 1973. He was accused by the Justice Department of violations of the Fair Housing Act in the operation of 39 buildings, including false "no vacancy" statements, and sham leases presenting higher rents to minority applicants, to facilitate the denial of housing to racial minorities. But Trump accused the DOJ of targeting his company in order to force it to rent to welfare recipients. After an unsuccessful countersuit filed by attorney Roy Cohn, Trump settled the charges in 1975 without admitting guilt, saying he was satisfied that the agreement did not "compel the Trump organization to accept persons on welfare as tenants unless as qualified as any other tenant." Years later, the Trump Organization was again in court for violating terms of that settlement.

The Trump Organization owns, operates, develops, and invests in real estate around the world such as Trump Ocean Club International Hotel and Tower, in Panama City, Panama.

Trump had an option to buy and made plans to develop the Penn Central Transportation Company property, which was in bankruptcy. This included the 60th Street rail yard on the Hudson River—later developed as Riverside South—as well as the land around Grand Central Terminal, for which he paid $60 million with no money down. Later, with the help of a 40-year tax abatement from the New York City government and again with his father securing or guaranteeing loans, he turned the bankrupt

Commodore Hotel next to Grand Central into the Grand Hyatt and created The Trump Organization.

Trump promoted Penn Central's rail yard on 30th Street as a site for New York City's planned Jacob K. Javits Convention Center. Trump estimated his company could have completed the project for $110 million, but, while the city chose his site, it rejected his offer and Trump received a broker's fee on the sale of the property instead.

Repairs on the Wollman Rink for ice skating in Central Park, built in 1955, were started in 1980, but were not completed by 1986. Trump took over the management of the project without the city needing to pay anything, and completed it in three months for $1.95 million, which was $750,000 less than the initial budget.

Casinos

In 1988, Trump acquired the Taj Mahal Casino on the boardwalk in Atlantic City, New Jersey, in a transaction with Merv Griffin and Resorts International. The acquisition was funded by significant bank borrowing and was built at a total cost of nearly one billion dollars, financed with $675 million in junk bonds at a 14% interest rate. By 1989, Trump was unable to meet loan payments. Although he secured additional loans and postponed interest payments, increasing debt brought the Taj Mahal to bankruptcy in 1991. Banks and bondholders, facing potential losses of hundreds of millions of dollars, opted to restructure the debt. The Taj Mahal emerged from bankruptcy on October 5, 1991, with Trump ceding 50 percent ownership in the casino to the bondholders in exchange for lowered interest rates and more time to pay off the debt. He also sold his financially challenged Trump Shuttle airline and his 282-foot mega yacht, the *Trump Princess*.

The late 1990s saw a resurgence in Trump's financial situation. The will of Trump's father, who died in 1999, divided an estate estimated at $250–300 million equally among his four surviving children.

The Taj Mahal was repurchased in 1996 and consolidated into Trump Hotels & Casino Resorts, which then itself filed for bankruptcy in 2004 with $1.8 billion in debt, filing again for bankruptcy five years later with $50 million in assets and $500 million in debt. The restructuring ultimately left Trump with 10% ownership in the Trump Taj Mahal and other Trump casino properties. Trump served as chairman of the organization, which was renamed Trump Entertainment Resorts, from mid-1995 until early 2009, and served as CEO from mid-2000 to mid-2005.

Its sister property, Trump Plaza Hotel and Casino, closed in September 2014. In November 2014, the Trump Taj Mahal threatened to close and cease casino and hotel operations by the end of the year if the union would not drop its appeal of the casino's bankruptcy ruling, rebuffing their demand for continued health insurance and pension coverage. (This is similar to what is still going on at Trump's main hotel property in Las Vegas).

On December 18, 2014 the Trump Taj Mahal reached an agreement with its union and kept the casino open, but did not restore the contested benefits. By 2014, Trump retained 10% ownership of Trump Entertainment Resorts, which owns the Trump Taj Mahal and Trump Plaza Hotel and Casino, both in Atlantic City. Trump closed Trump Plaza indefinitely.

In February 2016, the Trump Taj Mahal and Trump Entertainment Resorts were purchased by billionaire Carl Icahn and exited Chapter 11 bankruptcy. Icahn kept Trump's name on the building even though Trump no longer had any ownership.

A Trump hotel in Las Vegas has failed to be approved for a gaming license and has no casino.

Other Trump buildings

In 2001, Trump completed Trump World Tower, a 72-story residential tower across from the United Nations Headquarters. Also, he began construction on Trump Place, a multi-building development along the Hudson River. Trump owns commercial space in Trump International Hotel and Tower, a 44-story mixed-use (hotel and condominium) tower on Columbus Circle. Trump owns several million square feet of prime Manhattan real estate

Trump has licensed his name and image for the development of many other Trump-branded properties, which he does not own. Two Trump-branded real estate projects in Florida have gone into foreclosure. The Turkish owner of Trump Towers Istanbul, who pays Trump for the use of his name, was reported in December 2015 to be exploring legal means to dissociate the property after the candidate's call to temporarily ban Muslims from entering the United States.

Trump has been unsuccessful developing properties in Russia.

Trump has also licensed his name to son-in-law Jared Kushner's fifty story Trump Bay Street, a Jersey City luxury development that has raised $50 million of its $200 million capitalization largely from wealthy Chinese nationals who, after making an initial down payment of $500,000 in concert with the government's expedited EB-5 visa program, can usually be expected to obtain U.S. permanent residency for themselves and their families after two years.

The EB-5 visa program, which does not require visa recipients to demonstrate marketable skills, has aroused concerns from the Homeland Security Department regarding inadequate background checks, with money laundering concerns and cases of identity fraud also noted by the General Accounting Office.

A spokesperson clarified that Trump is a partner with Kushner Properties only in name licensing and not in the building's financing.

Trump Tower

Trump Tower, at 725 Fifth Avenue, in Mid Manhattan is a 58-story, mixed-use building and the Equitable Life Assurance Company, and was designed by architect Der Scutt of Swanke Hayden Connell.[Trump Tower houses both his primary penthouse condominium residence and the headquarters of The Trump Organization. (Trump Tower is also the name of buildings that The Trump Organization has built in Baku, Azerbaijan; Istanbul, Turkey, and several other places.)

Trump Tower occupies the former site of the architecturally important Bonwit Teller flagship store, demolished in 1980. Art Deco bas-relief sculptures on its facade, supposed to go to the Metropolitan Museum of Art, were destroyed during demolition.

The demolition of the store employed use of some 200 undocumented Polish immigrant workers, who, during the rushed demolition process, were reportedly paid 4–5 dollars per hour for work in 12-hour shifts. Trump said in 1990 that he rarely visited the site (Trump lives there) and was unaware of the illegal workers, some of whom lived at the site and who were known as the "Polish Brigade." A judge ruled in 1991 that the builders engaged in "a conspiracy to deprive the funds of their rightful contribution", referring to the pension and welfare funds of the labor unions. The record was sealed when a long-running labor lawsuit was settled in 1999, after 16 years in court.

Golf courses

The Trump Organization operates many golf courses and resorts here and overseas.

In 2006, Trump bought the Menie Estate in Balmedie, Aberdeenshire, Scotland, creating a highly controversial golf resort, against the wishes of local residents, on an area designated as a Site of Special Scientific Interest. A 2011 independent documentary, *You've Been Trumped,* by British filmmaker Anthony Baxter, chronicled the golf resort's construction and the subsequent struggles between the locals and Donald Trump. Despite Trump's promises of 6,000 jobs, a decade later, by his own admission, the golf course has created only 200 jobs.

In April 2014, Trump purchased the Turnberry Hotel and golf resort in Ayrshire, Scotland, which is a regular fixture in the Open Championship rota. In June 2015, Trump's appeal objecting to an offshore wind farm (Aberdeen Bay Wind Farm) within sight of the golf links was denied. A year and a half after his purchase, Trump's attempt to prevent the wind farm being built within sight of his golf course was dismissed by five justices at the UK Supreme Court . During the Presidential campaign, Trump visited Turnberry the morning after Great Britain voted to leave the European Union and talked about how the devaluation of the British pound, as a result, was 'good for business' for his club.

Branding and licensing

Trump has marketed his name on a large number of building projects, commercial products and services, achieving mixed success for himself, his partners, and investors in the projects. His external entrepreneurial and investment ventures include Trump Financial (a mortgage firm), Trump Sales and Leasing (residential sales) and Trump International Realty (a residential and commercial real estate brokerage firm).

The Trump Entrepreneur Initiative (a highly controversial and litigated for profit business education company used to be known as Trump University *and has several class action suits against it still in 2016 and has been hit with fraud charges by several states attorney generals as well as a Federal case).*

There are also Trump Restaurants (located in Trump Tower and consisting of Trump Buffet, Trump Catering, Trump Ice Cream Parlor, and Trump Bar), GoTrump (an online travel search engine),

Select By Trump (a line of coffee drinks), Trump Drinks (an energy drink for the Israeli and Palestinian markets) Donald J. Trump Signature Collection (a line of menswear, men's accessories, and watches (*all* of which are made overseas), Donald Trump The Fragrance (2004).

Also, there is SUCCESS by Donald Trump (a second fragrance launched by The Trump Organization and the Five Star Fragrance Company released in March 2012), Trump Ice bottled water, the former *Trump Magazine*, Trump Golf, Trump Chocolate, Trump Home (home furnishings), Trump Productions (a television production company), Trump Institute, the failedTrump: The Game (1989 board game with a 2005 re-release version tied to The Apprentice),[Donald Trump's Real Estate Tycoon (a business simulation game), Trump Books, Trump Model Management (now accused of hiring improprieties and breaking immigration law), the failed Trump Shuttle, Trump Mortgage, Trump Network (a multi-level vitamin, cosmetic, and urinalysis marketing company deemed by many to be as much of a scam as Trump University), Trump Vodka, Trump Steakhouse and the failed Trump Steaks. Despite Trump showing many of these products at a press conference during his Presidential campaign, many of them no longer existing at the time of the press conference and were failures.

In addition, Trump reportedly received $1.5 million for each one-hour presentation he did for The Learning Annex. Trump also endorsed ACN Inc., a multi-level marketing telecommunications company. He has spoken at ACN International Training Events at which he praised the company's founders, business model and video phone. He earned $450,000 each for three speeches given for the company.

Trump's Actual Worth

Trump says it is $10 billion but many experts scoff at that amount, putting it at several billion less or even *under* a billion dollars.

Since Trump won't share any of his tax returns, it is impossible to know....particularly since some of Trump's wealth, he says, "is based on (his) feelings."

(see separate article in this book with more details and Newsweek's revelation about Trump's foreign financial entanglements).

.

Trump and Wrestling

From the WWE web site ......"Trump has also been making a consistent impact on WWE since the days when Andre the Giant was still king".

The Donald's Trump Plaza in Atlantic City, N.J., hosted both Wrestle Mania IV and V — the only venue to present The Show of Shows two years in a row. Trump has remained a familiar face in the front row of WWE events, but it wasn't until 2007 that the billionaire got in on the action.

In January of that year, The Donald interrupted Mr. McMahon's "Fan Appreciation Night" on Raw and dropped tens of thousands of dollars from the rafters of the arena onto the WWE fans below. Red-faced that a rival would steal the spotlight from him, Mr. McMahon challenged Trump to a "Battle of the Billionaires" at Wrestle Mania 23 with the stipulation that the loser of the bout would have their his head shaved bald.

A record number of viewers tuned in to watch The Donald back Bobby Lashley to victory over Mr. McMahon's Umaga and subsequently shave the WWE Chairman's signature mane in the center of the ring.

The business magnates locked horns again in June 2009 when Trump purchased Monday Night Raw and immediately announced that next week's show would air commercial-free and that every WWE fan that who purchased a ticket would be given a full refund.

The trademark Trump PR public relations flourish nearly made Mr. McMahon's head explode and forced him to buy his show back from The Donald for twice the price.

Since then, the WWE Hall of Famer focused on his ever-expanding real estate empire, his Emmy-nominated reality television show "The Apprentice" until NBC "fired" Trump and on running for President of the United States since June, 2015.

The Apprentice / Celebrity Apprentice

It began, with Trump as its star, with Episode 1: Meet the Billionaire, on January 8, 2004 through early 2015. Trump is most famous for his line, "you are fired' on the reality show, (which also featured his three adult children) Trump left the show in 2015 to run for the Republican presidential candidacy and since, NBC has made clear that because of his racist and other incendiary remarks, he would not be invited back on NBC.

Miss Universe Pageant

It's an annual international **beauty pageant** that is run by the Miss Universe Organization. Along with its rival contests, **Miss World** and **Miss Earth**, this pageant is one of the most important and publicized **beauty pageants** in the world. It is held in more than 190 countries worldwide and seen by more than half a billion people annually. The pageant was founded in 1952 by the **California**-based clothing company Pacific Knitting Mills, and the Miss Universe Organization and the brand is currently owned, along with **Miss USA** and **Miss Teen USA**, by **WME/IMG**. Miss

Universe Organization licenses local organizations that wish to select the Miss Universe contestant for their country, and approves the selection method for national delegates. The current Miss Universe logo – "the woman with stars" – was created in 1998.

In 2015, after **Donald Trump** made statements about illegal **immigrants** from Mexico in his U.S. presidential campaign kickoff speech, NBC and Univision decided to end its business relationship with him and stated that it would no longer air the Miss Universe or Miss USA pageants on its networks. (or have him as the star of Apprentice, either). In September 2015, Trump bought the entire stock of the Miss Universe Organization from NBC, becoming its sole owner for three days, then sold the entire stock to WME/IMG.

TRUMP the Birther

Trump pretty much entered the political world when he became known as head of the 'birthers."

The whole birther thing went back to 2008…when Trump seized it from conspiracy theorists and even some wacky fringe Democrats. In 2011, when he was vocally mulling over a possible presidential run, the then reality TV star spoke extensively about his 'questions' over whether Barak Obama was actually born in Hawaii like he (and the state of Hawaii) says he was (and an implied questioning of whether Obama was Muslim, not Christian.) Trump launched a public pursuit of Obama's birth certificate, announcing that he had sent private investigators to Hawaii to see what they could find. Trump never told us! And there was no evidence they ever went to Hawaii at all.

The President then released the long-form version of his birth certificate in response to the uproar that Trump had caused. After its release, Trump said that he was "proud of myself because I've accomplished something nobody has been able to accomplish."

In 2016, polls of Republicans find that 60-70% of them still believe that President Obama is a secret Muslim and was not born in the U.S. And that's even in spite of Trump himself finally putting the birther claims to rest in mid-September, 2016 with his 'President Obama was born in America.'

As Trump ran for President in 2015-2016, though he refused to directly talk about it, those around him stirred up the waters once again. Trump himself has always talked about and allied himself with many other conspiracy theories getting his 'news,' he said, from 'the shows' or the National Enquirer, Alex Jones or now, additionally, the new conspiracy-theorist head of his campaign, Steve Bannon . During the primaries, he implied that rival Ted Cruz' father was with Lee Harvey Oswald around the time of the Kennedy assassination and that Ted Cruz was not a citizen, either. Trump drops these conspiracies usually with the phrase "I've heard it' or 'someone said…"

Then, shockingly, in September 2016, Trump declared that President Obama *was* born in the United States. Days later, he was back to saying that wasn't true….he had just said it 'to get back to his campaign!"

Trump Books

Trump: The Art of the Deal was originally published November 1, 1987. It has been bragged about by Trump in the campaign. as being the 'biggest (non-fiction) business best-seller of all-time next to the Bible," which it wasn't, though it did have big sales. "Deal,' like most Trump books, were mostly ghost-written by others.

Credited to Trump and journalist Tony Schwartz, it was actually written entirely by Schwartz, not Trump.

In August, 2016, Schwartz was giving a lot of interviews on the writing of the book, the 18 months he spent with Trump and how he regrets it all and why (see separate Art of the Deal page)

Trump has written several other books since, credited to himself and co-authors.

Trump's Russian Connection?

In 2016, thanks to Trump's own statements, many questions and much speculation started swirling about Trump's ties to Russia and Putin.

Trump had said repeatedly that he admired Putin as a leader and that he knows him and then that he doesn't know him and never met him.

What we do know was that Trump negotiated with Russia over his beauty pageants and about building hotels in Russia.

We know too that in summer, 2016, Trump repeatedly asked publically for Russia to computer hack the Democratic campaign, which security people believed was happening. Also, Trump had said erroneous things about Russia and Ukraine, not seeming to know that Russia had already, two years before, gone into Crimea and Ukraine.

We also know that Trump campaign manager Paul Manafort had numerous lobbyist ties to both Russia and the former Russian-backed President of the Ukraine. It was confirmed that Manafort had been noted in Russian documents of being paid (or to be paid) over $12 million by them. As this book was being finished, Trump demoted Manafort, instead making the head of Breitbart media the new chief of his campaign. Newsweek revealed a lot more about Russian ties and other numerous overseas entanglements Trump has, in a lengthy September, 2016 investigative cover story.

Trump University

Trump University was in business from 2005-2010 and enrolled thousands of people in

'courses' to become wealthy from real estate. Never an actual university of any kind, it was run, according to Donald Trump, with major involvement from him. In active lawsuits from New York to California, it is accused of fleecing many people out of hundreds to mostly tens of thousands of dollars each. *(See full page on Trump U. in this book)*.

Trump politics

In June 2015, at his Trump Tower in New York and his 'political fame' largely based on his role as chief birther, Trump announced his candidacy for the Republican nomination for President. Trump's flame-throwing throughout the 2015-2016 primaries worked for a year. There was his mocking of a disabled reporter, his calling for stopping Muslims entering the country and for a Mexican border wall and much more you will find in this book, particularly in our very comprehensive *Trump A-Z section*. Trump defeated all fellow primary candidates, won 13 million votes, spurred mostly record viewership for debates and was always on TV, calling in to news shows constantly, writing mostly flame-throwing tweets that usually got much media attention or giving inciting speeches according to what he said worked in his Tony Schwartz' Deal" book; good or bad publicity to 'get attention.'

In the general election campaign after he had won the nomination, during and after the conventions, Trump was considered by most media and many Republicans as well as Democrats, to be imploding with one controversy after another that seemed to be losing him support instead of gaining it; letters from GOP security and foreign affairs people calling for his defeat or actually saying they'll vote for Hillary, a 3rd party Republican candidate to thwart Trump's chances in winning key state Utah, speculation about

Trump's love for Russia's Putin and his campaign manager's ties to Russia, federal and state lawsuits against him for Trump University proceeding, backlash against his mocking of the Muslim Goldstar Khan family, continued refusal to release his tax returns (even years of them not under audit), renewed speculation about his true personal wealth, Trump saying Russia wouldn't go into Ukraine when he had already 2 years before, Trump implying to many that after Hillary got elected, people could employ 'second amendment' remedies to stop her, plummeting national polls and polls in most swing states started consistently showing Clinton ahead by 6 to 15 points!

GOVERNOR MIKE PENCE

GOP 2016 VP Candidate

Mike Pence was born in Columbus, Indiana, graduated from Hanover College in 1981 and earned his Doctorate in Jurisprudence from Indiana University School of Law in 1986.

Following graduation from law school, Congressman Pence ran for Congress in 1988 and 1990. In 1991, Pence was named president of a conservative state think tank based in Fort Wayne known as the Indiana Policy Review Foundation.

In 1992, Pence started a career in radio broadcasting and, two years later, Network Indiana syndicated his show statewide. The Mike Pence Show aired weekdays on 18 radio stations. Pence also hosted a Sunday morning political television show in Indianapolis from 1995 to 1999.

Mike and his wife Karen have three children and reside in Columbus, Indiana. The Pence family lives in Arlington, Virginia, while Congress is in session.

Mike describes himself as "a Christian, a conservative and a Republican, in that order."

Congressman Pence was elected to Congress in November 2000 and was re-elected to represent the Sixth Congressional District, encompassing much of the eastern half of Indiana, for a fifth term in 2008. In November of 2008, he was elected to serve as Chairman of the House Republican Conference.

Governor Pence is most known for his history as Governor on health issues and on 'religious protections' in Indiana.

Medicaid Expansion

Pence is a vocal opponent of the Affordable Care Act, even after the federal law passed in 2010 and was upheld by the Supreme Court.

But to expand Medicaid in his state, he compromised with a conservative-friendly version of the expansion, requiring a monthly contribution, based on income, into a health savings account. Recipients who miss a payment can be bumped to a lower level of coverage, or lose it entirely, for six months.

The Healthy Indiana Plan, or HIP 2.0, has enrolled about 190,000 more people into health coverage

HIV Outbreak

Pence drew criticism from local and national infectious disease experts for his response to an urgent HIV crisis in Indiana. In February of 2015, the state reported an outbreak of HIV in Scott County, blamed on opioid addiction and needle sharing.

It got so bad that the CDC went to Indiana to investigate, and public health experts began calling for a needle exchange. At the time, syringe exchanges were illegal in the state, and Pence was opposed to changing that, at first. He later signed an emergency declaration allowing Scott County to start a needle exchange program. Pence later signed a bill that forces counties to ask permission to start a needle exchange.

Public Health Budgets

The HIV crisis also brought some attention to Indiana's lack of public health funding in general, Lawrence says.

"I think we are dealing with the consequences of the fact that that we don't have a strong infrastructure for public health in the state," she says.

As governor, Pence signed legislation that *cut* Indiana's budget for public health programs, despite the state's many pressing public health problems. Indiana has a high smoking rate, high obesity rate, and high infant mortality rate. The state is ranked nearly last for both federal and state public health funding. According to Trust for America's Health, Indiana spends just $12.40 per resident on public health. West Virginia, in contrast, spends more than $220.

Abortion Access

As a congressman, Pence was an early advocate for defunding Planned Parenthood, and women's health advocates have clashed with him again's since he's been governor.

Pence signed a bill that's been cited as one of the most restrictive in the U.S., barring abortion on the basis of disability, gender or race of the fetus. It requires women to get an ultrasound at least 18 hours before the procedure, and requires that the fetal remains be buried or cremated.

DISCRIMINATION

Governor Pence, while saying he 'abhored discrimination,' signed legislation that could legalize discrimination against lesbian, gay, bisexual and transgender individuals.

The Religious Freedom Restoration Act would allow any individual or corporation to cite its religious beliefs as a defense when sued by a private party. But many opponents of the bill, which included business leaders, argued that it could open the door to widespread discrimination. Business owners who don't want to serve same-sex couples, for example, could now have legal protections to discriminate.

'Today,' said Pence, 'many people of faith feel their religious liberty is under attack by government action. The bill received national attention, but Pence signed it with little fanfare in a ceremony closed to the public and the press.

The bill was greeted nationally by a firestorm of condemnation with major businesses threatening to leave Indiana or abort starting up there.

Democrats in the state Legislature were unimpressed. They repeated their call for full repeal.

But some legal experts have said that Indiana's law opens a wider berth for discrimination, partly because it allows businesses to claim religious protection in lawsuits brought by individuals, not just against government action.

He insisted that the law, in its current form, allows no such thing. And he said that people have "smeared" the law by claiming that it sanctions discrimination against gays or anyone else.

But he referred to a "harsh glare of criticism from around the country" since he signed the bill.

"We'll fix this, and we'll move forward," the governor, told reporters in Indianapolis. "I believe in my heart of hearts that no one should be harassed or mistreated because of who they are, who they love or what they believe."

Pence said that the law was meant to protect religious liberty, which he called "our first freedom." But opponents of the law, and some social conservatives who supported it, said that it would allow businesses to turn away gay customers on religious grounds.

The outcry has included a **broad spectrum of public figures**. Tim Cook, the openly gay CEO of Apple, opposed it, as did Mark Emmert, president of the NCAA, which was staging the Final Four in Indianapolis.

The Indianapolis Star ran an editorial across its entire front page with the giant headline: "FIX THIS NOW."

The CEO of Angie's List, the online listings service, which suspended plans to expand an Indiana facility because of the law, said he was encouraged by some of what Pence had to say.

If Pence makes clear that neither the religion law "nor any other Indiana law can be used to justify discrimination based upon sexual orientation or gender identity, he can fix this mess," CEO Bill Oesterle said.

Democrats in the state Legislature were unimpressed. They repeated their call for full repeal.

Legal experts have said that Indiana's law opens a wider berth for discrimination, partly because it allows businesses to claim religious protection in lawsuits brought by individuals, not just against government action.

The Republican leaders of the Indiana Legislature said on Monday that they would rush to clarify the law.

At a press conference, Pence was asked whether a Christian business should be required to provide services for gay weddings.

He said, "I don't support discrimination against anyone," then said that a free society always has to conduct "a careful balancing of interests. And the facts and circumstances of each case determine the outcome." But finally, under intense pressure, Pence promised to greatly fix the new state law.

The governor said that Indiana has a proud tradition of inclusion. "Hoosiers are a loving, kind, generous, decent people"

MELANIA TRUMP

Melania Trump (born **Melanija Knavs**, April 26, 1970; Germanized to **Melania Knauss**) is the Donald's current wife. Born in Slovenia, then part of the Socialist Federal Republic of Yugoslavia, she became a permanent resident of the United States in 2001 and a citizen in 2006.

Early life

She was born in Novo Mesto in southeastern Slovenia (then part of Yugoslavia) on April 26, 1970. Her father, Viktor Knavs, who managed car and motorcycle dealerships for a state-owned vehicle manufacturer, and was a member of the Slovenian Communist Party, came from the nearby town of Radeče. Her mother, Amalija (Ulčnik), came from the village of Raka and was a patternmaker at the children's clothing manufacturer Jutranjka in Sevnica. Melania has a sister, Ines, and an older half-brother, whom she has never met, from her father's previous relationship.

Trump grew up in a modest apartment in a concrete housing block in Sevnica, in Slovenia's Lower Sava Valley. When she was a teenager, the family moved to a two-story house near Sevnica and used a high-rise apartment in Ljubljana.

Trump attended the Secondary School of Design and Photography in Ljubljana and studied at the University of Ljubljana for one year before dropping out. Her own web site, until recently and before it was taken down, said falsely that she graduated from that university and had many other falsehoods in it.

She speaks five languages: her native Slovenian, Serbian, English, French, and German.

Immigration to the United States

Trump "seemed to confirm" that she came to the United States on an H-1B visa in 1996, and an agent for a modeling agency told the The Washington Post that his agency sponsored Trump for an H-1B visa in 1996. She became a permanent resident of the United States in 2001 and a citizen in 2006.

In August 2016, it was reported that Trump's account of her immigration status may have contained inconsistencies. Controversial photographs of Trump were re-published in the New York Post in the first week of August 2016. These photographs were originally taken in the United States during a photo shoot which puts her inside the United States in 1995, as does a biography published in February by Slovenian journalists. The photos themselves were published by the French men's magazine, Max, in January 1996. This causes a discrepancy in her timeline of being a legal resident of the United States: her purported immigration timeline has her entering the country in 1996 on a short-term travel visa, which would not have authorized her to work as a model. However, the photographer who took the pictures republished by the New York Post stated that Trump was not paid for her work.

With all these discrepancies about her visa and false university graduation, her own web site disappeared from the internet in July, 2016.

Career

Melania Trump began her modeling career at age 16 and at age 17 posed for Slovenian fashion photographer Stane Jerko. At 18, she signed with a modeling agency in Milan, Italy. She was named runner-up in the 1992 Jana Magazine "Look of the Year" contest, held in Ljubljana, which promised its top three contestants an international modeling contract.

After attending the University of Ljubljana and leaving after her freshman year, she then worked as a model for fashion houses in Milan and Paris, before relocating to New York City in 1996, her contract and visa negotiated by Italian businessman Paolo Zampolli. Working with photographers including Helmut Newton, Patrick Demarchelier, and Mario Testino, she subsequently appeared on the covers of Harper's Bazaar (Bulgaria), Ocean Drive, In Style Weddings, New York Magazine, Avenue, Allure, Vanity Fair (Italy), Vogue (following her marriage to Donald Trump), and GQ (UK). She was featured as a bikini model in the 2000 Sports Illustrated Swimsuit Issue. As a model, she was associated with Irene Marie Management Group and Donald Trump's Trump Model Management.

In the 2000s, she appeared in an advertisement for Aflac insurance in which she and the Aflac mascot, a duck, voiced at the time by comedian Gilbert Gottfried, exchange personalities via a Frankenstein-like mad experiment.

Marriage to Donald Trump

New York City, 2006

After moving to New York City in 1996, Melania met Donald Trump at a Fashion Week party in New York City in September 1998, while he was still married to, but separated from, Marla Maples; Donald attended the event with another date, Celina

Midelfart, and Melania initially refused to give Donald her phone number. Melania broke off the relationship shortly after it began, but the couple reconciled after a few months. Their relationship gained attention after a 1999 interview on The Howard Stern Show. In 2000, Melania appeared with Donald while he campaigned for that year's Reform Party presidential nomination. Their relationship gained additional publicity after the 2004 launch of Donald's successful business-oriented reality television show, The Apprentice. Donald described their long courtship in 2005: "We literally have never had an argument, forget about the word 'fight' ... We just are very compatible. We get along."

After becoming engaged in 2004, Donald and Melania were married on January 22, 2005, at The Episcopal Church of Bethesda-by-the-Sea in Palm Beach, Florida, followed by a reception in the ballroom at Donald's Mar-a-Lago estate.

The event was attended by celebrities such as Katie Couric, Matt Lauer, Rudy Giuliani, Heidi Klum, Star Jones, P. Diddy, Shaquille O'Neal, Barbara Walters, Conrad Black, Regis Philbin, Simon Cowell, Kelly Ripa, then-Senator Hillary Clinton, and former president Bill Clinton. At the reception, Billy Joel serenaded the crowd with "Just the Way You Are" and supplied new lyrics about Trump to the tune of "The Lady Is a Tramp".

The Trumps' wedding ceremony and reception were widely covered by the media. Trump wore a $200,000 dress made by John Galliano of the house of Christian Dior. The cake at the reception was a 50-pound orange Grand Marnier chocolate truffle cake, with a Grand Marnier butter-cream filling, covered with 3,000 roses created by the chef at Mar-a-Lago.

In 2006, Melania gave birth to a son named Barron William Trump. Donald suggested his first name and Melania his middle name. As an infant, Barron reportedly occupied his own floor in the Trumps' apartment in Trump Tower in Manhattan, but often slept in a crib in his parents' bedroom. He plays golf with his father and is reported to be fluent in Slovene. He is said to like wearing a suit and tie, and Melania's nickname for him is "Mini-Donald".

2016 presidential campaign

In November 2015, when asked about her husband's presidential campaign, Mrs. Trump said, "I encouraged him because I know what he will do and what he can do for America. He loves the American people and he wants to help them." When asked by The New York Times in 1999 what her role would be if Donald Trump were to become president, Trump replied: "I would be very traditional. Like Betty Ford or Jackie Kennedy. I would support him."

An anti-Donald Trump PAC in March 2016 published an attack ad featuring a nude photo of Melania that was published in 2000 as part of a British GQ magazine photo shoot. The photograph shows her handcuffed to a briefcase, lying on a fur blanket aboard Donald Trump's private jet.

In July 2016, Trump's official web site was redirected to Trump.com. On Twitter, she stated that her site was outdated and did not "accurately reflect [her] current business and professional interests." This change came after it was widely noted by the media that the website had falsely claimed for more than 10 years that she had a degree in architecture and design from the University of Ljubljana. Her biography in the 2016 Republican National Convention official program also incorrectly stated that she had obtained a degree in Slovenia.

Speech plagiarism controversy

On July 18, 2016, Mrs. Trump gave a speech on the first day of the 2016 Republican National Convention. The speech contained a paragraph that was nearly identical to a paragraph of Michelle Obama's speech at the 2008 Democratic National Convention. When asked about the speech, Melania Trump said she wrote the speech herself "with as little help as possible". Two days later, Trump staff writer Meredith McIver took responsibility for the plagiarism and apologized for the "confusion." Accused also of several lies on her own web site, Melania disappeared completely from Trump's campaign right through the end of September!

TRUMP CHILDREN BIOS

Two divorces and three marriages seem not too surprising if you're Donald Trump, a man who admits that he's married to his business.

Settled down (maritally speaking) for now, Trump has two sons, Donald Jr. and Eric, and a daughter, Ivanka, with first wife Ivana; a college-age daughter, Tiffany, with second wife Marla Maples; and a 9-year-old son, Barron, with current wife Melania.

Having grown up in the spotlight, his three eldest children managed to find success and happiness while sidestepping the usual celebrity kid drama. Meanwhile, 21-year-old Tiffany, an aspiring pop star who was raised in LA, is attending business school on the East Coast and hitting the town with Manhattan's so-called "Rich Kids of Instagram." And young Barron is busy just being a fourth-grader.

Here's all you need to know about each of the Trump children.

DONALD JR., 38, son of Ivana

Donald Jr. is a huge outdoorsman. He hunts deer with a bow and arrow and big game.

A father of five, Donald Jr. was 12 years old when Ivana and Donald Sr. divorced. Unlike his younger siblings, he was old enough to understand what the nasty divorce headlines meant — his classmates were, too.

As a child he was extremely close to his maternal grandfather, Milos, who passed away in 1990. The two would spend a couple of weeks every summer hunting and fishing in a town outside of Prague (Ivana is Czechoslovakian). The fast-talking Donald Jr. is fluent in Czech and named one of his sons Tristan Milos, after his grandfather.

After boarding school (Pennsylvania's prestigious Hill School), he followed in his father's footsteps — as most of the Trump kids have — to The Wharton School of the University of Pennsylvania, where he earned his bachelor's degree in finance and real estate.

Donald Jr. was 12 years old when Ivana and Donald Sr. split up.

A 2004 New York magazine profile noted Donald Jr.'s propensity for drinking and getting into "do-you-have-any-idea-who-I-am? fights" in college, but he later told Forbes that his love of hunting kept him on the straight and narrow. "[While] other people I knew were getting into trouble, I was somewhere in a deer stand or going to bed early so I could be up before dawn to hunt turkeys," he said.

In 2001, a year after he graduated from college, Donald Jr. went to work for his dad for the second time. (The first time was when he was 13 and earning minimum wage plus tips as a dock attendant at Trump Castle.) Now an executive vice president at The Trump Organization, he cut his teeth with the development of Trump

Place at West Side Yards and has gone on to spearhead projects in Chicago, Las Vegas, Scotland, and India.

Vanessa Trump is a former model. The couple has three boys and two girls.

Thanks to a fix-up from his dad, he met his wife, Vanessa, at a fashion show. He caught a lot of heat for proposing to her in front of a jewelry store with a bunch of photographers standing by. The rumor-mill called it a publicity stunt and claimed he'd gotten the $100,000 ring on trade. But as the happy couple has welcomed five children in the past seven years, that news story has long since been buried.

IVANKA, 34, daughter of Ivana

Early in her career, Ivanka reportedly declined a job offer from Vogue's Anna Wintour. Reuters/Lucas Jackson

Ivanka is the breakout success of the family. The same year that she and brothers Donald Jr. and Eric founded the Trump Hotel Collections, Ivanka launched a jewelry brand that has spawned clothing, shoe, and accessories lines carried by the likes of Nordstrom, Bloomingdale's, and Zappos.

An avid runner and former runway model, Ivanka is an executive vice president of acquisitions and development for The Trump Organization. But she didn't go straight from The Wharton School to an office at Trump Tower. She worked for real estate developer Bruce Ratner for a year after college. And a 2013 Forbes profile indicates that she politely declined a job offer from Vogue's Anna Wintour.

After covering Seventeen magazine in 1997, Ivanka had a brief career as a runway model for designers like Gianni Versace and Thierry Mugler.

Specializing in deal-making and design, Ivanka joined her dad's company in 2005. She was the lead negotiator on the purchase of Trump National Doral Miami, a $1 billion property that she scooped up for $150 million.

Ivanka is stealthily private about her personal life, but before tying the knot with real estate and publishing scion Jared Kushner she was linked to Greg Hersch (now a wealth management SVP at UBS) and is said to have gone on a date with "That '70s Show" star Topher Grace.

As this book was being published, Ivanka was being sued for stealing Italian fashion shoe designs. Her clothing, like her father's, is all made overseas.

Even though they both work in real estate, Jared and Ivanka keep their work lives separate. "My mother and father worked together," she once told New York magazine.

She met her match in Kushner. The two live in a $16 million penthouse atop Trump Park Avenue with their two children, Arabella Rose and Joseph Frederick Kushner. Ivanka converted to Orthodox Judaism before her 2009 wedding and the family keeps kosher and observes the Sabbath. "From Friday to Saturday we don't do anything but hang out with one another. We don't make phone calls," she told Vogue.

ERIC, 32, son of Ivana

"I have always preferred to 'fly under the radar' in terms of recognition and celebrity," Eric said in an interview with his alma mater.

For a long time, Eric was the six-foot-five, media-shy baby of the family. He told New York magazine that his brother Donald Jr. is like his mentor and Ivanka is like his second mother. "She took me under her wing and raised me, took me shopping, tried to make me cool," he said.

Unlike his brother and sister, he chose Georgetown over Wharton and went straight to work for his father after he graduated. He has the same EVP of acquisitions and development title as his sister, but his niche is said to be in construction.

Eric and Ivanka are incredibly close, but still fiercely competitive at work.

In 2012, he proposed to his then-girlfriend of five years, Lara Yunaska, at Seven Springs, his dad's $19.5 million Westchester estate, with a ring from sister Ivanka's fine jewelry collection. Yunaska is a former personal trainer and TV producer.

The couple was married in front of 400 guests at Trump's Mar-a-Lago Club in Palm Springs, Florida. Eric's brother-in-law Jared Kushner officiated the wedding, telling Yunaska, "You are not just gaining a family, you are getting six million Twitter followers."

Eric and wife Lara's miniature beagle, Charlie, served as ring bearer at their wedding.

Eric also owns and operates Trump Winery, Virginia's largest vineyard, and has pledged nearly $28 million to the St. Jude Children's Research Hospital through his Eric Trump Foundation.

He and Lara split their time between Westchester and Manhattan, where Eric owns a three-bedroom apartment at Trump Parc East that he bought from his father in 2007 for $2 million.

Eric and his brother have been busy tweeting and re-tweeting several white supremacist statements.

Tiffany

Unlike her half-siblings, she didn't grow up playing in her father's office — nor did she spend her summers helping him fix up the grounds of Seven Springs. Tiffany was raised by mother Marla Maples outside of LA. There, she attended Calabasas' $31,205-a-year Viewpoint School

Maples has said that she raised Tiffany as a "single parent."Reuters/Jeff Christensen

In an interview with Oprah.com, Maples remarked that a then-17-year-old Tiffany was "getting to an age where she is studying business" and that soon she would "be able to look to her father to guide her."

Fast-forward to today and Tiffany is studying at the University of Pennsylvania and hoping to break into either fashion or music. Her sister Ivanka reportedly helped her snag an internship at Vogue, and in 2011 she dropped the single for her debut song, "Like a Bird."

Tiffany is friends with media mogul Peter Brant's society-party-hopping son, Harry.

Last October the bubbly California Trump celebrated her birthday bash with a pack of young socialites dubbed "The Rich Kids of Instagram." This summer she's been popping up on the Hamptons party circuit. Some of her friends are Harry Brant (son of media mogul Peter Brant), Gaia Matisse (Henri Matisse's great-great-granddaughter), and EJ Johnson (Magic Johnson's son), star of E!'s "Rich Kids of Beverly Hills" show.

She loves to travel and her father's private jet comes in handy when she wants a change of scenery. We're sure her Wikipedia page will arise and fill up fast soon.

BARRON, 10, son of Melania

"He's a great boy, he's working hard, he's starting the school thing," Donald told E! News last year.

From the way Melania describes her 9-year-old son, he may be the more like his father than any of his siblings. "He loves to build something and tear it down and build something else ... Sometimes I call him little Donald," she told Parenting.com.

The young heir is said to prefer suits to sweatpants and has an entire floor to himself at his parents' Trump Tower penthouse. Melania famously told ABC News that she slathers Barron in caviar moisturizer (from her skin care line, priced at $50-$150 per product) every night.

Barron celebrated his fourth birthday with his entire preschool class at Manhattan's Intrepid Sea-Air-Space Museum, where the kids ate a cake shaped like Donald's private jet and went on submarine and airplane tours.

Melania says he plays baseball and tennis, but has a proclivity for his dad's favorite sport: golf. His parents keep him out of the public eye as much as possible, but he regularly attends the Trump Invitational Grand Prix at Mar-a-Lago and, when he was younger, Melania always took him to the Upper East Side's hottest children's social of the year, the Memorial-Sloan Kettering Bunny Hop.

TRUMP ANNOUNCES CANDIDACY June 16, 2015 at Trump Tower in New York City

Wow. Whoa. That is some group of people. Thousands.

So nice, thank you very much. That's really nice. Thank you. It's great to be at Trump Tower. It's great to be in a wonderful city, New York. And it's an honor to have everybody here. This is beyond anybody's expectations. There's been no crowd like this.

And, I can tell, some of the candidates, they went in. They didn't know the air-conditioner didn't work. They sweated like dogs.

They didn't know the room was too big, because they didn't have anybody there. How are they going to beat ISIS? I don't think it's gonna happen.

Our country is in serious trouble. We don't have victories anymore. We used to have victories, but we don't have them. When was the last time anybody saw us beating, let's say, China in a trade deal? They kill us. I beat China all the time. All the time.

When did we beat Japan at anything? They send their cars over by the millions, and what do we do? When was the last time you saw a Chevrolet in Tokyo? It doesn't exist, folks. They beat us all the time.

When do we beat Mexico at the border? They're laughing at us, at our stupidity. And now they are beating us economically. They are not our friend, believe me. But they're killing us economically.

The U.S. has become a dumping ground for everybody else's problems.

Thank you. It's true, and these are the best and the finest. When Mexico sends its people, they're not sending their best. They're not sending you. They're not sending you. They're sending people that have lots of problems, and they're bringing those problems with us. They're bringing drugs. They're bringing crime. They're rapists. And some, I assume, are good people.

But I speak to border guards and they tell us what we're getting. And it only makes common sense. It only makes common sense. They're sending us not the right people.

It's coming from more than Mexico. It's coming from all over South and Latin America, and it's coming probably— probably— from the Middle East. But we don't know. Because we have no protection and we have no competence, we don't know what's happening. And it's got to stop and it's got to stop fast.

Islamic terrorism is eating up large portions of the Middle East. They've become rich. I'm in competition with them.

They just built a hotel in Syria. Can you believe this? They built a hotel. When I have to build a hotel, I pay interest. They don't have to pay interest, because they took the oil that, when we left Iraq, I said we should've taken.

So now ISIS has the oil, and what they don't have, Iran has. And in 19— and I will tell you this, and I said it very strongly, years ago, I said— and I love the military, and I want to have the strongest military that we've ever had, and we need it more now than ever. But I said, "Don't hit Iraq," because you're going to totally destabilize the Middle East. Iran is going to take over the Middle East, Iran and somebody else will get the oil, and it turned out that Iran is now taking over Iraq. Think of it. Iran is taking over Iraq, and they're taking it over big league.

We spent $2 trillion in Iraq, $2 trillion. We lost thousands of lives, thousands in Iraq. We have wounded soldiers, who I love, I love — they're great — all over the place, thousands and thousands of wounded soldiers.

And we have nothing. We can't even go there. We have nothing. And every time we give Iraq equipment, the first time a bullet goes off in the air, they leave it.

Last week, I read 2,300 Humvees— these are big vehicles— were left behind for the enemy. 2,000? You would say maybe two, maybe four? 2,300 sophisticated vehicles, they ran, and the enemy took them.

Last quarter, it was just announced our gross domestic product— a sign of strength, right? But not for us. It was below zero. Whoever heard of this? It's never below zero.

Our labor participation rate was the worst since 1978. But think of it, GDP below zero, horrible labor participation rate.

And our real unemployment is anywhere from 18 to 20 percent. Don't believe the 5.6. Don't believe it.

That's right. A lot of people up there can't get jobs. They can't get jobs, because there are no jobs, because China has our jobs and Mexico has our jobs. They all have jobs.

But the real number, the real number is anywhere from 18 to 19 and maybe even 21 percent, and nobody talks about it, because it's a statistic that's full of nonsense.

Our enemies are getting stronger and stronger by the way, and we as a country are getting weaker. Even our nuclear arsenal doesn't work.

It came out recently they have equipment that is 30 years old. They don't know if it worked. And I thought it was horrible when it was broadcast on television, because boy, does that send signals to Putin and all of the other people that look at us and they say, "That is a group of people, and that is a nation that truly has no clue. They don't know what they're doing. They don't know what they're doing."

We have a disaster called the big lie: Obamacare. Obamacare.

Yesterday, it came out that costs are going for people up 29, 39, 49, and even 55 percent, and deductibles are through the roof. You have to be hit by a tractor, literally, a tractor, to use it, because the deductibles are so high, it's virtually useless. It's virtually useless. It is a disaster.

And remember the $5 billion website? $5 billion we spent on a website, and to this day it doesn't work. A $5 billion website.

I have so many websites, I have them all over the place. I hire people, they do a website. It costs me $3. $5 billion website.

Well, you need somebody, because politicians are all talk, no action. Nothing's gonna get done. They will not bring us— believe me— to the promised land. They will not.

As an example, I've been on the circuit making speeches, and I hear my fellow Republicans. And they're wonderful people. I like them. They all want me to support them. They don't know how to bring it about. They come up to my office. I'm meeting with three of them in the next week. And they don't know— "Are you running? Are you not running? Could we have your support? What do we do? How do we do it?"

I like them. And I hear their speeches. And they don't talk jobs and they don't talk China. When was the last time you heard China is killing us? They're devaluing their currency to a level that you wouldn't believe. It makes it impossible for our companies to compete, impossible. They're killing us.

But you don't hear that from anybody else. You don't hear it from anybody else. And I watch the speeches.

I watch the speeches of these people, and they say the sun will rise, the moon will set, all sorts of wonderful things will happen. And people are saying, "What's going on? I just want a job. Just get me a job. I don't need the rhetoric. I want a job."

And that's what's happening. And it's going to get worse, because remember, Obamacare really kicks in in '16, 2016. Obama is going to be out playing golf. He might be on one of my courses. I would invite him, I actually would say. I have the best courses in the world, so I'd say, you what, if he wants to— I have one right next to the White House, right on the Potomac. If he'd like to play, that's fine.

In fact, I'd love him to leave early and play, that would be a very good thing.

But Obamacare kicks in in 2016. Really big league. It is going to be amazingly destructive. Doctors are quitting. I have a friend who's a doctor, and he said to me the other day, "Donald, I never saw anything like it. I have more accountants than I have nurses. It's a disaster. My patients are beside themselves. They had a plan that was good. They have no plan now."

We have to repeal Obamacare, and it can be— and— and it can be replaced with something much better for everybody. Let it be for everybody. But much better and much less expensive for people and for the government. And we can do it.

So I've watched the politicians. I've dealt with them all my life. If you can't make a good deal with a politician, then there's something wrong with you. You're certainly not very good. And that's what we have representing us. They will never make America great again. They don't even have a chance. They're controlled fully— they're controlled fully by the lobbyists, by the donors, and by the special interests, fully.

Yes, they control them. Hey, I have lobbyists. I have to tell you. I have lobbyists that can produce anything for me. They're great. But you know what? it won't happen. It won't happen. Because we have to stop doing things for some people, but for this country, it's destroying our country. We have to stop, and it has to stop now.

Now, our country needs— our country needs a truly great leader, and we need a truly great leader now. We need a leader that wrote "The Art of the Deal."

We need a leader that can bring back our jobs, can bring back our manufacturing, can bring back our military, can take care of our vets. Our vets have been abandoned.

And we also need a cheerleader.

You know, when President Obama was elected, I said, "Well, the one thing, I think he'll do well. I think he'll be a great cheerleader for the country. I think he'd be a great spirit."

He was vibrant. He was young. I really thought that he would be a great cheerleader.

He's not a leader. That's true. You're right about that.

But he wasn't a cheerleader. He's actually a negative force. He's been a negative force. He wasn't a cheerleader; he was the opposite.

We need somebody that can take the brand of the United States and make it great again. It's not great again.

We need— we need somebody— we need somebody that literally will take this country and make it great again. We can do that.

And, I will tell you, I love my life. I have a wonderful family. They're saying, "Dad, you're going to do something that's going to be so tough."

You know, all of my life, I've heard that a truly successful person, a really, really successful person and even modestly successful cannot run for public office. Just can't happen. And yet that's the kind of mindset that you need to make this country great again.

So ladies and gentlemen...I am officially running... for president of the United States, and we are going to make our country great again.

It can happen. Our country has tremendous potential. We have tremendous people.

We have people that aren't working. We have people that have no incentive to work. But they're going to have incentive to work, because the greatest social program is a job. And they'll be proud, and they'll love it, and they'll make much more than they would've ever made, and they'll be— they'll be doing so well, and we're going to be thriving as a country, thriving. It can happen.

I will be the greatest jobs president that God ever created. I tell you that.

I'll bring back our jobs from China, from Mexico, from Japan, from so many places. I'll bring back our jobs, and I'll bring back our money.

Right now, think of this: We owe China $1.3 trillion. We owe Japan more than that. So they come in, they take our jobs, they take our money, and then they loan us back the money, and we pay them in interest, and then the dollar goes up so their deal's even better.

How stupid are our leaders? How stupid are these politicians to allow this to happen? How stupid are they?

I'm going to tell you— thank you. I'm going to tell you a couple of stories about trade, because I'm totally against the trade bill for a number of reasons.

Number one, the people negotiating don't have a clue. Our president doesn't have a clue. He's a bad negotiator.

He's the one that did Bergdahl. We get Bergdahl, they get five killer terrorists that everybody wanted over there.

We get Bergdahl. We get a traitor. We get a no-good traitor, and they get the five people that they wanted for years, and those people are now back on the battlefield trying to kill us. That's the negotiator we have.

Take a look at the deal he's making with Iran. He makes that deal, Israel maybe won't exist very long. It's a disaster, and we have to protect Israel. But...

So we need people— I'm a free trader. But the problem with free trade is you need really talented people to negotiate for you. If you don't have talented people, if you don't have great leadership, if you don't have people that know business, not just a political hack that got the job because he made a contribution to a campaign, which is the way all jobs, just about, are gotten, free trade terrible.

Free trade can be wonderful if you have smart people, but we have people that are stupid. We have people that aren't smart. And we have people that are controlled by special interests. And it's just not going to work.

So, here's a couple of stories happened recently. A friend of mine is a great manufacturer. And, you know, China comes over and they dump all their stuff, and I buy it. I buy it, because, frankly, I have an obligation to buy it, because they devalue their currency so brilliantly, they just did it recently, and nobody thought they could do it again.

But with all our problems with Russia, with all our problems with everything— everything, they got away with it again. And it's impossible for our people here to compete.

So I want to tell you this story. A friend of mine who's a great manufacturer, calls me up a few weeks ago. He's very upset. I said, "What's your problem?"

He said, "You know, I make great product."

And I said, "I know. I know that because I buy the product."

He said, "I can't get it into China. They won't accept it. I sent a boat over and they actually sent it back. They talked about environmental, they talked about all sorts of crap that had nothing to do with it."

I said, "Oh, wait a minute, that's terrible. Does anyone know this?"

He said, "Yeah, they do it all the time with other people."

I said, "They send it back?"

"Yeah. So I finally got it over there and they charged me a big tariff. They're not supposed to be doing that. I told them."

Now, they do charge you tariff on trucks, when we send trucks and other things over there.

Ask Boeing. They wanted Boeing's secrets. They wanted their patents and all their secrets before they agreed to buy planes from Boeing.

Hey, I'm not saying they're stupid. I like China. I sell apartments for— I just sold an apartment for $15 million to somebody from China. Am I supposed to dislike them? I own a big chunk of the Bank of America Building at 1290 Avenue of the Americas, that I got from China in a war. Very valuable.

I love China. The biggest bank in the world is from China. You know where their United States headquarters is located? In this building, in Trump Tower. I love China. People say, "Oh, you don't like China?"

No, I love them. But their leaders are much smarter than our leaders, and we can't sustain ourself with that. There's too much— it's like— it's like take the New England Patriots and Tom Brady and have them play your high school football team. That's the difference between China's leaders and our leaders.

They are ripping us. We are rebuilding China. We're rebuilding many countries. China, you go there now, roads, bridges, schools, you never saw anything like it. They have bridges that make the George Washington Bridge look like small potatoes. And they're all over the place.

We have all the cards, but we don't know how to use them. We don't even know that we have the cards, because our leaders don't understand the game. We could turn off that spigot by charging them tax until they behave properly.

Now they're going militarily. They're building a military island in the middle of the South China sea. A military island. Now, our country could never do that because we'd have to get environmental clearance, and the environmentalist wouldn't let our country— we would never build in an ocean. They built it in about one year, this massive military port.

They're building up their military to a point that is very scary. You have a problem with ISIS. You have a bigger problem with China.

And, in my opinion, the new China, believe it or not, in terms of trade, is Mexico.

So this man tells me about the manufacturing. I say, "That's a terrible story. I hate to hear it."

But I have another one, Ford.

So Mexico takes a company, a car company that was going to build in Tennessee, rips it out. Everybody thought the deal was dead. Reported it in the Wall Street Journal recently. Everybody thought it was a done deal. It's going in and that's going to be it, going into Tennessee. Great state, great people.

All of a sudden, at the last moment, this big car manufacturer, foreign, announces they're not going to Tennessee. They're gonna spend their $1 billion in Mexico instead. Not good.

Now, Ford announces a few weeks ago that Ford is going to build a $2.5 billion car and truck and parts manufacturing plant in Mexico. $2.5 billion, it's going to be one of the largest in the world. Ford. Good company.

So I announced that I'm running for president. I would...

... one of the early things I would do, probably before I even got in— and I wouldn't even use— you know, I have— I know the smartest negotiators in the world. I know the good ones. I know the bad ones. I know the overrated ones.

You get a lot of them that are overrated. They're not good. They think they are. They get good stories, because the newspapers get buffaloed. But they're not good.

But I know the negotiators in the world, and I put them one for each country. Believe me, folks. We will do very, very well, very, very well.

But I wouldn't even waste my time with this one. I would call up the head of Ford, who I know. If I was president, I'd say, "Congratulations. I understand that you're building a nice $2.5 billion car factory in Mexico and that you're going to take your cars and sell them to the United States zero tax, just flow them across the border."

And you say to yourself, "How does that help us," right? "How does that help us? Where is that good"? It's not.

So I would say, "Congratulations. That's the good news. Let me give you the bad news. Every car and every truck and every part manufactured in this plant that comes across the border, we're going to charge you a 35-percent tax, and that tax is going to be paid simultaneously with the transaction, and that's it.

Now, here's what is going to happen. If it's not me in the position, it's one of these politicians that we're running against, you know, the 400 people that we're (inaudible). And here's what's going to happen. They're not so stupid. They know it's not a good thing, and they may even be upset by it. But then they're going to get a call from the donors or probably from the lobbyist for Ford and say, "You can't do that to Ford, because Ford takes care of me and I take care of you, and you can't do that to Ford."

And guess what? No problem. They're going to build in Mexico. They're going to take away thousands of jobs. It's very bad for us.

So under President Trump, here's what would happen:

The head of Ford will call me back, I would say within an hour after I told them the bad news. But it could be he'd want to be cool, and he'll wait until the next day. You know, they want to be a little cool.

And he'll say, "Please, please, please." He'll beg for a little while, and I'll say, "No interest." Then he'll call all sorts of political people, and I'll say, "Sorry, fellas. No interest," because I don't need anybody's money. It's nice. I don't need anybody's money.

I'm using my own money. I'm not using the lobbyists. I'm not using donors. I don't care. I'm really rich. I (inaudible).

And by the way, I'm not even saying that's the kind of mindset, that's the kind of thinking you need for this country.

So— because we got to make the country rich.

It sounds crass. Somebody said, "Oh, that's crass." It's not crass.

We got $18 trillion in debt. We got nothing but problems.

We got a military that needs equipment all over the place. We got nuclear weapons that are obsolete.

We've got nothing. We've got Social Security that's going to be destroyed if somebody like me doesn't bring money into the country. All these other people want to cut the hell out of it. I'm not going to cut it at all; I'm going to bring money in, and we're going to save it.

But here's what's going to happen:

After I'm called by 30 friends of mine who contributed to different campaigns, after I'm called by all of the special interests and by the— the donors and by the lobbyists— and they have zero chance at convincing me, zero— I'll get a call the next day from the head of Ford. He'll say. "Please reconsider," I'll say no.

He'll say, "Mr. President, we've decided to move the plant back to the United States, and we're not going to build it in Mexico." That's it. They have no choice. They have no choice.

There are hundreds of things like that. I'll give you another example.

Saudi Arabia, they make $1 billion a day. $1 billion a day. I love the Saudis. Many are in this building. They make a billion dollars a day. Whenever they have problems, we send over the ships. We say "we're gonna protect." What are we doing? They've got nothing but money.

If the right person asked them, they'd pay a fortune. They wouldn't be there except for us.

And believe me, you look at the border with Yemen. You remember Obama a year ago, Yemen was a great victory. Two weeks later, the place was blown up. Everybody got out— and they kept our equipment.

They always keep our equipment. We ought to send used equipment, right? They always keep our equipment. We ought to send some real junk, because, frankly, it would be— we ought to send our surplus. We're always losing this gorgeous brand-new stuff.

But look at that border with Saudi Arabia. Do you really think that these people are interested in Yemen? Saudi Arabia without us is gone. They're gone.

And I'm the one that made all of the right predictions about Iraq. You know, all of these politicians that I'm running against now— it's so nice to say I'm running as opposed to if I run, if I run. I'm running.

But all of these politicians that I'm running against now, they're trying to disassociate. I mean, you looked at Bush, it took him five days to answer the question on Iraq. He couldn't answer the question. He didn't know. I said, "Is he intelligent?"

Then I looked at Rubio. He was unable to answer the question, is Iraq a good thing or bad thing? He didn't know. He couldn't answer the question.

How are these people gonna lead us? How are we gonna— how are we gonna go back and make it great again? We can't. They don't have a clue. They can't lead us. They can't. They can't even answer simple questions. It was terrible.

But Saudi Arabia is in big, big trouble. Now, thanks to fracking and other things, the oil is all over the place. And I used to say it, there are ships at sea, and this was during the worst crisis, that were loaded up with oil, and the cartel kept the price up, because, again, they were smarter than our leaders. They were smarter than our leaders.

There is so much wealth out there that can make our country so rich again, and therefore make it great again. Because we need money. We're dying. We're dying. We need money. We have to do it. And we need the right people.

So Ford will come back. They'll all come back. And I will say this, this is going to be an election, in my opinion, that's based on competence.

Somebody said — thank you, darlin'.

Somebody said to me the other day, a reporter, a very nice reporter, "But, Mr. Trump, you're not a nice person."

That's true. But actually I am. I think I am a nice person. People that know me, like me. Does my family like me? I think so, right. Look at my family. I'm proud of my family.

By the way, speaking of my family, Melania, Barron, Kai, Donnie, Don, Vanessa, Tiffany, Evanka did a great job. Did she do a great job?

Great. Jared, Laura and Eric, I'm very proud of my family. They're a great family.

So the reporter said to me the other day, "But, Mr. Trump, you're not a nice person. How can you get people to vote for you?"

I said, "I don't know." I said, "I think that number one, I am a nice person. I give a lot of money away to charities and other things. I think I'm actually a very nice person."

But, I said, "This is going to be an election that's based on competence, because people are tired of these nice people. And they're tired of being ripped off by everybody in the world. And they're tired of spending more money on education than any nation in the world per capita, than any nation in the world, and we are 26th in the world, 25 countries are better than us in education. And some of them are like third world countries. But we're becoming a third word country, because of our infrastructure, our airports, our roads, everything. So one of the things I did, and I said, you know what I'll do. I'll do it. Because a lot of people said, "He'll never run. Number one, he won't want to give up his lifestyle."

They're right about that, but I'm doing it.

Number two, I'm a private company, so nobody knows what I'm worth. And the one thing is that when you run, you have to announce and certify to all sorts of governmental authorities your net worth.

So I said, "That's OK." I'm proud of my net worth. I've done an amazing job.

I started off— thank you— I started off in a small office with my father in Brooklyn and Queens, and my father said — and I love my father. I learned so much. He was a great negotiator. I learned so much just sitting at his feet playing with blocks listening to him negotiate with subcontractors. But I learned a lot.

But he used to say, "Donald, don't go into Manhattan. That's the big leagues. We don't know anything about that. Don't do it."

I said, "I gotta go into Manhattan. I gotta build those big buildings. I gotta do it, Dad. I've gotta do it."

And after four or five years in Brooklyn, I ventured into Manhattan and did a lot of great deals— the Grand Hyatt Hotel. I was responsible for the convention center on the west side. I did a lot of great deals, and I did them early and young. And now I'm building all over the world, and I love what I'm doing.

But they all said, a lot of the pundits on television, "Well, Donald will never run, and one of the main reasons is he's private and he's probably not as successful as everybody thinks."

So I said to myself, you know, nobody's ever going to know unless I run, because I'm really proud of my success. I really am.

I've employed— I've employed tens of thousands of people over my lifetime. That means medical. That means education. That means everything.

So a large accounting firm and my accountants have been working for months, because it's big and complex, and they've put together a statement, a financial statement, just a summary. But everything will be filed eventually with the government, and we don't [use] extensions or anything. We'll be filing it right on time. We don't need anything.

And it was even reported incorrectly yesterday, because they said, "He had assets of $9 billion." So I said, "No, that's the wrong number. That's the wrong number. Not assets."

So they put together this. And before I say it, I have to say this. I made it the old-fashioned way. It's real estate. You know, it's real estate.

It's labor, and it's unions good and some bad and lots of people that aren't in unions, and it's all over the place and building all over the world.

And I have assets— big accounting firm, one of the most highly respected— 9 billion 240 million dollars.

And I have liabilities of about $500 million. That's long-term debt, very low interest rates.

In fact, one of the big banks came to me and said, "Donald, you don't have enough borrowings. Could we loan you $4 billion"? I said, "I don't need it. I don't want it. And I've been there. I don't want it."

But in two seconds, they give me whatever I wanted. So I have a total net worth, and now with the increase, it'll be well-over $10 billion. But here, a total net worth of—net worth, not assets, not— a net worth, after all debt, after all expenses, the greatest assets— Trump Tower, 1290 Avenue of the Americas, Bank of America building in San Francisco, 40 Wall Street, sometimes referred to as the Trump building right opposite the New York— many other places all over the world.

So the total is $8,737,540,00.

Now I'm not doing that...

I'm not doing that to brag, because you know what? I don't have to brag. I don't have to, believe it or not.

I'm doing that to say that that's the kind of thinking our country needs. We need that thinking. We have the opposite thinking.

We have losers. We have losers. We have people that don't have it. We have people that are morally corrupt. We have people that are selling this country down the drain.

So I put together this statement, and the only reason I'm telling you about it today is because we really do have to get going, because if we have another three or four years— you know, we're at $8 trillion now. We're soon going to be at $20 trillion.

According to the economists— who I'm not big believers in, but, nevertheless, this is what they're saying— that $24 trillion— we're very close— that's the point of no return. $24 trillion. We will be there soon. That's when we become Greece. That's when we become a country that's unsalvageable. And we're gonna be there very soon. We're gonna be there very soon.

So, just to sum up, I would do various things very quickly. I would repeal and replace the big lie, Obamacare.

I would build a great wall, and nobody builds walls better than me, believe me, and I'll build them very inexpensively, I will build a great, great wall on our southern border. And I will have Mexico pay for that wall.

Mark my words.

Nobody would be tougher on ISIS than Donald Trump. Nobody.

I will find — within our military, I will find the General Patton or I will find General MacArthur, I will find the right guy. I will find the guy that's going to take that military and make it really work. Nobody, nobody will be pushing us around.

I will stop Iran from getting nuclear weapons. And we won't be using a man like Secretary Kerry that has absolutely no concept of negotiation, who's making a horrible and laughable deal, who's just being tapped along as they make weapons right now, and then goes into a bicycle race at 72 years old, and falls and breaks his leg. I won't be doing that. And I promise I will never be in a bicycle race. That I can tell you.

I will immediately terminate President Obama's illegal executive order on immigration, immediately.

Fully support and back up the Second Amendment.

Now, it's very interesting. Today I heard it. Through stupidity, in a very, very hard core prison, interestingly named Clinton, two vicious murderers, two vicious people escaped, and nobody knows where they are. And a woman was on television this morning, and she said, "You know, Mr. Trump," and she was telling other people, and I actually called her, and she said, "You know, Mr. Trump, I always was against guns. I didn't want guns. And now since this happened"— it's up in the prison area— "my husband and I are finally in agreement, because he wanted the guns. We now have a gun on every table. We're ready to start shooting."

I said, "Very interesting."

So protect the Second Amendment.

End— end Common Core. Common Core should— it is a disaster. Bush is totally in favor of Common Core. I don't see how he can possibly get the nomination. He's weak on immigration. He's in favor of Common Core. How the hell can you vote for this guy? You just can't do it. We have to end education has to be local.

Rebuild the country's infrastructure.

Nobody can do that like me. Believe me. It will be done on time, on budget, way below cost, way below what anyone ever thought.

I look at the roads being built all over the country, and I say I can build those things for one-third. What they do is unbelievable, how bad.

You know, we're building on Pennsylvania Avenue, the Old Post Office, we're converting it into one of the world's great hotels. It's gonna be the best hotel in Washington, D.C. We got it from the General Services Administration in Washington. The Obama administration. We got it. It was the most highly sought after— or one of them, but I think the most highly sought after project in the history of General Services. We got it. People were shocked, Trump got it.

Well, I got it for two reasons. Number one, we're really good. Number two, we had a really good plan. And I'll add in the third, we had a great financial statement. Because the General Services, who are terrific people, by the way, and talented people, they wanted to do a great job. And they wanted to make sure it got built.

So we have to rebuild our infrastructure, our bridges, our roadways, our airports. You come into La Guardia Airport, it's like we're in a third world country. You look at the patches and the 40-year-old floor. They throw down asphalt, and they throw.

You look at these airports, we are like a third world country. And I come in from China and I come in from Qatar and I come in from different places, and they have the most incredible airports in the world. You come to back to this country and you have LAX, disaster. You have all of these disastrous airports. We have to rebuild our infrastructure.

Save Medicare, Medicaid and Social Security without cuts. Have to do it.

Get rid of the fraud. Get rid of the waste and abuse, but save it. People have been paying it for years. And now many of these candidates want to cut it. You save it by making the United States, by making us rich again, by taking back all of the money that's being lost.

Renegotiate our foreign trade deals.

Reduce our $18 trillion in debt, because, believe me, we're in a bubble. We have artificially low interest rates. We have a stock market that, frankly, has been good to me, but I still hate to see what's happening. We have a stock market that is so bloated.

Be careful of a bubble because what you've seen in the past might be small potatoes compared to what happens. So be very, very careful.

And strengthen our military and take care of our vets. So, so important.

Sadly, the American dream is dead.

But if I get elected president I will bring it back bigger and better and stronger than ever before, and we will make America great again.

Thank you. Thank you very much.

"I know words. I have the best words."

Donald Trump

Donald Trump 2016 RNC Acceptance speech

Friends, delegates and fellow Americans: I humbly and gratefully accept your nomination for the presidency of the United States.

Together, we will lead our party back to the White House, and we will lead our country back to safety, prosperity, and peace. We will be a country of generosity and warmth. But we will also be a country of law and order.

Our Convention occurs at a moment of crisis for our nation. The attacks on our police, and the terrorism in our cities, threaten our very way of life. Any politician who does not grasp this danger is not fit to lead our country.

Americans watching this address tonight have seen the recent images of violence in our streets and the chaos in our communities. Many have witnessed this violence personally, some have even been its victims.

I have a message for all of you: the crime and violence that today afflicts our nation will soon come to an end. Beginning on January 20th 2017, safety will be restored.

The most basic duty of government is to defend the lives of its own citizens. Any government that fails to do so is a government unworthy to lead.

It is finally time for a straightforward assessment of the state of our nation.

I will present the facts plainly and honestly. We cannot afford to be so politically correct anymore.

So if you want to hear the corporate spin, the carefully-crafted lies, and the media myths the Democrats are holding their convention next week.

But here, at our convention, there will be no lies. We will honor the American people with the truth, and nothing else.

These are the facts:

Decades of progress made in bringing down crime are now being reversed by this Administration's rollback of criminal enforcement.

Homicides last year increased by 17% in America's fifty largest cities. That's the largest increase in 25 years. In our nation's capital, killings have risen by 50 percent. They are up nearly 60% in nearby Baltimore.

In the President's hometown of Chicago, more than 2,000 have been the victims of shootings this year alone. And more than 3,600 have been killed in the Chicago area since he took office.

The number of police officers killed in the line of duty has risen by almost 50% compared to this point last year. Nearly 180,000 illegal immigrants with criminal records, ordered deported from our country, are tonight roaming free to threaten peaceful citizens.

The number of new illegal immigrant families who have crossed the border so far this year already exceeds the entire total from 2015. They are being released by the tens of thousands into our communities with no regard for the impact on public safety or resources.

One such border-crosser was released and made his way to Nebraska. There, he ended the life of an innocent young girl named Sarah Root. She was 21 years-old, and was killed the day after graduating from college with a 4.0 Grade Point Average. Her killer was then released a second time, and he is now a fugitive from the law.

I've met Sarah's beautiful family. But to this Administration, their amazing daughter was just one more American life that wasn't worth protecting. One more child to sacrifice on the altar of open borders. What about our economy?

Again, I will tell you the plain facts that have been edited out of your nightly news and your morning newspaper: Nearly Four in 10 African-American children are living in poverty, while 58% of African American youth are not employed. 2 million more Latinos are in poverty today than when the President took his oath of office less than eight years ago. Another 14 million people have left the workforce entirely.

Household incomes are down more than $4,000 since the year 2000. Our manufacturing trade deficit has reached an all-time high – nearly $800 billion in a single year. The budget is no better.

President Obama has doubled our national debt to more than $19 trillion, and growing. Yet, what do we have to show for it? Our roads and bridges are falling apart, our airports are in Third World condition, and forty-three million Americans are on food stamps.

Now let us consider the state of affairs abroad.

Not only have our citizens endured domestic disaster, but they have lived through one international humiliation after another. We all remember the images of our sailors being forced to their knees by their Iranian captors at gunpoint.

This was just prior to the signing of the Iran deal, which gave back to Iran $150 billion and gave us nothing – it will go down in history as one of the worst deals ever made. Another humiliation came when president Obama drew a red line in Syria – and the whole world knew it meant nothing.

In Libya, our consulate – the symbol of American prestige around the globe – was brought down in flames. America is far less safe – and the world is far less stable – than when Obama made the decision to put Hillary Clinton in charge of America's foreign policy.

I am certain it is a decision he truly regrets. Her bad instincts and her bad judgment – something pointed out by Bernie Sanders – are what caused the disasters unfolding today. Let's review the record. In 2009, pre-Hillary, ISIS was not even on the map.

Libya was cooperating. Egypt was peaceful. Iraq was seeing a reduction in violence. Iran was being choked by sanctions. Syria was under control. After four years of Hillary Clinton, what do we have? ISIS has spread across the region, and the world. Libya is in ruins, and our Ambassador and his staff were left helpless to die at the hands of savage killers. Egypt was turned over to the radical Muslim brotherhood, forcing the military to retake control. Iraq is in chaos.

Iran is on the path to nuclear weapons. Syria is engulfed in a civil war and a refugee crisis that now threatens the West. After fifteen years of wars in the Middle East, after trillions of dollars spent and thousands of lives lost, the situation is worse than it has ever been before.

This is the legacy of Hillary Clinton: death, destruction and weakness.

But Hillary Clinton's legacy does not have to be America's legacy. The problems we face now – poverty and violence at home, war and destruction abroad – will last only as long as we continue relying on the same politicians who created them. A change in leadership is required to change these outcomes. Tonight, I will share with you my plan of action for America.

The most important difference between our plan and that of our opponents, is that our plan will put America First. Americanism, not globalism, will be our credo. As long as we are led by politicians who will not put America First, then we can be assured that other nations will not treat America with respect. This will all change in 2017.

The American People will come first once again. My plan will begin with safety at home – which means safe neighborhoods, secure borders, and protection from terrorism. There can be no prosperity without law and order. On the economy, I will outline reforms to add millions of new jobs and trillions in new wealth that can be used to rebuild America.

A number of these reforms that I will outline tonight will be opposed by some of our nation's most powerful special interests. That is because these interests have rigged our political and economic system for their exclusive benefit.

Big business, elite media and major donors are lining up behind the campaign of my opponent because they know she will keep our rigged system in place. They are throwing money at her because they have total control over everything she does. She is their puppet, and they pull the strings.

That is why Hillary Clinton's message is that things will never change. My message is that things have to change – and they have to change right now. Every day I wake up determined to deliver for the people I have met all across this nation that have been neglected, ignored, and abandoned.

I have visited the laid-off factory workers, and the communities crushed by our horrible and unfair trade deals. These are the forgotten men and women of our country. People who work hard but no longer have a voice.

I AM YOUR VOICE.

I have embraced crying mothers who have lost their children because our politicians put their personal agendas before the national good. I have no patience for injustice, no tolerance for government incompetence, no sympathy for leaders who fail their citizens.

When innocent people suffer, because our political system lacks the will, or the courage, or the basic decency to enforce our laws – or worse still, has sold out to some corporate lobbyist for cash – I am not able to look the other way.

And when a Secretary of State illegally stores her emails on a private server, deletes 33,000 of them so the authorities can't see her crime, puts our country at risk, lies about it in every different form and faces no consequence – I know that corruption has reached a level like never before.

When the FBI Director says that the Secretary of State was "extremely careless" and "negligent," in handling our classified secrets, I also know that these terms are minor compared to what she actually did. They were just used to save her from facing justice for her terrible crimes.

In fact, her single greatest accomplishment may be committing such an egregious crime and getting away with it – especially when others have paid so dearly. When that same Secretary of State rakes in millions of dollars trading access and favors to special interests and foreign powers I know the time for action has come.

I have joined the political arena so that the powerful can no longer beat up on people that cannot defend themselves. Nobody knows the system better than me, which is why I alone can fix it. I have seen firsthand how the system is rigged against our citizens, just like it was rigged against Bernie Sanders – he never had a chance.

But his supporters will join our movement, because we will fix his biggest issue: trade. Millions of Democrats will join our movement because we are going to fix the system so it works for all Americans. In this cause, I am proud to have at my side the next Vice President of the United States: Governor Mike Pence of Indiana.

We will bring the same economic success to America that Mike brought to Indiana. He is a man of character and accomplishment. He is the right man for the job. The first task for our new Administration will be to liberate our citizens from the crime and terrorism and lawlessness that threatens their communities.

America was shocked to its core when our police officers in Dallas were brutally executed. In the days after Dallas, we have seen continued threats and violence against our law enforcement officials. Law officers have been shot or killed in recent days in Georgia, Missouri, Wisconsin, Kansas, Michigan and Tennessee.

On Sunday, more police were gunned down in Baton Rouge, Louisiana. Three were killed, and four were badly injured. An attack on law enforcement is an attack on all Americans. I have a message to every last person threatening the peace on our streets and the safety of our police: when I take the oath of office next year, I will restore law and order our country.

I will work with, and appoint, the best prosecutors and law enforcement officials in the country to get the job done. In this race for the White House, I am the Law And Order candidate. The irresponsible rhetoric of our President, who has used the pulpit of the presidency to divide us by race and color, has made America a more dangerous environment for everyone.

This Administration has failed America's inner cities. It's failed them on education. It's failed them on jobs. It's failed them on crime. It's failed them at every level.

When I am President, I will work to ensure that all of our kids are treated equally, and protected equally.

Every action I take, I will ask myself: does this make life better for young Americans in Baltimore, Chicago, Detroit, Ferguson who have as much of a right to live out their dreams as any other child America?

To make life safe in America, we must also address the growing threats we face from outside America: we are going to defeat the barbarians of ISIS. Once again, France is the victim of brutal Islamic terrorism.

Men, women and children viciously mowed down. Lives ruined. Families ripped apart. A nation in mourning.

The damage and devastation that can be inflicted by Islamic radicals has been over and over – at the World Trade Center, at an office party in San Bernardino, at the Boston Marathon, and a military recruiting center in Chattanooga, Tennessee.

Only weeks ago, in Orlando, Florida, 49 wonderful Americans were savagely murdered by an Islamic terrorist. This time, the terrorist targeted our LGBT community. As your President, I will do everything in my power to protect our LGBT citizens from the violence and oppression of a hateful foreign ideology. To protect us from terrorism, we need to focus on three things.

We must have the best intelligence gathering operation in the world. We must abandon the failed policy of nation building and regime change that Hillary Clinton pushed in Iraq, Libya, Egypt and Syria. Instead, we must work with all of our allies who share our goal of destroying ISIS and stamping out Islamic terror.

This includes working with our greatest ally in the region, the State of Israel. Lastly, we must immediately suspend immigration from any nation that has been compromised by terrorism until such time as proven vetting mechanisms have been put in place.

My opponent has called for a radical 550% increase in Syrian refugees on top of existing massive refugee flows coming into our country under President Obama. She proposes this despite the fact that there's no way to screen these refugees in order to find out who they are or where they come from. I only want to admit individuals into our country who will support our values and love our people.

Anyone who endorses violence, hatred or oppression is not welcome in our country and never will be.

Decades of record immigration have produced lower wages and higher unemployment for our citizens, especially for African-American and Latino workers. We are going to have an immigration system that works, but one that works for the American people.

On Monday, we heard from three parents whose children were killed by illegal immigrants Mary Ann Mendoza, Sabine Durden, and Jamiel Shaw. They are just three brave representatives of many thousands. Of all my travels in this country, nothing has affected me more deeply than the time I have spent with the mothers and fathers who have lost their children to violence spilling across our border.

These families have no special interests to represent them. There are no demonstrators to protest on their behalf. My opponent will never meet with them, or share in their pain. Instead, my opponent wants Sanctuary Cities. But where was sanctuary for Kate Steinle? Where was Sanctuary for the children of Mary Ann, Sabine and Jamiel? Where was sanctuary for all the other Americans who have been so brutally murdered, and who have suffered so horribly?

These wounded American families have been alone. But they are alone no longer. Tonight, this candidate and this whole nation stand in their corner to support them, to send them our love, and to pledge in their honor that we will save countless more families from suffering the same awful fate.

We are going to build a great border wall to stop illegal immigration, to stop the gangs and the violence, and to stop the drugs from pouring into our communities. I have been honored to receive the endorsement of America's Border Patrol Agents, and will work directly with them to protect the integrity of our lawful immigration system.

By ending catch-and-release on the border, we will stop the cycle of human smuggling and violence. Illegal border crossings will go down. Peace will be restored. By enforcing the rules for the millions who overstay their visas, our laws will finally receive the respect they deserve.

Tonight, I want every American whose demands for immigration security have been denied – and every politician who has denied them – to listen very closely to the words I am about to say.

On January 21st of 2017, the day after I take the oath of office, Americans will finally wake up in a country where the laws of the United States are enforced. We are going to be considerate and compassionate to everyone.

But my greatest compassion will be for our own struggling citizens. My plan is the exact opposite of the radical and dangerous immigration policy of Hillary Clinton. Americans want relief from uncontrolled immigration. Communities want relief.

Yet Hillary Clinton is proposing mass amnesty, mass immigration, and mass lawlessness. Her plan will overwhelm your schools and hospitals, further reduce your jobs and wages, and make it harder for recent immigrants to escape from poverty.

I have a different vision for our workers. It begins with a new, fair trade policy that protects our jobs and stands up to countries that cheat. It's been a signature message of my campaign from day one, and it will be a signature feature of my presidency from the moment I take the oath of office.

I have made billions of dollars in business making deals – now I'm going to make our country rich again. I am going to turn our bad trade agreements into great ones. America has lost nearly-one third of its manufacturing jobs since 1997, following the enactment of disastrous trade deals supported by Bill and Hillary Clinton.

Remember, it was Bill Clinton who signed NAFTA, one of the worst economic deals ever made by our country.

Never again.

I am going to bring our jobs back to Ohio and to America – and I am not going to let companies move to other countries, firing their employees along the way, without consequences.

My opponent, on the other hand, has supported virtually every trade agreement that has been destroying our middle class. She supported NAFTA, and she supported China's entrance into the World Trade Organization – another one of her husband's colossal mistakes.

She supported the job killing trade deal with South Korea. She has supported the Trans-Pacific Partnership. The TPP will not only destroy our manufacturing, but it will make America subject to the rulings of foreign governments. I pledge to never sign any trade agreement that hurts our workers, or that diminishes our freedom and independence. Instead, I will make individual deals with individual countries.

No longer will we enter into these massive deals, with many countries, that are thousands of pages long – and which no one from our country even reads or understands. We are going to enforce all trade violations, including through the use of taxes and tariffs, against any country that cheats.

This includes stopping China's outrageous theft of intellectual property, along with their illegal product dumping, and their devastating currency manipulation. Our horrible trade agreements with China and many others, will be totally renegotiated. That includes renegotiating NAFTA to get a much better deal for America – and we'll walk away if we don't get the deal that we want. We are going to start building and making things again.

Next comes the reform of our tax laws, regulations and energy rules. While Hillary Clinton plans a massive tax increase, I have proposed the largest tax reduction of any candidate who has declared for the presidential race this year – Democrat or

Republican. Middle-income Americans will experience profound relief, and taxes will be simplified for everyone.

America is one of the highest-taxed nations in the world. Reducing taxes will cause new companies and new jobs to come roaring back into our country. Then we are going to deal with the issue of regulation, one of the greatest job-killers of them all. Excessive regulation is costing our country as much as $2 trillion a year, and we will end it. We are going to lift the restrictions on the production of American energy. This will produce more than $20 trillion in job creating economic activity over the next four decades.

My opponent, on the other hand, wants to put the great miners and steel workers of our country out of work – that will never happen when I am President. With these new economic policies, trillions of dollars will start flowing into our country.

This new wealth will improve the quality of life for all Americans – We will build the roads, highways, bridges, tunnels, airports, and the railways of tomorrow. This, in turn, will create millions more jobs. We will rescue kids from failing schools by helping their parents send them to a safe school of their choice.

My opponent would rather protect education bureaucrats than serve American children. We will repeal and replace disastrous Obamacare. You will be able to choose your own doctor again. And we will fix TSA at the airports! We will completely rebuild our depleted military, and the countries that we protect, at a massive loss, will be asked to pay their fair share.

We will take care of our great Veterans like they have never been taken care of before. My opponent dismissed the VA scandal as being not widespread – one more sign of how out of touch she really is. We are going to ask every Department Head in government to provide a list of wasteful spending projects that we can eliminate in my first 100 days. The politicians have talked about it, I'm going to do it. We are also going to appoint justices to the United States Supreme Court who will uphold our laws and our Constitution.

The replacement for Justice Scalia will be a person of similar views and principles. This will be one of the most important issues decided by this election. My opponent wants to essentially abolish the 2nd amendment. I, on the other hand, received the early and strong endorsement of the National Rifle Association and will protect the right of all Americans to keep their families safe.

At this moment, I would like to thank the evangelical community who have been so good to me and so supportive. You have so much to contribute to our politics, yet our laws prevent you from speaking your minds from your own pulpits.

An amendment, pushed by Lyndon Johnson, many years ago, threatens religious institutions with a loss of their tax-exempt status if they openly advocate their political views.

I am going to work very hard to repeal that language and protect free speech for all Americans. We can accomplish these great things, and so much else – all we need to do is start believing in ourselves and in our country again. It is time to show the whole world that America Is Back – bigger, and better and stronger than ever before.

In this journey, I'm so lucky to have at my side my wife Melania and my wonderful children, Don, Ivanka, Eric, Tiffany, and Barron: you will always be my greatest source of pride and joy. My Dad, Fred Trump, was the smartest and hardest working man I ever knew. I wonder sometimes what he'd say if he were here to see this tonight.

It's because of him that I learned, from my youngest age, to respect the dignity of work and the dignity of working people. He was a guy most comfortable in the company of bricklayers, carpenters, and electricians and I have a lot of that in me also. Then there's my mother, Mary. She was strong, but also warm and fair-minded. She was a truly great mother. She was also one of the most honest and charitable people I have ever known, and a great judge of character.

To my sisters Mary Anne and Elizabeth, my brother Robert and my late brother Fred, I will always give you my love you are most special to me. I have loved my life in business.

But now, my sole and exclusive mission is to go to work for our country – to go to work for all of you. It's time to deliver a victory for the American people. But to do that, we must break free from the petty politics of the past.

America is a nation of believers, dreamers, and strivers that is being led by a group of censors, critics, and cynics.

Remember: all of the people telling you that you can't have the country you want, are the same people telling you that I wouldn't be standing here tonight. No longer can we rely on those elites in media, and politics, who will say anything to keep a rigged system in place.

Instead, we must choose to Believe In America. History is watching us now.

It's waiting to see if we will rise to the occasion, and if we will show the whole world that America is still free and independent and strong.

My opponent asks her supporters to recite a three-word loyalty pledge. It reads: "I'm With Her". I choose to recite a different pledge.

My pledge reads: "I'M WITH YOU – THE AMERICAN PEOPLE."

I am your voice.

So to every parent who dreams for their child, and every child who dreams for their future, I say these words to you tonight: I'm With You, and I will fight for you, and I will win for you.

To all Americans tonight, in all our cities and towns, I make this promise: We Will Make America Strong Again.

We Will Make America Proud Again.

We Will Make America Safe Again.

And We Will Make America Great Again.

THANK YOU.

Don Fass

REPUBLICAN NATIONAL SECURITY LETTER ABOUT TRUMP

We the undersigned, members of the Republican national security community, represent a broad spectrum of opinion on America's role in the world and what is necessary to keep us safe and prosperous. We have disagreed with one another on many issues, including the Iraq war and intervention in Syria. But we are united in our opposition to a Donald Trump presidency. Recognizing as we do, the conditions in American politics that have contributed to his popularity, we nonetheless are obligated to state our core objections clearly:

His vision of American influence and power in the world is wildly inconsistent and unmoored in principle. He swings from isolationism to military adventurism within the space of one sentence.

His advocacy for aggressively waging trade wars is a recipe for economic disaster in a globally connected world.

His embrace of the expansive use of torture is inexcusable.

His hateful, anti-Muslim rhetoric undercuts the seriousness of combating Islamic radicalism by alienating partners in the Islamic world making significant contributions to the effort. Furthermore, it endangers the safety and Constitutionally guaranteed freedoms of American Muslims.

Controlling our border and preventing illegal immigration is a serious issue, but his insistence that Mexico will fund a wall on the southern border inflames unhelpful passions, and rests on an utter misreading of, and contempt for, our southern neighbor.

Similarly, his insistence that close allies such as Japan must pay vast sums for protection is the sentiment of a racketeer, not the leader of the alliances that have served us so well since World War II.

His admiration for foreign dictators such as Vladimir Putin is unacceptable for the leader of the world's greatest democracy.

He is fundamentally dishonest. Evidence of this includes his attempts to deny positions he has unquestionably taken in the past, including on the 2003 Iraq war and the 2011 Libyan conflict. We accept that views evolve over time, but this is simply misrepresentation.

His equation of business acumen with foreign policy experience is false. Not all lethal conflicts can be resolved as a real estate deal might, and there is no recourse to bankruptcy court in international affairs.

Mr. Trump's own statements lead us to conclude that as president, he would use the authority of his office to act in ways that make America less safe, and which would diminish our standing in the world. Furthermore, his expansive view of how presidential power should be wielded against his detractors poses a distinct threat to civil liberty in the United States. Therefore, as committed and loyal Republicans, we are unable to support a Party ticket with Mr. Trump at its head. We commit ourselves to working energetically to prevent the election of someone so utterly unfitted to the office.

Ken Adelman
David Adesnik
Michael Auslin
Mike Baker
Christopher Barton
Kevin W. Billings
Robert D. Blackwill
Daniel A. Blumenthal

Don Fass

Max Boot
Ellen Bork
Anna Borshchevskaya
Joseph A. Bosco
Michael Chertoff
Patrick Chovanec
James Clad
Eliot A. Cohen
Gus Coldebella
Carrie Cordero
Michael Coulter
Chester A. Crocker
Patrick M. Cronin
Seth Cropsey
Tom Donnelly
Daniel Drezner
Colin Dueck
Eric Edelman
Joseph Esposito
Charles Fairbanks
Richard A. Falkenrath
Peter D. Feaver
Niall Ferguson
Richard Fontaine
Aaron Friedberg
Dan Gabriel
Greg Garcia
Jana Chapman Gates
Jeffrey Gedmin
Reuel Marc Gerecht
James K. Glassman
David Gordon
Christopher J. Griffin
Mary R. Habeck
Paul Haenle
Melinda Haring
Robert Hastings
Rebeccah Heinrichs
Francis Q. Hoang
Rachel Hoff
Jeffrey W. Hornung
William C. Inboden
Jamil N. Jaffer

Ash Jain
Marc C. Johnson
Myriah Jordan
Robert G. Joseph
Tim Kane
Kate Kidder
Robert Kagan
Rep. Jim Kolbe
David Kramer
Stephen Krasner

Matthew Kroenig
Frank Lavin
Philip I. Levy
Philip Lohaus
Mary Beth Long
Peter Mansoor
John Maurer
Matthew McCabe
Bryan McGrath
Richard G. Miles
Paul D. Miller
Charles Morrison
Michael B. Mukasey
Scott W. Muller
Lester Munson
Andrew S. Natsios
Michael Noonan

Tom Nichols
John Noonan
Roger F. Noriega
Stephen E. Ockenden
John Osborn
Robert T. Osterhaler
Mackubin T. Owens
Daniel Pipes
Everett Pyatt
Martha T. Rainville
Stephen Rodriguez
Marc A. Ross
Nicholas Rostow
Michael Rubin
Daniel F. Runde

Don Fass

Benjamin Runkle
Richard L. Russell
Andrew Sagor
Kori Schake
Randy Scheunemann
Gary J. Schmitt
Gabriel Schoenfeld
Russell Seitz
Kalev I. Sepp
Vance Serchuk
David R. Shedd
Gary Shiffman
Kristen Silverberg
Michael Singh
Ray Takeyh
Jeremy Teigen
William H. Tobey
Frances F. Townsend
Jan Van Tol
Daniel Vajdich
Ruth Wedgwood
Albert Wolf
Julie Wood
Dov S. Zakheim
Roger Zakheim
Sam Zega
Philip Zelikow
Robert B. Zoellick
Laurence Zuriff

Number of Signatories: 121

The statement above was coordinated by Dr. Eliot A. Cohen, former Counselor of the Department of State (2007–8), and Bryan McGrath, Managing Director of The FerryBridge Group, a defense consultancy. They encourage other members of the Republican foreign policy and national security communities wishing to sign the declaration to contact them.

REAR ADMIRAL JOHN HUTSON (Ret) SPEECH AT DEMOCRATIC CONVENTION July, 2016

Good evening. My name is John Hutson, and unlike Donald Trump, there are two things I know an awful lot about: law and order. For 11 years, I was a law school dean. And for 30 years, I served proudly in the United States Navy, including as Judge Advocate General.

Donald Trump calls himself the "law-and-order candidate," but he'll violate international law. In his words, he endorses torture "at a minimum." He'll order our troops to commit war crimes like killing civilians. And he actually said, "You have to take out their families." And what did he say when he was told that's illegal? He said our troops "won't refuse, believe me." This morning, he personally invited Russia to hack us! That's not law and order. That's criminal intent!

Donald Trump would abandon our allies and let more countries get nuclear weapons. He lies about donating to our veterans and called the military I served in a "disaster." It's embarrassing enough that he's the face of one of our political parties. The real disaster is what would happen if we let Donald Trump become the face of the country we love.

More than 120 Republican national-security leaders recently warned that Donald Trump would, in their words, "make America less safe." He even mocks our POWs, like John McCain. I served in the same Navy as John McCain. I used to vote in the same party as John McCain. Donald, you're not fit to polish John McCain's boots!

But America, we have a better choice. Hillary Clinton is the only candidate who knows how to work with our allies and who has a specific plan to defeat ISIS. She is smart and steady. She has the experience, temperament, and spine to be a superb Commander-in-Chief. She knows what makes us the envy of the world. It's not our abundant natural resources, our resilient economy, or even that we have the strongest military on earth. Our strength comes from who we are, our humanity. If we lose our humanity, we lose the battle and the war.

ISIS and other radical Islamic groups have no humanity. That is their weakness. Our enemy can't defeat us militarily. Victory won't be found on the battlefield. For them, victory is to make us more like them: people who torture, who destabilize the international order, who target innocents because they don't look like them or don't pray like them. Donald Trump is a walking, talking recruiting poster for terrorists. That's not hyperbole. ISIS literally used Trump in a commercial.

You know, you can tell a lot about a person by whom they admire. Eleanor Roosevelt, Nelson Mandela, Dorothy Rodham – these are Hillary Clinton's heroes. Donald Trump admires Donald Trump and Saddam Hussein and Kim Jong-un. And of Vladimir Putin, he said, and I quote, "in terms of leadership he's getting an 'A.'"

I taught national security law. Praising dictators is an automatic "F" in my class. In the 2008 election, as the dean of the University of New Hampshire School of Law School, I invited each presidential candidate to talk about terrorism with me and other retired admirals and generals. Of all the candidates we met with, Hillary Clinton was by far the best prepared and most knowledgeable. She listened carefully and tested our arguments. We had more than 500 years of collective experience, and we learned from her. This was before she served as our Secretary of State. Before she brokered a cease-fire in Gaza, rallied the world to sanction Iran, advised President Obama to take out bin Laden, and restored our reputation in the world.

Anyone who's served with the young men and women of our armed forces knows how serious it is to send them into harm's way. When you're a soldier, sailor, airman, or marine, you don't get to choose your commanders. But when you're a citizen – you have the responsibility to choose the Commander-in-Chief who will keep us safe, strong, and secure. Choose Hillary.

FORMER SECRETARY OF DEFENSE ROBERT GATES
September, 2016

As of Fall, 2016, Gates, who served under 8 administrations, pretty much voiced his conclusion about Trump that echoes the Rear Admiral. *(see Gates remarks in our Others About Trump section).*

Don Fass

MICHAEL BLOOMBERG SPEECH AT THE DNC ON TRUMP

Now, I'm not here as a member of any party, or to endorse any party platform. I am here for one reason, and one reason only: to explain why I believe it is imperative that we elect Hillary Clinton as the next President of the United States. And to ask you to join with me in supporting her this November.

When the Founding Fathers arrived here in Philadelphia to forge a new nation, they didn't come as Democrats or Republicans, or to nominate a presidential candidate. They came as patriots who feared party politics. I know how they felt. I've been a Democrat, I've been a Republican, and I eventually became an Independent because I don't believe either party has a monopoly on good ideas or strong leadership.

When I enter the voting booth each time, I look at the candidate, not the party label. I have supported elected officials from both sides of the aisle. Probably not many people in this room can say that, but I know there are many watching at home who can. And now, they are carefully weighing their choices. I understand their dilemma.

I know what it's like to have neither party fully represent my views or values. Too many Republicans wrongly blame immigrants for our problems, and they stand in the way of action on climate change and gun violence. Meanwhile, many Democrats wrongly blame the private sector for our problems, and they stand in the way of action on education reform and deficit reduction.

There are times when I disagree with Hillary. But whatever our disagreements may be, I've come here to say: We must put them aside for the good of our country. And we must unite around the candidate who can defeat a dangerous demagogue.

I believe it's the duty of all American citizens to make our voices heard by voting in this election. And, if you're not yet registered to vote, go online. Do it now! It's just too important to sit this out.

Now, we've heard a lot of talk in this campaign about needing a leader who understands business. I couldn't agree more. I've built a business, and I didn't start it with a million-dollar check from my father. Because of my success in the private sector, I had the chance to run America's largest city for 12 years, governing in the wake of its greatest tragedy.

Today, as an Independent, an entrepreneur, and a former mayor, I believe we need a president who is a problem-solver, not a bomb-thrower; someone who can bring members of Congress together, to get big things done. And I know Hillary Clinton can do that, because I saw it firsthand!

I was elected mayor two months after 9/11, as a Republican — and I saw how Hillary Clinton worked with Republicans in Washington to ensure that New York got the help it needed to recover and rebuild. Throughout her time in the Senate, we didn't always agree — but she always listened. And that's the kind of approach we need in Washington today, and it just has to start in the White House!

Given my background, I've often encouraged business leaders to run for office because many of them share that same pragmatic approach to building consensus, but not all. Most of us who have created a business know that we're only as good as the way our employees, clients, and partners view us. Most of us don't pretend that we're smart enough to make every big decision by ourselves. And most of us who have our names on the door know that we are only as good as our word, but not Donald Trump.

Throughout his career, Trump has left behind a well-documented record of bankruptcies, thousands of lawsuits, angry shareholders and contractors who feel cheated, and disillusioned customers who feel ripped off. Trump says he wants to run the nation like he's run his business. God help us.

I'm a New Yorker, and New Yorkers know a con when we see one! Trump says he'll punish manufacturers that move to Mexico or China, but the clothes he sells are made overseas in low-wage factories. He says he wants to put Americans back to work, but he games the U.S. visa system so he can hire temporary foreign workers at low wages. He says he wants to deport 11 million undocumented people, but he seems to have no problem in hiring them. What'd I miss here?!

Truth be told, the richest thing about Donald Trump is his hypocrisy. He wants you to believe that we can solve our biggest problems by deporting Mexicans and shutting out Muslims. He wants you to believe that erecting trade barriers will bring back good jobs. He's wrong on both counts.

We can only solve our biggest problems if we come together and embrace the freedoms that our Founding Fathers established right here in Philadelphia, which permitted our ancestors to create the great American exceptionalism that all of us now enjoy. Donald Trump doesn't understand that; Hillary Clinton does. And we can only create good jobs if we make smarter investments in infrastructure, and do more to support small businesses — not stiff them. Donald Trump doesn't understand that; Hillary Clinton does.

I understand the appeal of a businessman president. But Trump's business plan is a disaster in the making. He would make it harder for small businesses to compete, do great damage to our economy, threaten the retirement savings of millions of Americans, lead to greater debt and more unemployment, erode our influence in the world, and make our communities less safe.

The bottom line is: Trump is a risky, reckless, and radical choice. And we can't afford to make that choice!

Now, I know Hillary Clinton is not flawless; no candidate is. But she is the right choice — and the responsible choice — in this election. No matter what you may think about her politics or her record, Hillary Clinton understands that this is not reality television; this is reality. She understands the job of president. It involves finding solutions, not pointing fingers, and offering hope, not stoking fear.

Over the course of our country's proud history, we have faced our share of grave challenges, but we have never retreated in fear. Never. Not here in Philadelphia in 1776, not at Gettysburg in 1863, not through two World Wars and a Great Depression, not at Selma or Stonewall, and not after 9/11 — and we must not start now.

America is the greatest country on Earth — and when people vote with their feet, they come here. The presidency of the United States is the most powerful office in the world, and so I say to my fellow Independents: Your vote matters now. Your vote will determine the future of your job, your business, and our future together as a country.

To me, this election is not a choice between a Democrat and a Republican. It's a choice about who is better to lead our country right now: better for our economy, better for our security, better for our freedom, and better for our future.

There is no doubt in my mind that Hillary Clinton is the right choice this November. So tonight, as an Independent, I am asking you to join with me — not out of party loyalty, but out of love of country. And together, let's elect Hillary Clinton as the next President of the greatest country in the world, the United States of America.

Don Fass

Don Fass

TRUMP'S NET WORTH

"I love debt. Debt is my friend."

-----Donald J. Trump

Millions or Billions?

According to a July 2015 press release Trump's "income" was $362 million ("which does not include dividends, interest, capital gains, rents and royalties").

According to *Fortune* magazine, the $362 million figure as stated on his FEC filings is not "income" but gross revenue before salaries, interest payments on outstanding debt, and other business-related expenses;

Trump's true income, sometimes Trump says *'based on (my feelings)'* was "most likely" about one-third of what Trump has publicly claimed.

According to public records, Trump received a $302 New York tax rebate in 2013 (and in two other recent years) given to couples earning less than $500,000 per year, who submit as proof their federal tax returns. Trump's campaign manager has suggested that Trump's tax rebate was an error. Trump has not publicly released his federal tax returns, saying he would not do so because of ongoing IRS audits, though most of his tax returns the last 20 years are *not* under audit.

In 2011, *Forbes'* financial experts estimated the value of the Trump brand at $200 million. Trump disputes this valuation, saying that his brand is worth about $3 billion. Many developers pay Trump to market their properties and to be the public face for their projects For that reason, Trump does not own many of the buildings that display his name According to *Forbes*, this portion of Trump's empire, actually run by his children, is by far his most valuable, having a $562 million valuation. According to *Forbes*, there are 33 licensing projects under development including seven "condo hotels" (the seven Trump International Hotel and Tower developments). In June 2015, as Trump announced his candidacy for the Presidency, Forbes pegged the Trump brand at $125 million as retailers like Macy's Inc. and Serta Mattresses began dropping Trump branded products, with Macy's saying they are "disappointed and distressed by recent remarks about immigrants from Mexico."

An analysis of Trump's business career by The Economist in 2016, concludes that his "...performance [from 1985 to 2016] has been mediocre compared with the stock market and property in New York," noting both his successes and bankruptcies. Any such analysis is difficult because, as the newspaper observed, "Information about Mr Trump's business is sketchy. He doesn't run a publicly listed firm..." Trump's early successes were partly commingled with those of his father so they omit them claiming, "The best long-term starting point is 1985, when Mr Trump first appeared in the rankings without his father."

Unlike past Presidential candidates, Trump has never publicly verified his income claims by releasing *any* of his tax returns and at the time of the 2016 Republican Convention, said he would not release his tax returns before the election, making him the only Presidential candidate of either party in decades to refuse to release any returns. "I try to pay as little tax as possible ... It's a little tax," Trump told an interviewer in January 2016 and failing to keep his promise to prepare his returns for release "in the near future." He claimed he had filed "big returns. Former GOP Presidential candidate Mitt Romney is among many who questioned Trump's purported wealth and his unwillingness to release his tax returns, suggesting Trump might be wary of revealing a potential electoral "bombshell"(now speculated to be Trump's alleged ties and his campaign manager's definite ties with the Russian Government.). Trump's excuse, during a February 25, 2016 debate, for not releasing returns was that he was currently subject to an Internal Revenue Service audit going back "two or three years," later saying the audit affected "four or five" years,[1] and that he had been audited every year for the past 12 years. Trump later told CNN he suspected the government's scrutiny was due to religion, because he was a "strong Christian." As he was "in the midst of negotiating and talking with the IRS" over tax obligations going back several years, he would neither reveal recent returns nor records for audited years he had "passed" because such records "mesh" and "interrelate" with current disputed IRS filings. Tax experts observed that the normal statute of limitations for IRS audits is three years, and an inquiry involving four or five years of returns might indicate substantial under-reporting or evidence of fraud, in which case normal statutes of limitations do not apply.

In April 2011, the Wikipedia bio says that amidst speculation whether Trump would run as a candidate in the U.S. presidential election of 2012, Politico quoted unnamed sources close to him stating that, if Trump should decide to run for president, he would file "financial disclosure statements that [would] show his net worth [was] in excess of $7 billion with more than $250 million of cash, and very little debt." (Presidential candidates are expected to disclose their finances after announcing their intentions to run.) Although Trump did not run as a candidate in the 2012 elections, his "professionally prepared" 2012 financial disclosure was published in his book which claimed a S7 billion net worth.

After accepting the Republican nomination for President in late July, 2016, Trump again said he would not release any of his tax returns before the election, despite the IRS reaffirming that its audits do not stop anyone from releasing their returns and many of Trump's returns not being under audit at all.

Trump was listed on the initial Forbes List of wealthy individuals in 1982 as having an estimated $200 million fortune, including a share of his father's estimated $200 million net worth After several years on the list, Trump's financial indiscipline in the 1980s caused him to be dropped from 1990 to 1995, and reportedly obliged him to borrow from his siblings' trusts in 1993; in 2005, *The New York Times* referred to Trump's "verbal billions" in a skeptical article about Trump's self-reported wealth.[At the time, three individuals with direct knowledge of Trump's finances told reporter Timothy L. O'Brien that Trump's actual net worth was between $150 and $250 million, though Trump then publicly claimed a net worth of $5 to $6 billion. Claiming libel, Trump sued the reporter (and his book publisher) for $5 billion, lost the case, and then lost again on appeal; Trump refused to turn over his unredacted tax returns despite his assertion they supported his case. In a sworn deposition, Trump testified that he once borrowed $9.6 million from his father, calling it "a very small amount of money," but could not recall when he did so; Trump has since told campaign audiences he began his career with "a small loan of one million dollars" from his father, which he paid back with interest: "it has not been easy for me," Trump told one New Hampshire crowd.

Unlike past Presidential candidates, Trump has never publicly verified his income claims by releasing *any* of his tax returns and at the time of the 2016 Republican Convention, said he would not release his tax returns before the election, making him the only Presidential candidate of either party in decades to refuse to release any returns. "I try to pay as little tax as possible ... It's a little tax," Trump told an interviewer in January 2016 and failing to keep his promise to prepare his returns for release "in the near future." He claimed he had filed "big returns. Former GOP Presidential candidate Mitt Romney is among many who questioned Trump's purported wealth and his unwillingness to release his tax returns, suggesting Trump might be wary of revealing a potential electoral "bombshell"(now speculated to be Trump's alledged ties and his campaign manager's definite ties with the Russian Government.). Trump's excuse, during a February 25, 2016 debate, for not releasing returns was that he was currently subject to an Internal Revenue Service audit going back "two or three years," later saying the audit affected "four or five" years,[1] and that he had been audited every year for the past 12 years. Trump later told CNN he suspected the government's scrutiny was due to religion, because he was a "strong Christian." As he was "in the midst of negotiating and talking with the IRS" over tax obligations going back several years, he would neither reveal recent returns nor records for audited years he had "passed" because such records "mesh" and "interrelate" with current disputed IRS filings. Tax experts observed that the normal statute of limitations for IRS audits is three years, and an inquiry involving four or five years of returns might indicate substantial under-reporting or evidence of fraud, in which case normal statutes of limitations do not apply. **Also see Newsweek's cover story about Trump foreign entanglements— near the end of this book. And ABC News, a week before the first debate has revealed that Trump has mega-millions tied up in Russia.**

BREAKING August 20, 2016

Companies belonging to Donald Trump have at least $650 million in debt, more than twice the amount shown in public filings made by his presidential campaign, the New York Times has reported.

The paper employed a property information firm to search publicly available data on more than 30 US properties connected to the Republican candidate, including offices and golf courses.

In addition to the $650 million liabilities, "a substantial portion of his wealth is tied up in three passive partnerships that owe an additional $2 billion to a string of lenders," the Times said about debt that could significantly affect Trump's wealth.

The billionaire tycoon campaigns on what he says is his spectacularly successful real estate record, claiming to be worth $10 billion and citing his business acumen as his major qualification for the presidency.

However, he has dismissed mounting pressure even from within his own party to disclose his tax returns or allow an independent valuation of his assets.

Trump's campaign filings show his businesses owed at least $315 million, the Times noted, saying they appear to be accurate and that Trump was not required to disclose all of his business activities.

Although the paper does not accuse him of any wrongdoing, the investigation "underscored how much of Mr Trump's business remains shrouded in mystery."

The probe "also found that Mr. Trump's fortunes depend deeply on a wide array of financial backers, including one he has cited in attacks during his campaign," the Times said.

His lenders include one of the largest banks in China -- which the Republican candidate accuses of being a US economic foe -- and the investment bank Goldman Sachs, which he says influences his Democratic White House rival Hillary Clinton.

As president, the Times said, Trump would be able to make decisions that would have a major influence on his business empire and net worth.

The strong possibility looms that Trump may not currently be under audit at all. The IRS does confirm that nothing bars the few years Trump claims are under audit are barred from being released.

In September, 2016, Newsweek also delivered a devastating cover story about all of Trump world's overseas entanglements that would corrupt his administration from the start, in nightmarish ways. Highlights of that story are near the end of this book.

Does it ever stop?

August 22-25, 2016

THE "*SOFTENING*"

The campaign was in hyper drive over a three day period.

Together with his new campaign manager and campaign CEO, Trump opened up attacks on Clinton on both her health and the Clinton Foundation.

Rudolph Guiliani went around everywhere where they'd let him with a lot of fake stuff about Clinton having seizures, dementia, a stroke, even syphilis. Most media repeated it all but laughed at it and pointed to her clean bill of health. However, it opened up a can of worms as it was repeatedly pointed out that Trump's own 'doctor's note was from a urologist who lied about some of his credentials and didn't offer any substance.

Trump also started a big attack on the Clintons for allegedly mixing together Secretary Clinton's work as Secretary of State with influence and funding connected to the Clinton Foundation and Clinton Global Initiative. That produced an announcement that the Foundation, benefiting millions of people in other countries and saving lives, would close if Hillary was elected President or at least stop accepting foreign contributions.

The big initiative by Trump then became courting African-Americans and Hispanics, which in record numbers aren't supporting him. Speaking to African-Americans but at repeatedly almost all-white venues and cities and suburbs, Trump kept asking 'what have you got to lose?"

In voting for him. But the effort was failing as Trump was criticized for saying/implying that most black people don't have jobs, decent living spaces and communities and walk down the street 'afraid of being shot.' Trump also said that American cities need more police, not less.

(see full quotes in our Trump A-Z section).

But what was really deemed 'The Softening' (Trump's own term but played up by the media and often laughed at by pundits) was Trump seeming to dramatically change his stance on undocumented immigrants, though his surrogates looked straight into cameras with straight faces and said that nothing had changed. Trump indicated he no longer wanted deportation squads and to ship 11 million people out of the country but to only get rid of 'the bad ones.' He repeated, however, that there still would be no amnesty and that he would still build a wall.

Trump was attacked by former fellow GOP primary candidates who had said that Trump's deportation position would change and that he couldn't be trusted and by all manner of 'alt right' people who were now feeling betrayed. Some even suggested they would retaliate against Trump with violence.

COULTER 'IN TRUMP WE TRUST;" NOT ANYMORE.

Trump supporter, conservative pundit and author Ann Coulter, within hours of her new book on trusting Trump being published, is now saying that she *doesn't* trust Trump anymore!

She was out promoting her new book, "In Trump We Trust" this week, making the case for Trump as president of the United States. In the midst of that tour, Trump went ahead and softened his stance on immigration, something Coulter wrote would be the only thing that could potentially damage his candidacy.

"There's nothing Trump can do that won't be forgiven," Coulter wrote in her new book. "Except change his immigration policies."

Since Trump's "softening" on deportation, Coulter has ripped into the GOP nominee on television and in a tweet storm. But the 'softening' apparently wasn't really one or last very long.

TRUMP GOES SOUTH OF THE BORDER

Donald Trump made a quick, surprise visit to Mexico August 31, hours before a new immigration speech to clarify his positions which appeared to be changing and then changing back again, bewildering analysts and even some of Trump's own campaign people.

Trump had called Mexican illegal immigrants rapists and criminals when he launched his campaign in June, 2015 and said he would expel all of the estimated 11 million people living in the country illegally with a "deportation force"

The meeting with President Enrique Pena Nieto, who had compared the billionaire candidate to Hitler, was a sudden acceptance of the invitation that the Mexican President had given to both Trump and Hillary Clinton.

Trump has suggested recently that he might be open to "softening" his stance as he tries to win over more moderate general election voters, especially Latinos.

Mexican President Enrique Peña Nieto says the Mexican people have been hurt by Donald Trump's past comments that painted them in a negative light.

Following a closed-door meeting, Peña Nieto told reporters in Spanish that "misinterpretation or assertions" had negatively impacted perceptions of Trump's candidacy. He said the "Mexican people have been hurt by the comments that had been made." But he also said he's sure that "Trump is genuinely interested in building a relationship that will benefit both countries."

He challenged the Republican presidential nominee's characterization of the situation on the U.S.-Mexican border and noted that the number of immigrants crossing the border illegally is down significantly "even to the point of being negative to a net effect."

While Peña Nieto says the countries have shared challenges, he says that there exists "an incomplete vision of the border issues," with weapons and cash flowing south from the U.S. and fueling violence. He's also stressing U.S. exports to Mexico and the number of jobs reliant on the countries' trade relationship. He says the Mexican people are people of "good will" who "deserve everybody's respect."

Republican nominee Donald Trump says that both countries "must respect the others' right to build a border wall on their soil to stop the movement of people, illegal drugs and weapons."

Trump says he and the Mexican President did not talk about Trump's insistence that Mexico pay for a border wall. Trump said "that'll be for a later date." Trump claims that having a secure border is a "sovereign right and mutually beneficial." Mexicans have been outraged by the proposal. He that the next president "will find in Mexico and its government" a neighbor who "wants to work constructively to strengthen even more" the relationship between their nations.

Trump flew to the Mexican President's residence near the airport by helicopter, rather than cross town in a motorcade.

At least two demonstrations were planned in Mexico City as Mexicans expressed anger about the Trump visit.

Former first lady Margarita Zavala wrote in a tweet aimed at Trump: "Even though you may have been invited, we want you to know you're not welcome. We Mexicans have dignity, and we reject your hate speech." She's considered a potential presidential candidate for 2018.

Leading historian Enrique Krauze also addressed Trump in a tweek, saying "We Mexicans expect nothing less than an apology for calling us "criminals and rapists". Krauze told the Televisa TV network that, "Tyrants are to be confronted, not pacified."

Meanwhile, Democratic vice presidential nominee Tim Kaine says Donald Trump has "put his feet in concrete" on his immigration positions, regardless of what the Republican nominee says in an immigration-focused speech later Wednesday night after Trump's visit to Mexico City.

Kaine was visiting a Hispanic community center in Bethlehem, Pennsylvania, hours before Trump is set to speak and about his immigration plans. Trump's speech is being closely watched to see if he softens proposals to deport millions of people living in the United States illegally.

Kaine says Trump's words and actions have been "frightening" to Hispanics and he doesn't expect to hear a change in tone. Hillary Clinton was tweaking Trump's decision to travel to Mexico, saying it takes more to make up for a "year of insults and insinuations" than a quick trip to America's southern neighbor. She said "it certainly takes more than trying to make up for a year of insults and insinuations by dropping in on our neighbors for a few hours and then flying home again. That is not how it works."

After Trump's Mexico visit and Phoenix speech, at least half his Hispanic advisors quit.

In other news, days after Hillary Clinton criticized the Trump campaign for promoting groups and individuals associated with preserving "white identity," Donald Trump Jr. has retweeted an adherent of the "alt-right" movement that Clinton singled out for criticism.

Donald Trump's oldest son this week retweeted a post from Kevin MacDonald, a former professor at California State University Long Beach. MacDonald said last week that white people in America are becoming a victimized minority. He has been accused of anti-Semitism by critics, including the Southern Poverty Law Center.

MacDonald's tweet had to do with Clinton's State Department and perceived favoritism for UBS, a global financial services company that donated to the Clinton Foundation.

Trump Jr.'s retweet prompted Richard Spencer, a leader of the alt-right movement, to tweet "Wow. Just wow."

On September 3, Trump did his first African-American community outreach at a black church in Detroit. That didn't go well either as it was criticized for being 'far too little too late' and most of the church's congregation boycotted Trump's speech.

ALT-*RIGHT?*

'Alt-right' definitions are now everywhere in media. Glenn Beck amazingly appeared on MSNBC to say how afraid of the alt-right he now was.

Even Hillary did a whole speech on the alt-right in Reno August 25 which The New York Times called a "blistering denunciation" of Trump. She said that he embraced the "alt-right" political philosophy and was an especially ominous turn in a presidential election full of them.

Clinton directly connected the Trump campaign to an unprecedented turn in modern politics to white nationalists, neo-Nazis, anti-semites, militias and the conservative fringe.

"He is taking hate groups mainstream and helping a radical fringe take over the Republican Party," she said. Asserting that a racially charged and "paranoid fringe" had always existed in politics, she said, "It's never had the nominee of a major party stoking it, encouraging it and giving it a national megaphone. Until now."

Trump even had French and British spokes people for the alt-right at his rallies, yet he simultaneously called Clinton 'a bigot.'

The Clinton speech came just a week after Trump named Stephen K. Bannon, the executive chairman of Breitbart News, as his campaign chief. Mr. Bannon has bragged that the site is "the platform for the alt-right" — a loosely defined and contested term often associated with white nationalist and anti-immigrant sentiment and the many conspiracy news trolls like Jones and Icke and all the fake news sites that pop up on your Facebook feed, often with patriot or fed in their titles. The August 29, 2016 issue of Time magazine had a cover story titled 'Hate Is Taking Over the Internet." About who is trolling the web, it's well worth reading.

TRUMP University

From Amazon, Trump University said, about itself:

Trump University promotional materials said:

"Our mission is to teach you success.

"The best courses and programs + an impressive list of been-there, done-that faculty + an ironclad guarantee = a really powerful resource for business education and professional development. Some educational resources have great content.

Some have a smart and eclectic community of members. Some offer educational experiences you can immediately apply to the real world and yield results.

We combine all three: Smart content. A thriving community. A learn by doing approach.

We've been here since 2005, and we're always looking ahead. Business people demand education they can apply to the real world, today.

We teach real-world education differently than traditional educational institutes do. We believe people absorb more efficiently and faster when they learn by doing."

The New York Times reported in specifics that former managers of Trump University, which never was a licensed or accredited university, portray it as "an unscrupulous business that relied on high-pressure sales tactics, employed unqualified instructors, made deceptive claims and exploited vulnerable students willing to pay tens of thousands for Mr. Trump's insights."

"Ronald Schnackenberg, (a sales rep for Trump U), "recounted how he was reprimanded for not pushing a financially struggling couple hard enough to sign up for a $35,000 real estate class, despite his conclusion that it would endanger their economic future. He watched with disgust, he said, as a fellow Trump University salesman persuaded the couple to purchase the class anyway," reports The Times.

"I believe that Trump University was a fraudulent scheme," Mr. Schnackenberg wrote in his testimony, "and that it preyed upon the elderly and uneducated to separate them from their money."

Unsealed documents from a California lawsuit, released by court order, are from just one of many ongoing lawsuits stretching across the U.S. to New York by dissatisfied Trump University students.

Trump himself started the university in 2005 which was active through 2010. Trump owned 93 percent.. He acted as its chief promoter, "selling it as a tool of financial empowerment," the Times says, "that would improve life for thousands of ordinary Americans" and according to Trump, would "teach you better than the best business school," according to Trump in his own promotional video.

Included in lawsuit documents were internal employee guides encouraging customers with little money to pay for the tuition with their credit cards. "We teach the technique of using OPM ... Other People's Money," explained instructions for salespeople "Let them know you've found an answer to their problems," sales people were instructed.

Among the lawsuits written testimony from many former employees, Corrine Sommer, an event manager, recounted how colleagues encouraged students to open up as many credit cards as possible to pay for classes that many of them could not afford, as much for some as $35,000.

Trump never showed up for the classes but at one point offered a cardboard cutout of Trump that students could pose for.

Meanwhile, in New York, New York Attorney General Eric Schneiderman stepped up his attacks on Donald Trump's Trump University business venture, alleging the businessman and presumptive Republican nominee ran a thoroughly fraudulent enterprise.

"In New York, we have laws against business fraud, we have laws against consumer fraud." New York state filed a lawsuit against Trump in 2013, the first of several across the country. "We have a law against running an illegal unlicensed university. This never was a university. The fraud started with the name of the organization." without actually qualifying and registering, so it was really a fraud from beginning to end,." said Schneiderman.

The initial estimates are that Trump personally pocketed $5 million from this.

"It's fraud. This is just straight up fraud. It's like selling people something you say is a Mercedes and it turns out to be a Volkswagen," he said. "And even if some people say, 'Well I actually kind of like Volkswagen, it's still fraud, 'cause it's not a Mercedes. This is not a university, " Schneiderman said.

TRUMP AND RELIGION

(also see Pope, abortion, Planned Parenthood in our Trump A-Z)

Trump claims to be a Presbyterian since attending a Presbyterian church at an early age.

He later says he joined the late Norman Vincent Peale's ("Power of Positive Thinking") Marble Collegiate Church in Manhattan. That church says they have no record of Trump being a member or a *regular* attendee.

Trump has appealed to and is doing quite well with evangelicals. The full list of board members of Trump's Evangelical committee:

- Michele Bachmann — former U.S. House member
- A.R. Bernard — senior pastor and CEO, Christian Cultural Center
- Mark Burns — pastor, Harvest Praise and Worship Center
- Tim Clinton — president, American Association of Christian Counselors
- Kenneth and Gloria Copeland — founders, Kenneth Copeland Ministries
- James Dobson — author, psychologist and host, "My Family Talk"
- Jerry Falwell Jr. — president, Liberty University
- Ronnie Floyd — senior pastor, Cross Church
- Jentezen Franklin — senior pastor, Free Chapel
- Jack Graham — senior pastor, Prestonwood Baptist Church
- Harry Jackson — senior pastor, Hope Christian Church
- Robert Jeffress — senior pastor, First Baptist Church of Dallas
- David Jeremiah — senior pastor, Shadow Mountain Community Church
- Richard Land — president, Southern Evangelical Seminary

- James MacDonald — founder and senior pastor, Harvest Bible Chapel

Donald Trump has had to work a little harder to convince Evangelical voters of his biblical bona fides.

On August 21, 2015, Trump called his own book, the Art of the Deal, his second favorite book of all time next to the Bible.

When pressed a few days later in a Bloomberg TV interview, Trump declined to share his favorite Bible verses, saying: *"I wouldn't want to get into it. Because to me, that's very personal.... The Bible means a lot to me, but I don't want to get into specifics."* And when asked if he prefers the Old or New Testament, Trump responded, *"Probably equal. I think it's just incredible."*

Another occasion, Trump was ridiculed for incorrectly naming "Two Corinthians" as his choice.

A few weeks later, in an interview on the Christian Broadcasting Network, Trump expanded on his appreciation of the Bible:

There's so many things that you can learn from it. Proverbs, the chapter 'never bend to envy.' I've had that thing all of my life where people are bending to envy. Actually it's an incredible book, so many things you can learn from the Bible and you can lead your life. I'm not just talking in terms of religion; I'm talking in terms of leading a life even beyond religion. There are so many brilliant things in the Bible.

The Bible, is special, the Bible — the more you see it, the more you read it, the more incredible it is. I don't like to use this analogy, but like a great movie, a great, incredible movie. You'll see it once it will be good. You'll see it again. You can see it 20 times and every time you'll appreciate it more. The Bible is the most special thing.

Trump appears to have relented to requests for his favorite passages in the Bible by sharing, "Proverbs, the chapter 'never bend to envy.'"

But the trouble is that it's not entirely clear that Trump's favorite Bible verse is actually in the Bible. His campaign later clarified that he was referring to Proverbs 24:1-2, which admonishes readers to "not envy the wicked." Whether or not he got the Bible passage wrong, Trump's repeated references to the Bible as a movie raise questions regarding whether he has actually read it or just has film versions of the Bible in mind.

On September 25, 2015, Trump brought his childhood Bible to the Values Voters Summit, showing off the hand-written dedication by his mother written in the inside flap. But that was it. He showed he owns a Bible and has kept it for sentimental reasons.

Trump's most recent attempt to show his legitimate Bible chops came on December 29 before a crowd of would-be Evangelical supporters in Iowa. As the rally opened, Trump waved his Bible and displayed the kind of rhetorical skill that has marked his entire campaign and made him the Republican front runner:

"I even brought my Bible — the evangelicals, ok?" Trump said as the rally opened. "We love the evangelicals and we're polling so well. This Bible was given to me by my mother, going to Sunday school. ... So, we love the Bible. It's the best. We love 'The Art of the Deal,' but the Bible is far, far superior, yes."

Among many other clergy, Max Lucado, the noted speaker, radio personality, pastor and author has made a statement warning about electing Trump and Tony Campolo, noted evangelical author and speaker has stated he is no longer calling himself an 'evangelical' because of Trump.

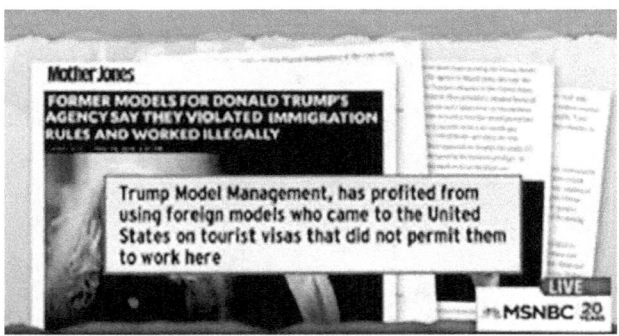

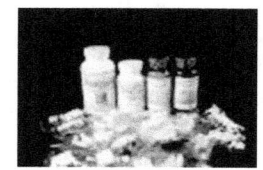

FAILED!

FAILED!

FAILED!

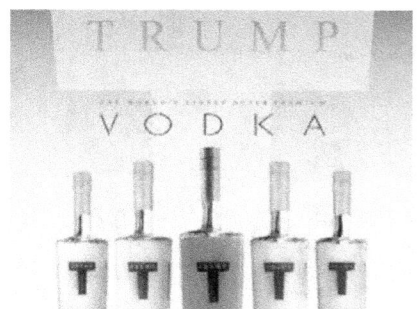

FAILED!

EDITORIALS AND OP-EDS ABOUT TRUMP

HOUSTON ★ CHRONICLE

EDITORIAL ON TRUMP July 29, 2016

For just the second time in a very long while and atypically ahead of schedule in a decision year, the major territorial daily paper Houston Chronicle issued a support of Hillary Clinton on 29 July 2016.

In 2008, the Houston Chronicle broke with custom and supported then Senator Barack Obama, selecting a Democrat interestingly since 1964. Distributed on 19 October 2008 by the paper's Editorial Board, the support held:

Obama seems to have the devices to go up against our heap and overwhelming issues. He's keen and systematic. He has met his rivals' assaults with quiet and contemplated reactions. Viewers of the verbal confrontations saw a balanced, all around arranged conceivable president with all around enunciated positions on the bread-and-spread issues that a great many polls demonstrate are the genuine worries of voters. While Arizona Sen. John McCain and his running mate Alaska Gov. Sarah Palin have struck an undeniably individual and negative tone in their addresses, Obama has kept on discussing issues of substance.

The reality of the matter is that Obama has served not exactly a term in the U.S. Senate and that his past elective experience is limited to the Illinois Legislature. In any case, amid that open administration and his past part as a group coordinator in the city of Chicago, he has built up a thankfulness and comprehension of the genuine worries of center and low-pay Americans.

On the Iraq war, Obama was an early voice of resistance to the underlying attack and his arrangement for a staged withdrawal of battle powers has been grasped by American and Iraqi policymakers. His accomplice on the ticket, Biden, is one of the main remote strategy specialists in Congress. They vow to modify America's lessened remaining on the planet and reestablish our notoriety for being the main shield of vote based system and human rights.

In October 2012, the Board embraced Mitt Romney, who went ahead to lose that decision to the officeholder President Obama. Their July 2016 support of Clinton varied somewhat from those two past supports, embracing a tenor of concern and earnestness not present in past decision cycles and depicting rival Donald Trump as "a threat to the Republic." Citing essential verbal confrontation vital under various situations, the Chronicle's Board went ahead to clarify:

The Chronicle article page does not ordinarily support ahead of schedule in a decision cycle; we lean toward sitting tight for the battle to play out and for issues to rise and be tended to. We make an exemption in the 2016 presidential race, on the grounds that the decision between Hillary Clinton and Donald Trump is not only political. It is something significantly more fundamental than gathering inclination.

A race between the Democrat Clinton and, suppose, the Republican Jeb Bush or John Kasich or Marco Rubio, even the hyper-ideological Ted Cruz, would start a genuinely necessary civil argument about the part of government and the country's future, about every applicant's experience and capacities. Be that as it may, those Republican hopefuls have been vanquished. To pick the competitor who vanquished them – decently and unequivocally, we ought to bring up – is to deny the most fundamental ideas of fitness and ability.

Any of Trump's not as much as sterling qualities – his unpredictable demeanor, his dodgy business hones, his bigotry, his Putin-like strongman slants and false populist demagoguery, his hatred for the tenet of law, his lack of awareness – is sufficient to exclude. His tradition discourse remark, "only i can settle it," ought to make each American shiver. He is, we trust, a risk to the Republic.

In the wake of tending to various arrangement contrasts amongst Trump and Clinton, the underwriting finished on the subject of "demeanor":

We could go ahead with issues, including her arrangements for sensible firearm security and for combatting terrorism – her approach positions are laid out in point of interest on her crusade site – however issues in this race are verging on optional to inquiries of character and reliability. We dismiss the "toon variant" of Hillary Clinton (again to acquire her significant other's expression) for a presidential applicant who has the demeanor, the capacity and the experience to lead this country.

These are unsettling times, regardless of the possibility that they're not the dim, tragic end times that Trump lays out. They require a consistent hand. That is not Donald Trump.

The times likewise require a man who imagines a cheerful future for this country, a man who has confidence in the solid, prosperous and sure America we would like to pass on our youngsters and grandchildren, as first woman Michelle Obama so persuasively imagined in Philadelphia. That is not Donald Trump's America.

Romney, embraced by the paper in 2012, had not himself focused on any underwriting starting 30 July 2016. Another outlet gave an account of late comments amid which Romney induced Trump had a chance at the White House:

"To be completely forthright, it's extremely conceivable in my perspective that Trump wins," Romney said. "I wouldn't think it'd be by a surprising margin, yet I think he could win. I think he could lose, I think he could lose by an embarrassing margin. In any case, I don't know which it will be and a ton of that relies on upon what happens to Hillary Clinton. Is there an emergency minute, or some implosion or some likeness thereof?"

The previous GOP chosen one went ahead to say that he discovers Clinton inauthentic, and that she is endeavoring act like her better half, previous President Bill Clinton, with a specific end goal to pick up votes, calling her a "dreadful competitor."

"You can't overlook that Hillary Clinton is a player also, and she's a terrible competitor. Individuals don't believe her, they don't care for in my perspective she seems to be not being at all real," Romney said.

The Dallas
Morning News

EDITORIAL

What does it mean to be a Republican?

For generations, the answer had been clear: A belief in individual liberty. Free markets. Strong national defense.

But what does it mean to be a Republican *today*? With Donald Trump as the party's new standard-bearer, it's impossible to say.

Even before Trump's name reached the top of the GOP presidential ticket, the party was pulled in different directions. Many

Republicans held fast to the good-governing principles of the past, while a growing wing of the party yanked hard from the right to force a conscripted definition of conservatism.

Inexplicably, the presidential candidate who emerged from that ideological tug of war was the one who thumbed his nose at conservative orthodoxy altogether. Trump is — or has been — at odds with nearly every GOP ideal this newspaper holds dear.

Donald Trump is no Republican and certainly no conservative.

Individual liberty? Trump has displayed an authoritarian streak that should horrify limited-government advocates. This impulsive, unbridled New York real estate billionaire and reality-TV star wants to deport people who were born in the U.S. and don't meet his standard for loyalty. He has proposed banning all Muslims from entering the country, even those escaping Islamist rule, and won't rule out creating a database of Muslims already living here.

His open admiration of Russia's Vladimir Putin is alarming.

Free markets? Economic conservatism? Ronald Reagan once said that "protectionism is destructionism." Trump, on the other hand, has called the Trans-Pacific Partnership "a rape of our country."

Businesses who invest overseas, he says, should pay a hefty fine on imports. (We'll leave aside for a moment his hypocrisy in pretending that investing in hotels abroad, as he does, is somehow different from a manufacturer investing in foreign car factories.) His protectionism would likely force the U.S. into trade wars, increase the deficit and sink the U.S. economy back into a recession.

Trump's idea of fiscal conservatism is reducing expenses by financing mountains of soul-crushing debt.

Strong national defense? Trump pledges to make our military "so big, so powerful, so strong that nobody — absolutely nobody — is going to mess with us." But what does he want to do with that military? He says he <u>supports killing the families of Muslim terrorists</u> and allowing interrogation methods "a hell of a lot worse than waterboarding." And if the military balks at obeying such orders? "If I say do it, they're gonna do it," he says.

His isolationist prescriptions put sound bites over sound policy: Invite the Russians into our elections. Bomb the Middle East into dust. Withdraw from NATO.

It's not easy to offer a shorthand list of such tenets, since Trump flips from one side to the other, issue after issue, sometimes within a single news cycle. Regardless, his ideas are so far from Republicanism that they have spawned a new description: Trumpism.

We have no interest in a Republican nominee for whom all principles are negotiable, nor in a Republican Party that is willing to trade away principle for pursuit of electoral victory.

Trump doesn't reflect Republican ideals of the past; we are certain he shouldn't reflect the GOP of the future.

Donald Trump is not qualified to serve as president and does not deserve your vote.

The New York Times

EDITORIAL

Donald Trump ascended the dais on Thursday night as the most improbable of Republican presidential nominees.

What historical shift, what tremors in American culture, yielded up Mr. Trump's moment from the depths of the national id? How did a braggadocious Manhattan billionaire with a history of dodgy business deals convince 13 million people feeling battered by a changing world that he is their solution? Chutzpah, reality TV and a hyperactive Twitter account are part of the answer. But Mr. Trump's nomination is also a referendum on the Republican Party, delivered by working people fed up with leaders who want their votes but don't address their struggles.

Given a chance to replace the empty sloganeering and self-aggrandizement of his primary campaign with solid proposals worthy of Americans' trust, Mr. Trump made clear that he instead intends to terrify voters into supporting him, who will protect them from violence, a word that occurs over and over in his remarks.

Asserting that his nomination comes at a moment of national crisis, of "poverty and violence at home, war and destruction abroad," Mr. Trump offered no solutions beyond his messianic portrayal of himself. "Every day I wake up determined to deliver a better life for the people all across this nation that have been neglected, ignored, and abandoned," he says in advance excerpts from his speech.

The dark vision of America advanced by Mr. Trump is one in which immigrants, including immigrant families, are prime sources of "violence in our streets and the chaos in our communities." Abroad, America is a disrespected, humiliated nation.

This is not only factually false, it's a wildly distorted view of all the nation stands for. One would think that if Mr. Trump believed this dystopia existed, he would have a clear and detailed plan for change. But, as always, he has only his empty sales pitch to offer — "I'm with you, I will fight for you, and I will win for you," he says.

Mr. Trump trounced 16 rivals and won 37 states by crude, boastful force. Refusing ever to acknowledge error, he has aimed to "knock the hell" out of all who rejected his vision of an America made great again, denying inconvenient facts or inventing convenient ones.

The more he was dismissed by Republican politicians, the more he fired up voters angered by the same treatment. In the end virtually nobody in active Republican leadership stood up to him. He dispatched Jeb Bush, scion of the party's old guard, early on. When the House speaker, Paul Ryan, didn't immediately endorse Mr. Trump, he lashed out, saying that Mr. Ryan was "not ready" to support his big-think agenda. Soon after, Mr. Ryan crumpled, and now, almost daily, he offers weak defenses of Mr. Trump's ideas and conduct.

Ted Cruz, Mr. Trump's chief primary rival, has emerged as one of the few Republicans to look beyond this political cycle, consider his own honor, and refuse to truckle to the nominee. Mr. Trump savaged Mr. Cruz during the primaries, sowing doubts about his citizenship, encouraging misogynistic attacks on his wife, and implying that his father was involved in John F. Kennedy's assassination. Mr. Cruz used his prime-time convention speaking slot on Wednesday to exact revenge, speaking for more than 20 minutes without endorsing Mr. Trump, while the candidate stewed.

It was doubtless a calculated move on Mr. Cruz's part, but it was refreshing to see Mr. Trump at last reap some consequences for his vile tactics.

The consequences for the Republican Party still lie ahead. Mr. Trump emerged as a political force with the racist claim that President Obama was not born in the United States. He has since sought advantage by playing to disaffected people's worst instincts, inventing scapegoats and conspiracy theories, waging and inciting vicious attacks on those who disagree with him. He is a poisonous messenger for a legitimate demand: that an ossified party dedicate itself to improving working people's lives, instead of serving the elite.

The Washington Post

Donald Trump: The candidate of the apocalypse

By <u>Editorial Board</u> July 21

THESE ARE anxious times in America. Despite a steadily, if slowly, growing economy and the absence of a major war, people remain troubled by a sense of national underperformance and myriad social ills, most recently the surge in racially tinged fatal shootings committed <u>by law enforcement officers</u> and <u>against them</u>. A new Gallup poll reports that <u>only 17 percent of Americans feel satisfied with the way things are going</u>, the lowest percentage since October 2013 — and down 12 points in just the past month.

For many, of course, a cause of concern is Donald Trump, who accepted the Republican presidential nomination Thursday evening. Belligerent and erratic, Mr. Trump nevertheless has a serious chance to win in November. In his acceptance speech, he sought to enhance his political prospects the only way he knows how: by inflaming public angst, so as to exploit it.

Mr. Trump took real challenges and recast them in terms that were not only exaggerated but also apocalyptic. "The attacks on our police, and the terrorism in our cities, threaten our very way of life," he claimed. Though he addressed issues ranging from public safety, to immigration, to trade, Mr. Trump's proposed solutions all shared a common premise: the way to overcome difficulty is through force. To American companies that exercise their right to move production abroad, the Trump administration will administer unspecified "consequences." A giant wall will block migrants and drug traffickers along the Mexico border. And "law and order" — an old trope of Richard Nixon and George Wallace that Mr. Trump brought out of retirement — will be restored.

Perhaps politically effective because of their simplicity, Mr. Trump's now-familiar formulations would fail as actual policies — because they are simplistic. There is no practical prospect, for example, of constructing the wall he insistently touts; even if built, drug traffickers and others could eventually tunnel under it. And, as per usual, last night he added no details to this plan that might convince anyone otherwise.

As for law and order, the president has at most indirect influence over thousands of law enforcement agencies across the country. To the extent it can be taken seriously at all, Mr. Trump's assertion that "safety will be restored" on the day of his inauguration implies a vast federalization of a traditional state and local function, contrary to long-standing law and custom — not to mention the small-government doctrine of the Republican Party that has so unwisely and hypocritically hitched its wagon to Mr. Trump's star. To tense communities in need of the nuanced toughness that police chiefs such as David O. Brown of Dallas have successfully applied, a President Trump would project from the White House a repressive attitude, unbuffered by a shred of sensitivity, racial or otherwise. Less safety, not more, could be the result.

A MAJOR theme of the Republican convention so far has been that a vote for Donald Trump is a vote to restore America's position in world affairs, which President Obama has, in the GOP view, deliberately undermined. Mr. Trump "will rebuild our military and stand with our allies," vice presidential nominee Mike Pence proclaimed. He also said: "We cannot have four more years of apologizing to our enemies and abandoning our friends."

In reality, Mr. Trump's political rise has already disturbed traditional American allies and encouraged adversaries such as Russia, because of the candidate's own disparagement of U.S. security alliances with Europe, Japan and South Korea. And in the midst of the Cleveland get-together — nearly overlapping with his running mate's remarks, in fact — Mr. Trump was giving an interview to the New York Times that was giving the lie to his supporters and reinforcing doubts about his potential policies abroad.

Stand with our allies? No, Mr. Trump told the Times, we "always have to be prepared to walk," lest they rip us off for the costs of defending them. In his transactional world, there is no such thing as a long-term U.S. investment that pays for itself many times over in global stability. Chillingly, Mr. Trump even seemed to place conditions on NATO's ironclad mutual security guarantee, saying he would honor it in the event of a Russian attack on the Baltic states if the victim of that attack had, in his opinion, "fulfilled their obligations to us."

This is an extraordinary willingness to question 70 years of bedrock political consensus on U.S. foreign policy — one that includes Mr. Obama, who has dispatched U.S. troops to defend the Baltics. Of course, there is no such thing as an unquestionable policy. What's astonishing about Mr. Trump, though, is the obvious casualness with which he muses about such matters — as if the words of even a potential commander in chief do not influence world affairs the moment they are uttered.

But they do. Equally remarkable was Mr. Trump's unilateral surrender of the moral high ground when it comes to the global cause of democracy and human rights. Republicans love to denounce Mr. Obama for allegedly going on "apology tours" around the world. Never in his most self-critical moments, however, has Mr. Obama failed to assert the United States' right to defend democracy abroad based not on our perfection but on our willingness as a people to pursue betterment.

Mr. Trump, by contrast, said this, apropos the undeniably ugly events in cities such as Baltimore and Ferguson, Mo., of late: "When the world looks at how bad the United States is, and then we go and talk about civil liberties, I don't think we're a very good messenger. .... I don't know that we have a right to lecture." This is music to the ears of dictators everywhere, from Xi Jinping of China to Recep Tayyip Erdogan of Turkey, whose sweeping crackdown in the wake of a failed coup was the specific context Mr. Trump addressed.

Where Ronald Reagan saw his country as a shining city on a hill, Mr. Trump, apparently, perceives the moral equivalent of a low-rent district.

Contrary to his apologists in Cleveland, Mr. Trump does not understand the value of American global leadership or the moral ground upon which it ultimately rests. If he becomes president, the retreat of U.S. influence for which Republicans now hold Mr. Obama culpable will likely turn into a rout.

www.weeklystandard.com

The Worst Nominee

Jul 25, 2016 | By William Kristol

Hillary Clinton may or may not be the all-around worst presidential nominee in the history of the Democratic party. That party has, over the years, thrown up some pretty unappealing characters. It's also nominated candidates whose policies did (James Buchanan, Jimmy Carter) or would have done (George McClellan, George McGovern) great harm to the nation.

The Republican party has, on the whole, had higher standards or at least better luck. Since its first convention in 1856, it has nominated 27 men to serve as president of the United States. Not all have been of sterling quality. Even the most loyal Republican will acknowledge that there have been times when perhaps GOP nominees fell short of the standard for the presidency set forth in *Federalist* 68, that "it will not be too strong to say, that there will be a constant probability of seeing the station filled by characters pre-eminent for ability and virtue." It would not perhaps even shock a loyal Republican to say that over the long history of the GOP there have been times when it was perhaps as well that the Republican nominee did not prevail in the general election.

But we do think it fair to say, tipping our hat to recent revisionist studies of Warren G. Harding, and making allowances for a few unfortunate stumbles by Richard M. Nixon, that none of the previous GOP nominees was an embarrassment or a disgrace. I can say, as someone who has cast votes for the Republican presidential nominee in the eleven elections of my adult lifetime, that in no case have I felt it necessary to engage in serious second thoughts about the propriety of my choice.

But now the presumptive nominee of the Republican party, heir to the distinguished mantle of Abraham Lincoln and Ronald Reagan, of Ulysses S. Grant and Dwight D. Eisenhower, and, yes, of Tom Dewey and Gerald Ford and John McCain and Mitt Romney, is one Donald J. Trump. If Trump is nominated on Thursday, it will not be a grand day for a grand old party. For it will have nominated the worst nominee in its history.

There were many moments over the past year when this fate could have been avoided. The weakness not to say debility of several elements of the Republican party is an important topic for another day. For now, the last chance to save the Grand Old Party from itself rests with the delegates to the 41st Republican Convention. If they succeed, all honor to them. If they fall short, their failure will merely mark the final act of the Lamentable & Extraordinary Republican Tragedie of 2016.

At this melancholy moment for Republicans and conservatives, the conclusion of Winston Churchill's great speech in the House of Commons of March 24, 1938, comes to mind. Not because we think Donald Trump's nomination is in any way comparable to the Anschluss. And not because we think this era is comparable to the eve of World War II. But because we do think, for all of its farcical aspects, it is a moment of some gravity.

Here's Churchill:

For five years I have talked to the House on these matters, not with very great success. I have watched this famous island descending incontinently, fecklessly the stairway which leads to a dark gulf. It is a fine broad stairway at the beginning, but after a bit the carpet ends. A little further on there are only flagstones, and a little further on still these break beneath your feet.

For our part, we have watched the party descend a stairway. Now the carpet has ended. The flagstones are broken beneath our feet. A dark gulf awaits.

Perhaps the party, and the principles for which it stands, can emerge from this episode without lasting damage. After all, a distinguished party's traditions are not undone in a day or a year. They will remain available to us as a source of education and encouragement. Donald J. Trump may become the 2016 Republican nominee. He cannot be allowed to define the future of a great party that can, we trust, be made great again.

The NY Post endorses Donald Trump

By Post Editorial Board

April 14, 2016

Donald Trump is a rookie candidate — a potential superstar of vast promise, but making rookie mistakes. The nominee Republicans need for the fall campaign is often hard to make out amid his improvisations and too-harsh replies to his critics.

Here's how we see it.

Should he win the nomination, we expect Trump to pivot — not just on the issues, but in his manner. The post-pivot Trump needs to be more presidential: better informed on policy, more self-disciplined and less thin-skinned.

Yet the promise is clearly there in the rookie who is, after all, leading the field as the finals near.

Trump has electrified the public, drawing millions of new voters to the polls and inspiring people who'd given up on ever again having a candidate who'd fight for them.

That's the work of the Donald Trump we know — a New Yorker, born and bred.

Trump is now an imperfect messenger carrying a vital message. But he reflects the best of 'New York values' — and offers the best hope for all Americans who rightly feel betrayed by the political class.

A plain-talking entrepreneur with outer-borough, common-sense sensibilities.

Trump is a do-er. As a businessman, he's created jobs for thousands. And he's proven how a private-sector, can-do approach can rip through government red tape and get things done.

These last 10 months, he's ripped through a different morass — the nation's stale, insider-driven politics.

And he's done it by appealing to the public's anger at a government that's eternally gridlocked when it comes to serving the people — but always able to deliver for the connected.

He's slammed the system for being rigged — and he's right.

To those fed up with the rule of lobbyists and an insular political class, to those who've seen their government ignore their needs — seen it continually degrade the quality not just of their economic lives, but of their plaace in society — Trump offers hope.

But then there are those rookie mistakes.

Start with policies that seem made on the fly.

No, pulling US troops out of Japan and South Korea — and pushing both countries to go nuclear to defend themselves — is not remotely a good idea. American commitments may need rethinking — but careful rethinking.

Yes, controlling the border is one of Washington's fundamental duties — but "Build the Wall" is far too simplistic a policy for a nation of immigrants.

By all means, get the best trade deals for America — but remember that trade means cheaper goods for the less well-off, and challenge US industries to improve.

Trump's language, too, has too often been amateurish, divisive — and downright coarse.

But what else to expect from someone who's never been a professional politician and reflects common-man passions?

Indeed, his political incorrectness is one of his great attractions — it proves he's not one of "them." He's challenging the victim culture that has turned into a victimizing culture.

In the general election, we'd expect Trump to stay true to his voters — while reaching out to those he hasn't won yet.

Trump is now an imperfect messenger carrying a vital message. But he reflects the best of "New York values" — and offers the best hope for all Americans who rightly feel betrayed by the political class.

He has the potential — the skills, the know-how, the values — to live up to his campaign slogan: to make America great again.

For those reasons, The Post today endorses Donald Trump in the GOP primary.

NATIONAL ENQUIRER

ENDORSES TRUMP

Don Fass

Los Angeles Times

LOS ANGELES TIMES EDITORIAL

Donald Trump plays the fear card at the Republican convention

The Times Editorial Board

Donald J. Trump accepted the Republican presidential nomination Thursday evening with a speech that was frightening in more ways than one.

Trump's overarching intention was to sow fear in America's voters: Fear of uncontrolled crime and terrorism that "threaten our very way of life." Fear of immigrants, including refugees from the civil war in Syria. Fear of Muslims, although instead of the "total and complete shutdown of Muslims entering the United States" he proposed last year, Trump said he would suspend immigration from countries that have been "compromised by terrorism." Fear of foreign trading partners that, thanks to "disastrous trade deals supported by Bill and Hillary Clinton," have destroyed American manufacturing.

Finally, Trump warned that Americans should fear Hillary Clinton, whom he described as a corrupt politician whose legacy as secretary of State amounted to "death, destruction and weakness."

But Trump's speech was frightening in a second sense: By softening his strident rhetoric, by (selectively) citing statistics, by couching cruel policies in the language of compassion, Trump managed to make an extreme agenda sound not only plausible but necessary.

This seemingly more restrained Trump said that he wakes up every day "determined to deliver for the people I have met all across this nation that have been neglected, ignored and abandoned." He spoke with feeling about victims of crime, impoverished Latinos and African-Americans, and the LGBTQ community, which was victimized by the recent attack on a nightclub in Orlando, Fla. All Americans, he suggested, would benefit from a Trump administration that would restore law and order and "add millions of new jobs and trillions in new wealth that can be used to rebuild America."

Even in his attacks on Clinton, he moderated his tone and elevated his vocabulary. He dropped the reference to "Crooked Hillary," and when some in the crowd shouted "Lock her up," he countered: "Let's defeat her in November." The underlying slander, however, was the same. Notwithstanding the FBI's conclusion that Clinton's use of a private email server to transmit classified material was extremely careless and negligent but not worthy of criminal prosecution, Trump claimed to know better: "These terms are minor compared to what she actually did. They were just used to save her from facing justice for her terrible crimes."

Trump's speech was frightening in a second sense: He managed to make an extreme agenda sound not only plausible but necessary.

In the hours and days ahead, fact-checkers will dissect Trump's speech and call attention to omissions, oversimplifications and distortions. For example, although the murder rate has jumped in some cities in the last year, long-term trends show that homicide in urban areas has been declining. And the loss of manufacturing jobs in this country is the result of myriad factors (including automation), not just free-trade agreements.

If Trump's dire diagnosis of the country's problems was deceptive, so were his proposed solutions. For example, he promised that "the crime and violence that today afflicts our nation will soon come to an end," adding, "Beginning on January 20th 2017, safety will be restored." But how? Trump said he would "work with, and appoint, the best and brightest prosecutors and law enforcement officials in the country to get the job done." But most prosecutors and law enforcement officers are local, and the federal government plays little or no role in their daily work.

When Trump fleetingly addressed foreign policy in his speech, he said he would replace "globalism" with "Americanism" — whatever that means. One interpretation, suggested by Trump's recent interview with the New York Times, is that a Trump administration would be willing abandon NATO allies if they didn't spend enough on their own defense. In his speech, Trump warned that "the countries that we protect, at a massive loss, will pay their fair share."

Other assertions in Trump's speech will be subjected to similar scrutiny, but many of those who watched it on television will never catch up with the corrections. They will remember that they saw a nominee who spoke in somber tones and seemed resolute about rescuing America from a nightmare of crime, terrorism and economic stagnation. Never mind that Trump still lacks an elementary grasp of domestic and foreign affairs, that he still wants to build a wall on the Mexican border and withdraw the U.S. from engagement with the world, and that he still has no words of comfort for victims of police brutality.

The challenge for Hillary Clinton is to rescue reality from the illusion Trump created in this perversely powerful speech.

Bloomberg
NEWS

Donald Trump's Dark Vision

July 21, 2016

Donald Trump was true to form Thursday in his speech accepting the Republican Party's nomination for president of the United States. He stoked fears by painting a dark, dystopian image of a country overwhelmed by violent crime and under siege by illegal immigrants. He made pie-in-the-sky promises that were divorced from both reality and rationality. He called for a new era of isolationism in which America would retreat from the world order that generations of citizens sacrificed so much to build and sustain. And beyond the slogan he never tires of repeating, he offered no sense of faith in America's great strengths.

In short: It was the most disturbing, demagogic and deluded acceptance speech by any major party nominee in the modern political era. It's no wonder so many Republicans -- including Senator Ted Cruz of Texas and Ohio Governor John Kasich -- are refusing to endorse Trump. When the idea of "voting your conscience" becomes a source of division within a party, something is terribly wrong.

The primary election campaign made clear that Republicans are looking for a miracle worker, but with none in the field, they opted for the snake-oil salesmen instead. Trump pitches himself as an ultra-successful businessman, but scratching the story's surface makes clear that it is -- like so many others he tells -- a mirage. At a time when the U.S. needs a prudent and responsible manager, Trump most emphatically does not fit the bill.

Over the past year he has run a campaign that has been almost entirely devoid of substance and full of ill-conceived and ill-considered ideas. Just this week, for example, Trump indicated he would be willing to abandon America's commitment to its European allies in NATO. That ironclad principle -- an attack on any member country is an attack on all -- was essential to victory in the Cold War and it remains essential to discouraging Russia and other countries from disrupting the era of peace and democracy that has spread across Europe.

Trump's speech identified a few real problems: crumbling infrastructure, failing schools, excessive regulation, increasing safety concerns, high health-care costs. But, as on the campaign trail, he offered almost no details on how he would tackle them. Instead, he just preached doom and gloom.

Trump's campaign manager indicated that the speech would evoke Richard Nixon's 1968 acceptance speech, in which Nixon portrayed the country at the brink of chaos. It did, and not just by repeatedly using the phrase "law and order."

But the speech was more reflective of a line uttered by Nixon's Vice-President, Spiro Agnew, who said: "We have more than our share of nattering nabobs of negativism." That's still true. And now there is one at the top of the Republican ticket.

EDITORIALS

NEW YORK DAILY NEWS

Tuesday, August 9, 2016

Trump must go: Hinting at assassination is too much, even for him

Donald Trump must end his campaign for the White House in a reckoning with his own madness, while praying that nothing comes of his musing about an assassination of Hillary Clinton.

In the event that Trump fails to abandon his candidacy — as he seems determined to — the Republican Party, including vice presidential nominee Mike Pence, must instead abandon Trump for toying with political bloodshed.

Trump hurtled past offensiveness into dangerous recklessness on Tuesday by suggesting violence as a means to prevent Clinton from nominating U.S. Supreme Court justices.

Donald Trump's offensiveness, ignorance and instability have repulsed Americans, including Republicans, in increasing numbers.

At a rally in North Carolina, Trump leveled a standard accusation that Clinton intends to essentially repeal the Second Amendment by naming justices who would eviscerate the right to purchase and own firearms.

Donald Trump could be in hot water with Secret Service

Then, referring to gun owners, he said: "By the way, and if she gets the pick — if she gets the pick of her judges, nothing you can do, folks. Although the Second Amendment people, maybe there is, I dunno."

Trump can offer no apology sufficient to make up for insidiously making light of murder. Nor can he explain away or justify planting a notion that could spur a demented follower to kill a political rival, a President or Supreme Court justices.

"If she gets the pick of her judges, nothing you can do, folks. Although the Second Amendment people, maybe there is, I dunno," the GOP nominee said of Clinton.

Predictably, his campaign claimed that he "was obviously talking about American voters who are passionate about their Second Amendment rights and advocating they use that power at the ballot box."

Which is not at all what he said.

Donald Trump has gone too far by hinting at violence against Hillary Clinton.

Since the Democratic convention, Trump's offensiveness, ignorance and instability have repulsed Americans, including Republicans, in increasing numbers. Leading GOP national security experts have deemed him unfit to serve as commander in chief.

With notable exceptions, Republican officials have stayed uneasily with Trump while disowning his words and actions. Now, he has left them no choice but to dump Trump.

Wall Street Journal: Trump faces 'moment of truth'

In a scathing editorial in August, 2016, the conservative-leaning The Wall Street Journal declared that Republican presidential nominee Donald Trump's "window for a turnaround is closing" and telling Trump to either get a grip or get out of the race.

The paper's editorial board declared the GOP nominee "has alienated his party and he isn't running a competent campaign."

It points to Trump's poor polling numbers in swing states, as well as his lack of organization and ground game.

"Those who sold Mr. Trump to GOP voters as the man who could defeat Hillary Clinton now face a moment of truth," the editorial board wrote, name-checking top Trump allies Newt Gingrich, Chris Christie, Rudy Giuliani and campaign manager Paul Manafort.

The piece, entitled *"Trump's Self-Reckoning,"* argues that the mogul's slip in the polls "underlies how his bombastic style continues to alienate him from crucial undecided voters. Trump has been warring with and blaming the media for much of the past week, but even though *WSJ* agreed that there is a liberal bias to the press, it doesn't excuse Trump from the same challenges that **Ronald Reagan**, **George H.W. Bush**, and **George W. Bush** had to face themselves."

After further critiquing the organization of the Trump campaign's ground game, the op-ed also seemed to express similar concerns that *The New York Times* did with how Trump's staffers have lost hope of making him more disciplined and presidential.

"Trump's advisers and his family want the candidate to deliver a consistent message making the case for change. They'd like him to be disciplined. They want him to focus on growing the economy and raising incomes and fighting terrorism.

They think he should make the election a referendum on Hillary Clinton, not on himself. And they'd like him to spend a little time each day — a half hour even — studying the issues he'll need to understand if he becomes President."

Is that so hard? Apparently so. Mr. Trump prefers to watch the cable shows rather than read a briefing paper."

"If they can't get Mr. Trump to change his act by Labor Day, the GOP will have no choice but to write off the nominee as hopeless and focus on salvaging the Senate and House and other down-ballot races," the editorial board continued.

"As for Mr. Trump, he needs to stop blaming everyone else and decide if he wants to behave like someone who wants to be President—or turn the nomination over to Mike Pence."

TRUMP

AROUND

THE

WORLD

TRUMP OVERSEAS

Courtesy of Think Progress, Huffington Post and several others

SOUTH AFRICA

"Momma doesn't want the baby. The machine begat a monster. It's doomsday time for the Grand Old Party." The Daily Maverick

South Africa's the New Age called Trump "arguably the most successful internet troll in today's political spectrum, He reads like a laundry list of troll tactics."

The Daily Maverick in South Africa wrote "Exit polls demonstrated voters felt that eight years of Democratic administration were enough and that, instead, the country now needed someone who wasn't, in the words of responses to the exit pollsters, 'soft on nuclear armed dictators', 'global terrorists' — and who had not 'cheated on the country's classified information,'" the piece satirically commented. "But on the day of the actual inauguration itself, before half a million Americans standing in front of the Capitol Building (many pro and some not), television channels around the world showed split screen pictures of violent demonstrations in many different locations, juxtaposed with the actual ceremony taking place in Washington. While the Washington police managed to keep the crowds in the capital relatively calm, demonstrators across the U.S. held smaller demonstrations in sympathy with those anti-Trump events taking place throughout the world."

The Daily Maverick has also published a variety of other pieces on Trump, including ones calling him the "dark side of American Populism" and describing his rise as a product of the Republican party.

The City Press has published pieces on how members of the Republican party are going through the five stages of grief, the likelihood of Trump actually building the wall he wants between the U.S. and Mexico, and a psychiatrist's two-part analysis on "the tricks and techniques Trump uses to sell his own brand of flimflam. God help us all if Trump wins. The answer to a possible far-right takeover of the White House will not be to 'look East', as some of our politicians will suggest," wrote Mondli Makhanya. "It will be to bolster our diplomatic capabilities so as to penetrate sectors of American power and bypass the White House for most of our dealings."

The Daily Maverick said "In 2016, the American and South African elections will see powerful political parties humbled. Both will survive better than they deserve, on paper. But both will be forced into introspection, out of which both may rebuild their former glory. But only if they recognise where they lost their way and offer something that makes more sense to the ordinary voter." Rand Daily Mail compared Trump to Julius Malema, the leader of the Economic Freedom Fighters (EFF) in South Africa, with one piece focusing on the violence at both their rallies. A piece a few days earlier, however, noted Trump's similarity to President Jacob Zuma. "They're peas in a pod, our President Jacob Zuma and Republican front-runner Donald Trump, both of them macho men whose opinion of women is stuck in the stygian gloom of the dark ages," wrote Charmain Naidoo for the paper.

The Sunday Times also compared Trump to Julius Malema. "If Trump's symbol is the figurative middle finger, then Malema's is an expletive outrage, not fit for a family newspaper. Like Trump, he burrows deep into the zeitgeist of the marginalised and the left-behinds." New Age Editor-In-Chief Moegsien Williams also called Malema South Africa's "very own Donald Trump" in February, claiming EEF similarly intimidated media in the country.

CANADA

"The fact is, Cape Breton is lovely all times of the year and if people do want to make choices that perhaps suit their lifestyles better, Canada is always welcoming and opening." **Canadian Prime Minister Justin Trudeau** when asked about Americans leaving the country if Trump is elected.

"A man of unmatched ego and wealth has passed himself off as a savior to the weak and the demoralized." The Toronto Star.

Canadian Prime Minister Justin Trudeau has been referred to as the "anti-Trump," a Canadian island jokingly said it would accept Americans fleeing a Trump presidency, and Google searches on "moving to Canada" spiked after Super Tuesday.

As such, it's no surprise that Canadian media has had a lot to say about the Republican presidential candidate.

Canadian newspaper Toronto Star has published a number of articles on Trump, including ones that called him a "historically unpopular" candidate, described Trump's rallies as a "testosterone rage," and noted that Trump is actually "an epic illusion."

Toronto Star columnist Vinay Menon wrote that Trump is actually following a condominium development script, where "you hook people on the idea of owning a piece of the sky." "If there are hiccups in construction—if there's no way to actually build a wall or bring China to the bargaining table by declaring it a currency manipulator or remove from the income tax rolls more than 50 percent of all U.S. households—well, too bad, his four years are up. You should have read the fine print before signing," Menon wrote. "Trump is the front-runner in a party he claims not to need. He's become a leader to people who, on balance, wouldn't be allowed in his servant quarters. A man of unmatched ego and wealth has passed himself off as a saviour to the weak and the demoralized."

Toronto Star sportswriter Bruce Arthur also offered refuge to Americans in his backyard following those Super Tuesday wins:

The Globe and Mail documented the significant increase in American tourism to Canada's Cape Breton, described Trump rallies as an "uneasy mixture of anger and excitement," and highlighted a top Canadian real estate executive's comments that Trump's popularity highlights the "stark differences in opportunity and attitude" between the U.S. and Canada.

Globe and Mail's conservative columnist Margaret Wente noted that a majority of Americans "would rather swallow arsenic than vote for Mr. Trump" and predicted his fall. "If Donald Trump were a stock, my advice would be to sell it now," she wrote. "The one thing that has to happen is that Mr. Trump will have to change. And he can't. His most deadly foe is himself. Mr. Trump has no situational awareness. He has no ability to take advice, or build bridges, or learn from others, or direct a team."

CBC's *The Fifth Estate* devoted an entire episode to documenting Trump's campaign, called "The Fire Breather: The Rise and Rage of Donald Trump," as has documentary series *The Passionate Eye*, in an episode called "The Mad World of Donald Trump." Last month, CBC asked audience members why Trump has been so popular, and received answers ranging from his charisma, to the increasing polarization in the United States, to the role of celebrities in American culture.

Canadian media has also discussed Trump's business ventures in Canada including Toronto's Trump International Hotel and Tower's desire to disassociate from the Trump brand, and the construction worker that flew a Mexican flag over Vancouver's Trump International Hotel and Tower, claiming that it the building was only standing because of Mexican workers.

"Just months ago, Trump as the presumptive nominee was a punchline — now it's reality," journalist Lyndsay Duncombe said Wednesday on the Canadian Broadcasting Corporation's "World Report" radio program.

Also from the CBC, the "World Report" radio program's Lyndsay Duncombe summed up the state of the race.

"Just months ago, Trump as the presumptive nominee was a punchline; now it's reality, setting up a general election contest between a man widely condemned as sexist, and most likely the first female nominee for the White House."

Canada's **Toronto Star** assessed what led voters to choose Trump, " He is the single most unpopular nominee in the modern history of polling. A plurality of Republican voters didn't care. Furious with the polished figures of the political establishment, eager for simpler times and receptive to Trump's anti-Muslim, anti-illegal-immigration, anti-free-trade message, they had chosen the insult-spewing businessman in almost every part of the country."

Canada's CBC reported on Trump's likely nomination with news reports and analysis pieces underscoring the fractured state of the Republican establishment and the new phase of the presidential race. Washington correspondent Keith Boag wrote about how far the GOP has veered away from its establishment's control:

The Republican establishment decided after the last election in 2012 that it couldn't rely on simply mobilizing its base anymore, that its future lay in expanding that base. Those Republicans wanted a party that would reach out to Hispanics, for example, and not threaten to round up their relatives, deport them back to Mexico and then wall them off.

MEXICO

"That's the way Mussolini arrived and the way Hitler arrived." **Mexican President Enrique Peña on Trump's rhetoric.**

"When an apple's red, it is red. When you say ignorant things, you're ignorant." **Mexico's top diplomat, Foreign Affairs Secretary Claudia Ruiz Massieu.**

"So Donald Trump … is ambitious but not exactly a very well-informed man, I don't want to say ignorant, but he is not very well informed." **Former Mexican president Felipe Calderon**

"This nation [the U.S.] is going to fail if it goes into the hands of a crazy guy." **Former Mexican president Vicente Fox.**

"A lot of people in Mexico and Latin America are worried about this. It's not just the substance of what Trump says, but it's the style. It's a familiar and worrisome style to us." **Former Mexican foreign minister Jorge Castaneda.**

"The man who managed to make us miss the Bush clan." wrote Milenio. Mexico's *El Pulso de la Republica*, a satirical news show, has also covered Trump's rise with humor, but he noted that you can only make fun of the candidate so much. "I'm tired of talking about Trump, because it's always the same, you know?" he recently told BBC News. "It's just stupid, so let's move on. As a comedian, you want a fresh kick. And with Trump it's just the same every time, you know?"

Mexican academic Sergio Aguayo compared the anti-Mexican sentiment of Trump and many of his supporters to the fear of communism in the United States in the 20th century, referring to it as a new "brown panic" in Mexico City newspaper La Reforma. "We must answer again and again Donald Trump, and make the U.S. government understand that we're not willing to continue being pointed out as the only ones responsible for problems that are also caused by the United States," Aguayo wrote, as translated by the Associated Press.

In September 2015, Genaro Lozano, a columnist for La Reforma, told Politico that what worries him most is "the kind of xenophobia that Trump's comments generate in the United States." He added, "I lived and studied in the United States for five years, and I've seen prejudice and racism towards Mexicans and immigrants in general firsthand. Trump's comments resonate so much, because they express feelings the feelings of many Americans. His candidacy can make those stronger."

"Trump thought he was attacking those who have always been vulnerable, those who remain silent in the shadows—and that his bravado was politically correct," read a piece in La Jornada in summer 2015 "But he was wrong. He attacked an entire community that has finally begun to come forward and defend themselves and denounce these covert racists." Daily newspaper Excelsior declared that "Trump unites Mexicans in the United States" and documented the increase in Mexicans applying for dual citizenship with the United States in order to stop the Republican candidate from possibly winning the presidency.

RUSSIA

"Both (Putin and Trump) are an anti-mainstream and self-confident people who don't feel constrained by political correctness." Moscow Times

Trump has previously bragged that he would "get along very well with Putin." And after Putin called Trump "a bright and talented person without any doubt" in December, Trump returned the praise, calling the Russian president "a man so highly respected within his own country and beyond."

Russian journalist Ivan Nechepurenko published a piece in English-language news site the Moscow Times, which noted the similarities between Trump and Putin. "Both are anti-mainstream and self-confident people who don't feel constrained by political correctness," he wrote. "Both belong to closely knit systems: Putin is a graduate of the Soviet security apparatus, Trump belongs to the American corporate world. Both want to be portrayed as genuine men who are not part of the establishment."

Trump told state-owned Russia Today's Caleb Maupin that he was open to having closer U.S.-Russian relations. "I want a better relationship with everybody. And with Russia, yeah," he said. "If we can get along with Russia, that's very good." The head of state-owned news network, Rossiya Sedognya, also praised Trump. Dmitry Kiselyov, who was appointed to head the network by Putin himself, has described Trump as "anti-establishment" and said he "is not wanted and is even seen as harmful" due to his praise for Putin. Kiselyov has also previously called Trump a "rising star" in U.S. politics.

Putin's press secretary told Russian media that a video ad Trump posted to his Instagram account asking about the United States' toughest opponents, and showing Putin flipping a judo opponent onto the mat, demonized the country. "I saw this clip. I do not know for sure if Vladimir Putin saw it. [But] our attitude is negative. It's an open secret for us that demonizing Russia and whatever is linked to Russia is unfortunately a mandatory hallmark of America's election campaign. We always sincerely regret this and wish the electoral process was conducted without such references to our country."

ISRAEL

"Prime Minister Netanyahu rejects Donald Trump's recent remarks about Muslims." **A statement from Israeli Prime Minister Benjamin Netanyahu after Trump's proposed Muslim travel ban.**

"Trump's statements are shocking and disgusting." **Isaac Herzog, Israeli opposition leader, on Trump's proposed Muslim travel ban.**

"Trump is no more racist than mainstream Israeli policy" +972 Magazine

"As an Israeli Who Loves America, I Am Worried by Trump," wrote Ari Shavit in the liberal publication Haaretz "After the astounding victories of the vulgar populist in New Hampshire, South Carolina and Nevada, it is clear to all that America is no longer the country we have known. It is no longer a nation with a prudent economic establishment, a contented middle class and a stable political system. It is no longer a nation confident in itself, its identity and its future. It is a frightened, angry America. An America that has lost its way. To an Israeli who spends considerable time in debates about Israel between Boston and San Francisco, Trump is a relief. Suddenly Israeli politics seem a little less embarrassing."

A summer 2016 report from the Jerusalem Post earlier this month noted that Trump Vodka is actually not kosher. After the brand was discontinued in the U.S., it continued to be popular in Israel, where "Trump Vodka found a niche as one of the few kosher for Passover vodkas," according to the publication. But an investigation revealed that some bottles of the spirit currently being sold in Israel "are not kosher for Passover, despite being labeled as such."

Naomi Zeveloff published a piece in the Forward on how Trump's offensive style was actually winning many Israeli admirers. "If America elects a person who advocates discrimination and condescension and even resentment toward minorities, maybe we won't be so criticized by the West," Yaron Ezrahi, a professor emeritus of political science at The Hebrew University of Jerusalem, explained to Zeveloff regarding Israeli right-wing thinking on Trump. A month later, Dan Cohen, reporting for Mondoweiss, similarly noted a "love for Donald Trump" among many Israelis he spoke with.

Among Palestinians, there is a tendency to prefer Hillary Clinton over Trump, Adnan Abu Amer reported for Al-Monitor in March, "Our history with both Democratic and Republican administrations is long, and many previous presidents failed to fulfill the aspirations of the Palestinian people, namely the establishment of a state and liberation from occupation," Husam Zomlot, the Ramallah-based Executive Deputy Commissioner for Fatah's Commission for International Affairs, told Al-Monitor. "As Palestinians in general, we are not concerned with the U.S. electoral campaigns. "What concerns us is the political approach that the next president will adopt, irrespective of whether it will be Clinton or Trump. Much of what we hear these days is designed to gain the sympathy of U.S. public opinion and attract votes and funding, which mostly emanates from Jewish parties."

+972 Magazine, an independent blog-based website founded by Israeli and Palestinian writers, has criticized many of Trump's policy recommendations by comparing them to actual policies in Israel, like building a wall and different identification cards for Muslims. Last December, journalist Mairav Zonszein boldly claimed that "Trump is no more racist than mainstream Israeli policy."

+972 has also questioned pro-Netanyahu newspaper Israel Hayom's decision in March to put an interview with former New York City Mayor Rudy Giuliani on its front page, alongside the headline: "Giuliani says: 'Trump isn't afraid to say Islamic terror.'" The Hebrew-language paper, which was founded by the far-right billionaire Sheldon Adelson, also included a subheading of Giuliani's opinion that Clinton has "failed at everything she has ever done," sparking questions of whether the paper and Adelson were endorsing Trump for president.

Haaretz also noted "how unlikely, and bizarre, Trump's takeover of the GOP has been. Correspondent Chemi Shalev wrote on the unexpected and concerning rise of Trump, and how he has gained his support from projecting success and confidence. Many Americans had to pinch themselves on Tuesday night. It's the end of the world as we know it, they told themselves. The party of Abraham Lincoln, Ronald Reagan, Teddy Roosevelt and Dwight Eisenhower is about to anoint Donald Trump as its new leader.

Beyond his abrasive style and abusive rhetoric, his instinctive connection to white men's rage and his ability to change positions from one moment to the next, Trump owes his success to his success. In America, as in many other places, nothing succeeds like success. His early successes then created their own momentum, which led to ever-greater victories, until he turned invincible."

NORWAY

"A lot of what Donald Trump says makes for a more unstable world." **Norwegian Prime Minister Erna Solberg.**

AUSTRALIA

"I think Donald Trump's views are just barking mad on some issues." **Australian opposition leader Bill Shorten.**

GERMANY

"Whether Donald Trump, Marine le Pen or Geert Wilders — all these right-wing populists are not only a threat to peace and social cohesion, but also to economic development." **Germany's Vice Chancellor Sigmar Gabriel.**

"I can only hope that the election campaign in the USA does not lack the perception of reality." **Germany's Foreign Minister Frank-Walter Steinmeier** on Trump's use of the "America first" slogan.

"If a communist propaganda ministry had commissioned a gifted cartoonist to draw a typically-American rogue, he would have invented a figure like 'The Donald"   Frankfurter Allemeine Zeitung.

German media, like media elsewhere in the world, has expressed a lot of surprise at Trump's candidacy. In July 2015, German international broadcaster Deutsche Welle described Trump as "the presidential hopeful who baffles Europe." "He's leading some polls when it comes to Republican presidential candidates, but most Germans, and other Europeans, have a hard time taking 'The Donald' seriously," wrote Carla Bleiker. "That's because their expectations of politicians differ."

In August 2015, conservative newspaper Frankfurter Allgemeine Zeitung noted, as translated by WorldMeets.US, that Trump is "the outsized American version of a populist phenomenon that can also be observed in other Western states, especially in West Europe." Still, the author explained, Trump's rise is particular to the United States. "In American society, a political and social atmosphere has developed that rewards this type of bullying rhetoric. It is a milieu in which such rhetoric is appreciated, reflecting nothing but contempt for the political compromise that is the essence of democratic societies. In this context, it is regarded as a welcome counterbalance to Washington's 'normal' politics—in its institutions, practices and ways of communicating."

It had perhaps the best description of Trump. "If a communist propaganda ministry had commissioned a gifted cartoonist to draw a typically-American rogue, he would have invented a figure like 'The Donald': a man who embodies the wealthy, boorish philistine, from his self-important attitude to the way his hair is folded this way and that, and someone for whom nothing is sacred—other than money, bosoms, success and power," wrote Yascha Mounk, as translated by WorldMeets.US. "In Germany, Trump's unstoppable rise is seen mostly as a symptom of a distinctly American disease. In no other democracy in the world, it is said, could voters be so openly motivated by greed, show so little concern for less-privileged fellow citizens and be so politically ignorant. Only in hate-filled, under-educated 'Ami-land' could someone like Trump be successful."

After Trump mocked a disabled New York Times journalist in December, German national newspaper Die Welt said his candidacy revealed that the U.S. no longer has any red lines. "Whether mocking a Vietnam veteran like John McCain or spouting sexist talk, nothing seems to sink his poll numbers. Therefore, it is unlikely there will be any consequences for aping the disabled Kovaleski," Clemens Wergin wrote, as translated by WorldMeets.US. "The same type of enraged German citizen who cries 'lying press' — in the U.S. hoots with delight at Trump's political improprieties. After each of Trump's outbursts the mainstream media wonders when, at last, the red line will have been crossed. Now though, a growing number of disillusioned analysts are concluding that in the United States, there may no longer be any red lines."

German media has also explored the danger that would come from a Trump presidency. In February, German news site Spiegel Online labeled Trump the "World's Most Dangerous Man." In March, German business newspaper Handelsblatt noted that "the Trump candidacy has opened the door to madness: for the unthinkable to happen, a bad joke to become reality," as translated by the Associated Press. "What looked grotesque must now be discussed seriously." In late January, the print version also included the candidate on its cover with a burning American flag in the background and a one word headline: Madness.

IRAN

"The Trump Storm Is Coming," Shargh Daily

The popular reformist newspaper Shargh Daily wrote "He is noisy and at any moment, it is possible that he will start a brawl with his words."

Iranian newspaper Javan featured a photo of a fight that broke out during a Trump rally with the caption "American democracy! Trump rally turned into a boxing ring."

Tasnim News Agency declared Trump a fascist in a political cartoon portraying him as half-Donald Trump, half-Statue of Liberty. The accompanying caption noted that the Economist Intelligence Unit recently forecast that a possible Donald Trump presidency would be a major global risk.

Reformist weekly Seda, meanwhile, drew a comparison between Trump and former Iranian president Mahmoud Ahmadinejad this week in its front cover in a mock movie poster. The move, about whether the populists will unite, stars "Mahmoud and Donald."

The managing editor of conservative newspaper Kayhan, Hossein Shariatmadari, said that the smartest plan "crazy Trump" has is to rip up last year's Iranian nuclear deal. (It is not actually clear if Trump would do this, since like many other issues, he has made opposing statements about the deal.)

DENMARK

"He changes opinions like the rest of us change underwear."
Danish Foreign Minister Kristian Jensen.

NICARAQUA

"Trump reflects "the ultraconservative, racist, and war-like thinking that is incubated in the roots of the empire."
Nicaraguan President Daniel Ortega.

SAUDI ARABIA

"You [Trump] are a disgrace not only to the GOP but to all America. Withdraw from the U.S. presidential race as you will never win." Saudi Prince Alwaleed bin Talal Alsaud.

"For the life of me, I cannot believe that a country like the United States can afford to have someone as president who simply says, 'These people are not going to be allowed to come to the United States.' " Saudi Prince Turki al-Faisal, a former ambassador to the U.S., on Trump's proposed Muslim ban.

ECUADOR

"His discourse is so dumb, so basic." **Ecuadorian President Rafael Correa.**

CHINA

"Trump is an irrational type." **Chinese Finance Minister Lou Jiwei.**

"An unprecedented joke." Beijing Review

The English-language publication of the state-owned Global Times said that Trump has opened a "Pandora's box" in the U.S., noting Trump's "racist and extremist" comments and the fights that break out during his rallies. "Even if Trump is simply a false alarm, the impact has already left a dent. The U.S. faces the prospect of an institutional failure, which might be triggered by a growing mass of real-life problems," read the piece, which noted that leaders like Benito Mussolini and Adolf Hitler also came to power through Western democracy. "The U.S. had better watch itself for not being a source of destructive forces against world peace, more than pointing fingers at other countries for their so-called nationalism and tyranny."

The publication has also called Trump "the most beguiling part of the election process" and a master of "manipulating populists." A story in the Chinese-language version of Global Times gleefully noted that there had been violence at Trump's rallies, in what was supposedly one of the "most developed and mature democratic election systems" in the world, as translated by the Guardian.

A recent report from state-owned Xinhua similarly decried Western democracy, noting that Trump's success revealed "the limitations of the 'democracy' that Americans have long boasted about," as translated by the BBC. Another boldly claimed that Trump's rise "illustrates the malfunction of the self-claimed world standard of democracy."

Another recent story from national magazine Beijing Review noted that the Obama's fairy tales in U.S. political history are over, and Trump's success has now turned the presidential race into "an unprecedented joke," as translated by the Guardian.

China's state-controlled Xinhua News Agency ran an article criticizing Trump's views on international trade and rhetoric toward China, citing economic analysts who have derided the candidate's policies on trade:

U.S. Republican presidential front-runner Donald Trump's blunt accusation that China "raped" the United States in trade and committed "the greatest theft in the history of the world" was refuted by western media and experts for its naive logic.

Analysts also believe Trump's verbal attacks on China were merely a tactic to cater to blue-collar voters who have suffered loss of jobs and industry.

ITALY

"Trump solutions for me are false solutions, but they're not original. They're things that we have heard in Europe from extremist sections," **Sandro Gozi, undersecretary for European affairs in the Italian government.**

SWEDEN

"It's not a man I would vote for, I can tell you that [...] I hope that the American people, and I think they will, choose someone else who is better equipped for this task." **Swedish Defense Minister Peter Hultqvist.**

"If Donald Trump was to end up as president of the United States, I think we better head for the bunkers." **Carl Bildt, former foreign minister of Sweden.**

"He is very good at making speeches, but as a politician and a world leader? No, I don't think that's a very good idea." **Jimmie Akesson, leader of the far right Sweden Democrats.**

ALBANIA

"[The anti-Islam rhetoric of] Donald Trump and others in Europe are really the shame of our civilization." **Albanian Prime Minister Edi Rama.**

TURKEY

"A successful politician would not make such statement, as there are millions of Muslims living in the U.S." **Turkish President Recep Tayyip Erdogan on Trump's proposed ban on Muslim arrivals.**

FRANCE

"Mr Trump is so stupid, my God!" **Paris Mayor Anne Hidalgo.**

"Yes [the election of Donald Trump would be dangerous]. [It] would complicate relations between Europe and the United States." **French President Francois Hollande.**

"Trump, like others, stokes hatred and conflations." **Manuel Valls, prime minister of France**

"A *nightmare.*" Liberation

"Donald Trump faced with the choice of respectability," declared Le Monde after Trump's foreign policy speech, noting the candidate's restraint in recommending torture or a disproportionate use of force in the fight against terrorism, as he has repeatedly done in the past.

French newspaper Libération has devoted a significant amount of its covers to the Republican front-runner, calling him "the American nightmare," comparing him to French politician Le Pen, and asking what can bring him down. One of its more recent covers shows a cartoon Trump sitting on a world plagued by climate change, explosions, and nuclear war.

French media also criticized Trump after he claimed that the victims of the terrorist attacks in Paris last November would have been better off if they had guns. The Libération declared, "Well, finally, Donald Trump is a 'vulture,'" referring to a tweet by French Ambassador to the United States Gérard Araud.

In an interview with Valeurs Actuelles's Andre Bercoff, which the magazine said was his first interview with any European outlet, Trump decreed that the end of Europe was near. "What's happening in Europe can lead to its collapse. It's dramatic what [Merkel] has allowed to happen, this flood," Trump said, referring to the refugee crisis, as translated by the Telegraph. "If we don't deal with the situation competently and firmly, then yes, it's the end of Europe," he added, and Europe could see "real revolutions."

"Unfortunately, France isn't what it was, nor Paris," Trump claimed. (At least this time, Trump knew Paris was in France and not Germany.)

JAPAN

"The 'wild child' of a lost big power is engulfing people in his crazy whirlpool." Shukan Shincho

"There's a puzzling mood within the administration on the unexpected turn of events in the U.S. presidential election," the Evening Fuji reported in March, as translated by the Washington Post's Anna Fifield. "The foreign ministry has already made an internal document that compares Trump and Ronald Reagan."

"But the biggest concern for Japan is his foreign and security policies as he keeps saying things like 'China and Japan are taking jobs away from the U.S.' and 'We should demand Japan pay more for the support of U.S. forces in Japan,'" the paper added.

"What would become of Japan if 'President Trump' were born?" the Nikkan Gendai asked last month, as translated by Fifield. "We'd better think that Trump is simply speaking on the American people's behalf," former Japanese ambassador to Lebanon Naoto Amaki told the paper. "I won't deny there is a possibility that the U.S. will some day ask to review U.S.-Japan security treaty from scratch and dissolve the alliance." Thus, the piece concluded, Japan will be in trouble if Trump wins the presidency.

"The 'wild child' of a lost big power is engulfing people in his crazy whirlpool," Shukan Shincho wrote in March, as translated by Fifield. Trump "was a joker and considered as a buffoon in the beginning, but now he's jumped to a position of a probable winner," something that wouldn't be good for Japan.

After Trump said that U.S. troops should withdraw from Japan, and he would be open to allowing the country to develop its own nuclear arsenal, in an interview with the New York Times last month, the concern grew.

Japanese daily Yomiuri Shimbun referred to government concern about Trump's remarks. "If [Trump] becomes the U.S. president, it would be a problem for the Japan-U.S. national security system," it quoted an unnamed source close to the Japanese government as saying, as translated by AFP. The conservative daily paper Sankei Shimbun similarly called Trump's proposals "a grave threat to Japanese security."

Interestingly, however, not all of Japanese media is criticizing the candidate. As Fifield has reported, there are some who may even admire him. "Japanese writer Hidenori Sato, a writer for the RocketNews24 pop culture website, went to a fashionable beauty salon in Tokyo and asked them to make him look like Trump," she wrote. "It took some effort—and two rounds of bleach on his Japanese hair to achieve Trump's 'glittering blond'—but Sato came out with a very Donaldesque orange quiff [sic].

"'Leaving aside his ideals, I thought to myself: 'I want to become big like him so that I can be talked about internationally!'' Sato wrote. 'To make my appearance look like him at least, I went to a hair salon and asked: 'Please make me like Donald Trump!' I think I've become even closer than I expected to becoming a big star!'"

NETHERLANDS

"It's easier for the other monkeys in the group to make themselves subordinate to the alpha rather than join the 'losers'" De Volkskrant

Trump may not have said anything particularly offensive about the Netherlands, unlike some of the other countries on this list, but that hasn't stopped Dutch media from commenting.

Dutch newspaper De Volkskrant, or the People's Paper, created a "VoteWiser" tool, exposing Trump's inconsistent positions on issues like the Iraq War, undocumented immigrants, and even Fox News anchor Megyn Kelly. The newspaper asked readers to find out "which Donald Trump suits you best" with the tool, which showed on what day Trump agreed with the user's answers to a series of questions.

The newspaper published a piece on understanding Trump's popularity through our evolutionary history. "Monkeys live in groups with a clear hierarchical structure, whereby one dominant male, the alpha, is boss. The alpha-male decides who can eat, who can interact and who is allowed to pick his fleas," wrote Mark van Vugt as translated by WorldMeets.US. "Intimidation and bullying is part of his daily repertoire. It's easier for the other monkeys in the group to make themselves subordinate to the alpha rather than join the 'losers.'" Van Vugt delved into this evolutionary history, as well as psychology, to explain that Trump's popularity is due to his "narcissism, intimidation, anger, charisma and guinea pig hair," but ultimately concluded that he wouldn't win the Republican nomination. "Studies into monkeys and children show that the bully has a shaky power base because he makes too many enemies," he wrote.

Dutch political cartoonist Joep Bertrams also has some of the best cartoons on Trump, including this one: https://twitter.com/joepbertrams/status/702201899735498752

SPAIN

"The opportunism, unreliability and amorality that we have seen during the [Trump] campaign would be damaging for the world in general and hurt Europe in particular." **Ana Palacio, former Spanish foreign minister.**

El Pais newspaper covered Cruz's failure to mount a serious challenge to Trump's campaign, as well as what lies ahead as the race to the White House continues:

"In recent weeks, Trump's belligerent attitude, coupled with his lack of political experience and inflammatory rhetoric, had made Cruz look by comparison like a calm, level-headed candidate who is open to dialogue – itself a far cry from the early combative spirit that Cruz had displayed in the Senate.

But the strategy has proven futile. The results in Indiana confirmed Trump's advance with a 17-point victory that opinion polls had already been forecasting. Cruz was unable to avoid defeat despite his attempts at mobilizing voters with support from the governor of Indiana, his announcement of a running mate, and his surprising deal with Kasich by which the latter agreed not to campaign in that state."

UNITED KINGDOM

"Divisive, unhelpful and quite simply wrong." **Former British prime minister David Cameron on Trump's Muslim travel ban**.

"Donald Trump's ignorant view of Islam could make both our countries less safe: It risks alienating mainstream Muslims around the world and plays into the hands of the extremists." **London Mayor Sadiq Khan.**

"Some of the claims made during the campaign have been empty or just wrong." **Peter Westmacott, former British ambassador to the United States.**

"The orange prince of American self-publicity." **Marcus Fysh, British MP with the Conservative Party.**

"If he met one or two of my constituents in one of the many excellent pubs in my constituency, they may well tell him he is a wazzock." **Victoria Atkins, British MP with the Conservative Party.**

"The person you are dealing with may be a successful businessman, but he's also a buffoon." **Gavin Robinson, a British MP from Northern Ireland who represents the Democratic Unionist Party.**

"Mr. Trump is a promoter of paranoid fantasies, a xenophobe and an ignoramus." Financial Times

"Donald Trump embodies how great republics meet their end," wrote Martin Wolf, the chief economics commentator at the Financial Times of London, last month. "Mr. Trump is a promoter of paranoid fantasies, a xenophobe and an ignoramus. His business consists of the erection of ugly monuments to his own vanity. He has no experience of political office... Trump is grossly unqualified for the world's most important political office."

"Dear America, this Donald Trump thing? It's not all about you," declared a recent video in the Guardian, noting the ramifications his victory could have for the rest of the world. "If Trump actually makes it to the White House, there's only one thing you can predict about this wholly unpredictable man. There'll be a surge of what people will call anti-American-ism. People will mock the nation as dumb, vulgar, and aggressive. It'll be like it was in the George W. Bush years, only much, much worse."

The Guardian has also published pieces giving Trump emergency hair advice ("bleach it, cut it, or get a wig"), imagining what a "Keeping Up With The Trumps" television show would look like, and describing him as "an arrogant televangelist suspected of murder by Columbo."

After researchers in the United States found that Trump's grammar in his speeches is similar to that of an 11-year-old, the Independent invited readers to see if they were smarter than him. The British newspaper also told readers to "be very afraid" after Trump declared he would be his own foreign policy adviser in March. "He's a nativist, a mercantilist and a neo-isolationist, who is not afraid to turn long-term allies into enemies. And Trump will mainly be trusting his instinct," wrote Rupert Cornwell.

The Times said "The tycoon is now all but certain to be the Republicans' presidential nominee — a result that a year ago would have seemed even more outlandish than Leicester City winning the Premier League. Trump's campaign has proved hugely divisive for the party, with many believing that he is unelectable." (Leicester City had a 5,000-1 shot to win the U.K.'s soccer Premier League title, which it clinched.)

Weekly magazine the Big Issue featured a cartoon Trump on its front page in January for a story on what the candidate's incendiary rhetoric really means. "Rather than problems coming from overseas, those who'd do most damage are the indigenous hate groups mushrooming up across the States" emboldened by Trump's language, wrote the magazine.

Trump's first interview with UK media was on ITV News' *Good Morning Britain* just a few weeks ago, and Piers Morgan questioned the candidate on issues like the terrorist attacks in Brussels, the refugee crisis, and gun violence in the United States. After the interview, many British viewers took to social media to criticize Morgan for not pressing Trump on the issues—especially on whether he is anti-Muslim. (Trump said he's not racist, but he is "speaking my mind and it's just common sense.") Morgan didn't really comment on why he didn't press Trump harder, but it may have something to do with this descriptions of the Republican presidential candidate, who he has known for 10 years, as someone with "warmth," "good humor," and a "sense of perspective."

THE VATICAN

"A person who thinks only about building walls — wherever they may be — and not building bridges, is not Christian." **Pope Francis.**

Newspapers and media around the world have been closely covering the U.S. presidential election.

TRUMP

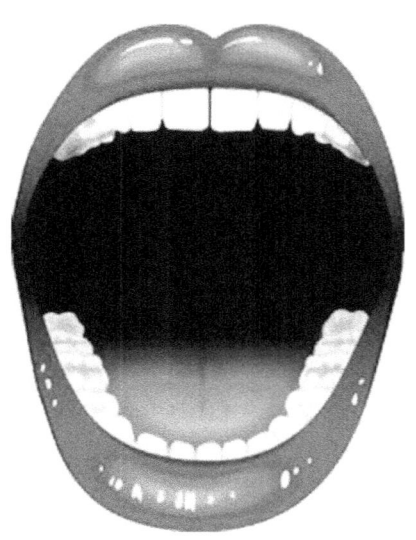

TRUMP A-Z

TRUMP ON ABORTION (also see Planned Parenthood)

(1999) "I'm very pro-choice I hate the concept of abortion. I hate it. I hate everything it stands for. I cringe when I listen to people debating the subject. But you still — I just believe in choice."

(March, 2016) "I'm pro-choice….I'm pro-life. I'm sorry.'

"This issue is unclear. It should be put back to the states. I am pro life, like Reagan."

"I would want to change the Republican platform for the three exceptions, I would."

"If abortion becomes illegal, women should face some sort of punishment. Well people in certain parts of the Republican party and conservatives Republicans would say, yes they should be punished."

TRUMP ON Arianna Huffington

Founder, The Huffington Post (also see media)

"dummy"

"liberal clown"

TRUMP ON African-Americans (also see Black Lives Matter, crime, guns)

"What do you have to lose by trying something new, like Trump?" "You're living in your poverty, your schools are no good, you have no jobs, 58 percent of your youth is unemployed — what the hell do you have to lose?"

"African-American youth are doing worse under Obama than under slavery."

"The slavery era was a good time."

"And I say to the African-American parent: You have a right to walk down the street of your city without having your child or yourself shot, and that's what's happening right now."

TRUMP ON Barack Obama

President of the United States

"failed"

"the worst president in U.S. history!"

"weak"

"looks and sounds so ridiculous"

"perhaps the worst president in U.S. history!"

"spends so much time speaking of the so-called Carbon footprint, and yet he flies all the way to Hawaii on a massive old 747"

"Is our president insane?"

"has a horrible attitude"

"he is just so bad!"

"I did much better on 60 Minutes last week than President Obama did tonight"

"terrible"

"horrible"

"incompetent leader"

"all talk & no action"

"hollowing out our military"

"weak & ineffective"

TRUMP ON Ben Carson

Republican Presidential candidate

"Ben Carson has an incurable pathological temper.

"He wrote a book and in the book, he said terrible things about himself. He said that he's pathological and he's got basically pathological disease ... I don't want a person that's got pathological disease."

"I said that if you're a child molester, a sick puppy, a child molester, there's no cure for that - there's only one cure and we don't want to talk about that cure, that's the ultimate cure. No there's two, there's death and the other thing. But if you're a child molester, there's no cure, they can't stop you. Pathological, there's no cure."

"I have a belt. If someone hits, you not going in, it moves this way, it moves that way, he hit the belt buckle. Believe me, it ain't going to work. And he plunged it into the belt and amazingly the belt stayed totally flat and the knife broke. How stupid are the people of Iowa? How stupid are the people of the country to believe this crap?"

TRUMP ON Bernie Sanders

United States senator

"Crazy"

"is lying when he says his disruptors aren't told to go to my events. Be careful Bernie, or my supporters will go to yours!"

"he would be so easy to beat!"

"wacko"

"a disaster"

"can't even defend his own microphone"

"Very sad!"

TRUMP ON Bill Clinton

Former president of the United States

"the WORST abuser of woman in U.S. political history"

"hypocrite"

"terrible, failed badly"

"was called a racist"

"DEMONSTRATED A PENCHANT FOR SEXISM"

"so inappropriate"

"Look at the trouble Bill Clinton got into with something that was totally unimportant. And they tried to impeach him, which was nonsense."

TRUMP ON Bill Kristol

Editor, The Weekly Standard (also see media)

"dummy"

"an embarrassed loser"

"dopey"

"even dumber"

"a sad case"

"his predictions are always wrong"

"Dopey"

"lost all credibility"

TRUMP ON Black Lives Matter (also see crime, guns, African-Americans)

"It's a massive crisis. It's a double crisis. What's happening and people. You know, I look at things. And I see it on television. And some horrible mistakes are made. At the same time, we have to give power back to the police because crime is rampant. And I'm a big person that believes in very big -- you know, we need police. The group's a threat essentially calling death to the police."

"Certainly, in certain instances they are a fuse-lighter in the assassinations of these police officers. They certainly have ignited people and you see that ... It's a very, very serious situation and we just can't let it happen."

TRUMP ON Bobby Jindal

"I only respond to people that register more than 1% in the polls. I never thought he had a chance and I've been proven right."

"I think he was stupid for using that term ('talk like adults"), because that term is so obnoxious, and so good for the other side. He should not have used that term. That term is going to be living now with the Republican Party for a long time, and they're going to have his face on television saying it for the next four years."

"Look, I speak ill of their negotiating abilities, I speak ill of certain things they make mistakes, but I want to tell you, I thought that term, used by the governor, was a disgrace and he shouldn't have used it. I thought it was very demeaning to the Republican party. "

TRUMP ON BREXIT (the vote for Britain to leave the EU)

(Editor's note: a month before the vote, Trump said he didn't know what Brexit was.)

(At his Scottish golf course, after the Brexit vote), "I said this was going to happen, and I think that it's a great thing."

"Basically they took back their country,"

"Look, if the pound goes down, they're going to do more business,"

"When the pound goes down, more people are coming to Turnberry (his golf course), frankly."

"People want to take their country back, they want to have independence in a sense, and you see it with Europe, all over Europe, and you're going to have more than just, in my opinion, more than just what happened last night."

TRUMP ON Brit Hume

Political Analyst, Fox News (also see media)

"a dope!"

"know nothing"

TRUMP ON Bush family (also see George W Bush, Jeb Bush)

"I think he did a terrible thing when he went into Iraq."

"The World Trade Center came down (Jeb) during your brother's reign. Remember that."

"Jeb Bush pushed Chief Justice Roberts through the brother. They were close. We have Obamacare because of Ted Cruz, Jeb Bush, and George Bush."

"It wasn't the Iraqis that knocked down the World Trade Center, we went after Iraq, we decimated the country. Iran's taking over. It wasn't the Iraqis, you will find out who really knocked down the World Trade Center. They have papers in there that are very secret, you may find it's the Saudis, okay? But you will find out."

"Eminent domain is a very important thing, Jeb Bush doesn't understand what it means, and if you look into the Bush family – I found this five minutes ago – they used eminent domain for the stadium in Texas, where they own, I guess, a piece of the Texas Rangers."

"That doesn't matter. It was the Bush family. They used private eminent domain. He didn't tell anybody this. So, I mean, he should have told people."

"Maybe – he probably doesn't know because I don't think he even knows what eminent domain is But I just found that out five minutes ago."

"Wow, Jeb Bush, whose campaign is a total disaster, had to bring in mommy to take a slap at me. Not nice!"

TRUMP ON Carly Fiorina

Former business executive, Republican candidate

"a running mate who was unable to catch on in her own failed campaign"

"a V.P.candidate who failed badly"

"campaign is dead"

"failing campaign"

"terrible at business"

"did such a horrible job"

"if you listen to Carly Fiorina for more than ten minutes straight, you develop a massive headache"

"has zero chance"   "Look at that face. Would anyone vote for that? Can you imagine that, the face of our next president?"

Charles Krauthammer

Columnist, Fox commentator (also see media)

"biased"

"a Fox News flunky"

"Iraq war monger"

"highly overrated"

"clown"

"dopey"

"should be fired"

"a dope"

"highly overrated"

TRUMP ON Chris Christie

Republican Governor of New Jersey

"(That Christie wasn't involved in Bridgegate) Does anybody believe that? Honestly?"Is there a 1% chance?"

"The taxes (under Christie in NJ) are through the roof,"

"I don't call it a hug (Christie's hug of President Obama as they toured Hurricane Sandy devastation) . I call it a hug mentally. "It was unbelievable. He was like a little boy: 'Oh, I'm with the president' like a "little child."

"I know you're happy he's up here (in New Hampshire), but, you know, the people of New Jersey want to throw him out of office."

"Get on the plane and go home"

"Here is the story: The George Washington Bridge, he knew about it. Christie can't win because of his past."

"Christie's appearance with Obama cost 2012 Republican presidential candidate Mitt Romney "a lot of votes."

"On Christie's watch, New Jersey's had nine credit downgrades."

Don Fass

TRUMP ON Chuck Todd

Moderator, "Meet the Press"   (also see media)

"sleepy eyes"

"totally biased"

"so dishonest in his reporting"

"no ratings"

"was going off the air until I came along"

"very dishonest"

"just hopeless"

"knows so little about politics"

"still not nice"

"I saved his job"

"sleepy eyes"

"sleepy eyes"

"will be fired like a dog"

"love watching him fail"

"killing Meet the Press"

"pathetic"

TRUMP ON Climate Change

Climate change is a hoax invented by the Chinese."

"The concept of global warming was created by and for the Chinese in order to make U.S. manufacturing non-competitive."

"Well, I think the climate change is just a very, very expensive form of tax. A lot of people are making a lot of money. I know much about climate change. I'd be — received environmental awards. And I often joke that this is done for the benefit of China. Obviously, I joke. But this is done for the benefit of China, because China does not do anything to help climate change. They burn everything you could burn; they couldn't care less. They have very — you know, their standards are nothing. But they — in the meantime, they can undercut us on price. So it's very hard on our business."

"Obama's talking about all of this with the global warming and … a lot of it's a hoax. It's a hoax. I mean, it's a money-making industry, okay? It's a hoax, a lot of it."

"NBC News just called it the great freeze — coldest weather in years. Is our country still spending money on the global warming hoax?"

"I'm not a big believer in man-made climate change."

TRUMP ON CNN Cable News (also see media)

"Don Lemon is a lightweight — dumb as a rock."

TRUMP ON Crime   (also see guns, African-Americans, second amendment)

"I am your law and order candidate."

"We need more police."

TRUMP ON David Brooks

Columnist, The New York Times   (also see media)

"a clown"

"dummy!"

"one of the dumbest of all pundits"

"he has no sense of the real world!"

"is closing in on being the dumbest of them all"

"doesn't have a clue"

TRUMP ON Elections (general and primary)

The American delegate system / Way of electing major party nominees "the system is rigged"

"the books are cooked"

"totally rigged"

"Don't let the bosses take your vote!"

"The rules DID CHANGE in Colorado shortly after I entered the race in June because the pols and their bosses knew I would win with the voters"

"great people being disenfranchised by politicians. Repub party is in trouble!"

"The people of Colorado had their vote taken away from them by the phony politicians."

"totally unfair!"

"I win a state in votes and then get non-representative delegates because they are offered all sorts of goodies by Cruz campaign. Bad system!"

TRUMP ON Elizabeth Warren

United States Senator

"one of the least productive senators"

"goofy"

"Very racist!"

"one of the least productive U.S. Senators"

"has a nasty mouth"

"All talk, no action!"

"Total hypocrite!"

"lowlife!"

"If it were up to goofy Elizabeth Warren, we'd have no jobs in America"

"she doesn't have a clue"

"failed Senator"

"goofy"

"gets nothing done"

"lied"

"Our Native American Senator"

"goofy couldn't care less about the American worker"

"does nothing to help!"

"using the woman's card"

"didn't have the guts to run for POTUS"

"phony Native American heritage"

"phony Native American heritage"

"one of the least effective Senators in the entire U.S. Senate"

"has done nothing!"

"weak and ineffective"

"All talk, no action -- maybe her Native American name?"

"phony Native American heritage"

"Pocahontas!"

"Hillary Clinton's flunky"

"has a career that is totally based on a lie"

"a fraud!"

TRUMP on Erick Erickson

Conservative commentator (also see media)

"got fired like a dog from RedState"

"ran Red State into the ground"

"no 'it' factor"

"total low life"

"will fade fast"

"just doesn't have IT!"

"a major sleaze and buffoon"

TRUMP ON Faith (see religion)

TRUMP on Frank Luntz

Don Fass

Political consultant / pollster

"a total clown" "where did you find that dumb panel"

"a low-class slob"

"knows nothing about me or my religion"

"came to my office looking for work"

"a clown"

TRUMP ON Freedom of Press / First Amendment (also see media)

"I love free press. I think it's great."

"We ought to open up the libel laws."

"I think the media is among the most dishonest groups of people I've ever met. They're terrible. If I become president, oh, do they have problems. They're going to have such problems."

"One of the things I'm going to do if I win, and I hope we do, and we're certainly leading, is I'm going to open up our libel laws so when they write purposely negative and horrible and false articles, we can sue them and win lots of money. We're going to open up those libel laws so that when The New York Times writes a hit piece, which is a total disgrace, or when The Washington Post, which is there for other reasons, writes a hit piece, we can sue them and win money instead of having no chance of winning because they're totally protected."

TRUMP ON Forgiveness (see religion)

TRUMP ON Gaddafi

"I made a lot of money with Gaddafi, if you remember. I dealt with Gaddafi. I rented him a piece of land. He paid me more for one night than the land was worth for two years, and then I didn't let him use the land."

"Let's not worry about that tent, I'm interested in having a meeting with Gaddafi and discuss business opportunities involving the Mediterranean waterfront and construction."

"We should go in (to Libya). We should stop this guy, which would be very easy and very quick."

"The (Libyan) intervention was a total mistake."

TRUMP ON Gary Johnson

Libertarian candidate for President, former Governor New Mexico

"I think he's a fringe candidate, you want to know the truth. Johnson got about 1 percent of the vote as the Libertarian candidate in 2012"

"I look at him and I watch him and I watch his motions and I watch what he says. I think that he is a fringe candidate."

TRUMP ON George W Bush (also see Bush family)

"George Bush lied about Iraq. Something was going on. He made the worst decision to invade Iraq. I was surprised that she (Pelosi) didn't do more in terms of Bush and going after Bush. It was almost -- it just seemed like she was going to really look to impeach Bush and get him out of office, which, personally, I think would have been a wonderful thing. Absolutely, for the war."

"Well, he lied. He got us into the war with lies. And, I mean, look at the trouble Bill Clinton got into with something that was totally unimportant. And they tried to impeach him, which was nonsense. And, yet, Bush got us into this horrible war with lies, by lying, by saying they had weapons of mass destruction, by saying all sorts of things that turned out not to be true."

TRUMP ON George Will

Columnist (also see media)

"one of the most overrated political pundits"

"lost his way long ago"

"made many bad calls"

"deadpan"

"BORING"

"dopey"

"broken down political pundit"

"wrong almost all of the time"

"broken down, boring and totally biased"

"should be thrown off Fox News"

"wrong on so many subjects"

TRUMP ON Glenn Beck

Television personality   (also see media)

"Your endorsement means nothing!"

"crying"

"dumb as a rock"

"failing"

"lost all credibility"

"irrelevant"

"wacko"

"sad"

"failing, crying, lost soul"

"very dumb and failing"

"has zero credibility"

"irrelevant"

"mental basketcase"

"viewers & ratings are way down"

"irrelevant"

"wacky"

"a real nut job"

"always seems to be crying"

TRUMP ON Guns (see crime, second amendment, violence)

"She [Hillary Clinton] talked about guns in classrooms. I don't want to have guns in classrooms although, in some cases, teachers should have guns in classrooms, frankly. Because, teachers are, you know, things that are going on in our schools are unbelievable. You look at some of our schools, unbelievable what's going on. But I'm not advocating guns in classrooms. But remember in some cases, and a lot of people have made this case, teachers should be able to have guns, trained teachers should be able to have guns in classrooms."

"This is another issue where you see the extremes of the two existing major parties. Democrats want to confiscate all guns, which is a dumb idea because only the law-abiding citizens would turn in their guns and the bad guys would be the only ones left armed. The Republicans walk the NRA line and refuse even limited restrictions. "

"I generally oppose gun control, but I support the ban on assault weapons and I support a slightly longer waiting period to purchase a gun."

"Hillary wants to abolish, essentially abolish, the Second Amendment. By the way, and if she gets to pick her judges, nothing you can do, folks. Although the Second Amendment people, maybe there is, I don't know. But I'll tell you what, that will be a horrible day."

With today's Internet technology we should be able to tell within seventy-two hours if a potential gun owner has a [criminal] record."

"We already have tremendous regulations. Now, if you look at my opponents, they're very weak on the Second Amendment. I'm very, very strong."

"No (to limiting guns). I am a 2nd amendment person. If we had guns in California on the other side where the bullets went in the different direction, you wouldn't have 14 or 15 people dead right now.If even in Paris, if they had guns on the other side, going in the opposite direction, you wouldn't have 130 people plus dead. So the answer is no."

TRUMP ON Healthcare (also see Obamacare)

"As far as single payer [universal health care], it works in Canada. It works incredibly well in Scotland. It could have worked in a different age, which is the age you're talking about here.

What I'd like to see is a private system without the artificial lines around every state. I have a big company with thousands and thousands of employees. And if I'm negotiating in New York or in New Jersey or in California, I have like one bidder. Nobody can bid...

I'm not arguing for a single-payer system. I don't think you heard me."

TRUMP ON Hillary Clinton

Former secretary of state, Democratic Presidential nominee

"Not capable!"

"Presidency would be catastrophic"

"ill-fit"

"bad judgment"

"Lying"

"Crooked"

"no sense of markets"

"such bad judgement"

"Disgraceful!"

"All talk, no action!"

"would be a disaster"

"maybe the most corrupt person ever to seek the presidency"

"will be a disaster for jobs and the economy!"

"defrauded America"

"Corrupt"

"dangerous"

"dishonest"

"judgement has killed thousands, unleashed ISIS and wrecked the economy."

"failed policies"

"totally unfit to be our president"

"really bad temperament"

"will be a disaster"

"total fraud!"

"record is so bad, unable to answer tough questions!"

"poor leadership skills"

"very bad and destructive track record"

"Not honest!"

"Bad performance"

"Reading poorly from the telepromter!"

"doesn't even look presidential!"

"no longer has credibility"

"too much failure in office"

"has made so many mistakes"

"zero natural talent"

"temperament is bad"

"decision making ability-zilch!"

"fraud"

"very stupid use of e-mails"

"not qualified"

"her judgement has been proven to be so bad!"

"Would be four more years of stupidity!"

"Wrong!"

"reckless and dangerous"

"very dishonest"

"has no chance!"

"zero imagination and even less stamina"

"ISIS, China, Russia and all would love for her to be president"

"a fraud"

"Can't believe she would misrepresent the facts!"

"pushing the false narrative that I want to raise taxes"

"corrupt"

"ZERO leadership ability"

"Constantly playing the women's card - it is sad!"

"said she is used to "dealing with men who get off the reservation." Actually, she has done poorly with such men!"

"perhaps the most dishonest person to have ever run for the presidency"

"one of the all time great enablers!"

"unqualified to be president"

"incompetent"

"has been involved in corruption for most of her professional life!"

"Who should star in a reboot of Liar Liar- Hillary Clinton or Ted Cruz? Let me know."

"a major national security risk"

"not presidential material"

"such bad judgement"

"lied last week"

"doesn't have the strength or stamina to be president"

"totally flawed candidate"

"stupidity"

"pathetic"

"LIED at the debate last night"

"SAD!"

"We need a #POTUS with great strength & stamina. Hillary does not have that."

"disloyal person"

"weak and ineffective"

"does not have the STRENGTH or STAMINA to be President"

"won't call out radical Islam"

"will be soundly defeated"

"afraid of Obama & the emails"

"corruption is what she's best at"

"totally incompetent as a manager and leader"

"no strength or stamina"

"she looked lost"

"She and Bill Clinton did pay for play with their Clinton Foundation."

"her record is so bad"

"the trade deal is a disaster, she was always for it!"

"100% CONTROLLED"

"Just can't read speeches!"

"Hillary wants to abolish, essentially abolish, the Second Amendment. By the way, and if she gets to pick her judges, nothing you can do, folks. Although the Second Amendment people, maybe there is, I don't know. But I'll tell you what, that will be a horrible day."

"She is a bigot. Hillary is a bigot."

"Barack Obama and Hillary Clinton founded ISIS"

"Hillary created the birther movement."

TRUMP ON Immigrants (see Mexico, Muslims, Syria, full August '16 speech following this section)

"No citizenship. They'll pay back taxes. They have to pay taxes.There's no amnesty, but we will work with them. We will get the bad ones out. People have told me 'Mr. Trump, I love you, but to take a person that has been here for 15 or 20 years and throw them and the family out, it's so tough, Mr. Trump."

"We MUST have strong borders and stop illegal immigration. Without that we do not have a country. Also, Mexico is killing U.S. on trade. WIN!"

"For all of those who want to #MakeAmericaGreatAgain, boycott @Macys. They are weak on border security & stopping illegal immigration."

"For those that don't think a wall (fence) works, why don't they suggest taking down the fence around the White House? Foolish people!"

TRUMP ON Internet

"We're losing a lot of people because of the Internet. We have to see Bill Gates and a lot of different people who really understand what's happening and maybe, in some ways, closing that Internet up in some ways. Somebody will say, 'Oh, freedom of speech, freedom of speech.' These are foolish people, we have a lot of foolish people. We've got to maybe do something with the Internet because they're recruiting by the thousands, they're leaving our country, and then when they come back, we take them back."

TRUMP ON Iran nuclear deal

International sanctions agreement

"terrible"

"horrendous"

"horrible"

"horribly negotiated"

"Really sad!"

"truly stupid"

"insane"

"incompetent"

"horrible"

"incompetent"

"one of the most incompetent ever made"

"terrible"

"is a catastrophe"

"will lead to at least partial world destruction"

"one of the dumbest & most dangerous misjudgments ever"

"poses a direct national security threat"

TRUMP ON Iraq

(September 11, 2002 to Howard Stern) "Yeah, I guess so. I'm for it (*supporting* the invasion) You know, I wish it was, I wish the first time it was done correctly." "Either you attack or you don't attack.

(Note the Iraq War started March 19, 2003)

(2003) "The war looks like a tremendous success from a military standpoint,"

"The question is whether or not we should have been in Iraq in the first place. I don't think that this president can do anything about that. He is really — he is on a course that has to stay."

"Hussein's capture was a "great thing" for the country, but there are a lot of people questioning" the wisdom of going to war with Iraq in the first place."

(April 2004) "the war was "a terrible mistake.""

"I said it loud and clear, 'You'll destabilize the Middle East.'"

"What was the purpose of this whole thing? Hundreds and hundreds of young people killed. And what about the people coming back with no arms and legs? Not to mention the other side. All those Iraqi kids who've been blown to pieces. And it turns out that all of the reasons for the war were blatantly wrong. All this for nothing!"

"I was the only one on this stage who knew that (to oppose the Iraq war) and had the vision to say it." The War in Iraq — I was the one that said, 'Don't go, don't do it, you're going to destabilize the Middle East,'"

"I fought very, very hard" against the invasion; there were "25 different stories" backing up his claim. "

"Look at the war in Iraq and the mess that we're in. I would never have handled it that way. Does anybody really believe that Iraq is going to be a wonderful democracy where people are going to run down to the voting box and gently put in their ballot."

"C'mon. Two minutes after we leave, there's going to be a revolution, and the meanest, toughest, smartest, most vicious guy will take over. And he'll have weapons of mass destruction, which Saddam didn't have."

"What was the purpose of the whole thing? Hundreds and hundreds of young people killed. And what about the people coming back with no arms and no legs? Not to mention the other side. All those Iraqi kids who've been blown to pieces. And it turns out that all of the reasons for the war were blatantly wrong. All this for nothing!"

(2007) "Anybody who stays in Iraq — look at what happened to McCain — he wants to show how tough he is, he's sunk, immediately, and that's with the Republicans."

(2008) "First, I'd get out of Iraq right now. And by the way, I am the greatest hawk who ever lived, a far greater hawk even than Bush. I am the most militant military human being who ever lived. I'd rebuild our military arsenal, and make sure we had the finest weapons in the world. Because countries such as Russia have no respect for us, they laugh at us. Look at what happened in Georgia, a place we were supposed to be protecting."

"I wish McCain would promise to get us out of Iraq faster. I am not in love with that aspect of what he represents."

"You know how they get out? They get out," That's how they get out. Declare victory and leave, because I'll tell you, this country is just going to get further bogged down. They're in a civil war over there, Wolf. There's nothing that we're going to be able to do with a civil war. They are in a major civil war."

(Note: The group that would become ISIS was founded in Jordan in 1999, and became devoted to holding territory in Iraq after the US invasion in 2003. It was President George W. Bush, who had negotiated for U.S. troops to leave Iraq in 2011 and Trump himself called for immediately leaving Iraq in 2007 and 2008.)

(August, 2016) "ISIS is honoring President Obama. He is the founder of ISIS. He is the founder of ISIS, okay? He is the founder. He founded ISIS. And I would say the cofounder would be crooked Hillary Clinton."

TRUMP ON ISIS

"I know more about Isis than the Generals do'"

"I'd bomb the s—" out of ISIS"ISIS is making a tremendous amount of money because they have certain oil camps, certain areas of oil that they took away. They have some in Syria, some in Iraq. I would bomb the s— out of 'em. I would just bomb those suckers. That's right. I'd blow up the pipes. ... I'd blow up every single inch. There would be nothing left. And you know what, you'll get Exxon to come in there and in two months, you ever see these guys, how good they are, the great oil companies? They'll rebuild that sucker, brand new – it'll be beautiful."

"Some of the candidates, they went in and didn't know the air conditioner didn't work and sweated like dogs, and they didn't know the room was too big because they didn't have anybody there. How are they going to beat ISIS?"

"I would do things that would be so tough that I don't even know if they'd be around to come to the table. ... I would bomb the hell out of those oil fields [in Iraq]. I wouldn't send many troops, because you won't need them by the time I got finished."

"ISIS headquarters in Syria should have been hit harder…"

"This is a war. They don't wear uniforms. The "cancer" of terrorism needs to be stopped before it "festers and festers and only gets worse."

"I love the idea" of teaming up with Russia to root out ISIS."

"The problem is, we want to get rid of Assad, but we don't know who we're getting rid of. It's not like we have 'George Washington' that we're backing. We're backing people who we have no idea who they are."

"I would knock out the source of their wealth, the primary source of their wealth, which is oil," "I would knock the hell out of them, but I'd put a ring around it and I'd take the oil for our country."

(Note: Trump talking in 1987 about how he thought the United States should invade Iran and take their oil, but abandon our other agendas there)

:

221

 **Donald J. Trump**
@realDonaldTrump

Eight Syrians were just caught on the southern border trying to get into the U.S. ISIS maybe? I told you so. WE NEED A BIG & BEAUTIFUL WALL!

RETWEETS 15,995   LIKES 28,731

8:11 AM - 19 Nov 2015

"ISIS is tremendously rich. They're rich, you know why? Because of the oil, they have the oil. That's why they're rich... They're building a hotel in Syria. Can you believe ISIS is building a hotel? They're in competition with me now. They're building a hotel – they have so much money. You bomb the hell out of the oil. Don't worry about the cities, the cities are terrible that they took over... And you kill them at the head."

"Barack Obama is the founder of ISIS. Hillary Clinton is the co-founder."

TRUMP ON Israel

"I'm not exactly thrilled by it [the United States funding the Palestinian Authority]. It's obvious. We have to help people that respect us, that want things to be done and properly done. Not just there (the Palestinian Authority), we're giving money to all sorts of groups and people and countries that take advantage of the United States, so it's something that I'm not thrilled about."

"You truly have a great prime minister in Benjamin Netanyahu. He's a winner, he's highly respected, he's highly thought of by all. Vote for Benjamin – terrific guy, terrific leader, great for Israel."

"I will be neutral. I doubt that it makes sense to hand Israel billions of dollars annually in military aid. I do not recognize Jerusalem as Israel's capital."

"We will move the American embassy to the eternal capital of the Jewish people, Jerusalem."

"The Republican platform is the most pro-Israel of all time! Support for Israel is an expression of Americanism. ... We reject the false notion that Israel is an occupier."

"A lot (peace negotiations) will have to do with Israel and whether or not Israel wants to make the deal – whether or not Israel's willing to sacrifice certain things."

"When I become president, the days of treating Israel like a second-class citizen will end on day one. I will meet with Prime Minister Netanyahu immediately. I have known him for many years and we'll be able to work closely together to help bring stability and peace to Israel and to the entire region."

"I will dismantle the disastrous (Iran) deal."

"I will enforce (the Iran deal) like you've never seen a contract enforced before."

"Barack Obama is possibly the worst thing to ever happen to Israel."

TRUMP ON Ivanka Trump

Oldest Trump daughter, business partner

"It would be really disappointing (if Ivanka posed for Playboy) — not really — but it would depend on what's inside the magazine."

"I don't think Ivanka would do that, although she does have a very nice figure. I've said if Ivanka weren't my daughter, perhaps I'd be dating her."

TRUMP ON Jeb Bush

Former Florida governor   (also see Bush family)

"failed presidential candidate"

"no honor!"

"low energy"

"just got contact lenses and got rid of the glasses. He wants to look cool, but it's far too late"

"hypocrite"

"Just another clueless politician!"

"has no clue"

"failed campaign"

"How can @JebBush beat Hillary Clinton- if he can't beat anyone else on the #GOPDebate stage with $150M?"

"lightweight"

"spending a fortune of special interest against me in SC"

"desperate and sad"

"Weak"

"Jeb failed as Jeb"

"gave up and enlisted Mommy and his brother"

"had to bring in mommy to take a slap at me"

"no chance"

"has gone nasty with lies"

"by far the weakest of the lot"

"Not a leader!"

"Sad!"

"A pathetic figure!"

"desperate"

"zero communication skills"

"spent a fortune of special interest money on a Super Bowl ad"

"total disaster"

"will do anything to stay at the trough"

"low energy guy"

"at the bottom of the barrel"

"he should go home and relax!"

"sad sack"

"chances of winning are zero"

"did poorly last night in the debate"

"weak & ineffective"

"campaign is a disaster"

"low-energy individual," "low-energy 'stiff'"

"a total embarrassment to himself and his family"

"took millions of $'s of hit ads on me"

"spent $59 million & done"

"failed candidate"

"ridiculous"

"SO SAD"

"poor"

"he's bottom (and gone), I'm top (by a lot)"

"really pathetic"

"phony"

"campaign is a disaster"

"a loser"

"can't win"

"terrible on Face the Nation"

"a basket case"

"ineffective"

"false advertising"

"campaign is a disaster"

"puppet"

"cratered"

"if Jeb Bush were more competent he could not have lost the skirmish with Marco" "stupid message"

"VERY weak on illegal immigration"

"campaign is in total disarray"

"paid ridiculous amounts of money"

"if he can't manage his campaign, how can he manage our countries finances?"

"had a tiny 300 person crowd"

"totally lost"

"too soft"

"our country needs more energy and spirit than you can provide!"

"pathetic"

"doubled Florida State debt"

"has been confused for forty years"

"policies in Florida helped lead to its almost total collapse"

"100% CONTROLLED"

"a failing campaign"

"just can't get it right!"

"weak on illegal immigration"

"bad on women's health issues"

"no more Bushes"

"is miserable"

"fell more than anybody"

"just doesn't get it"

"will never secure the border"

"will NEVER Make America Great Again"

TRUMP ON John Kasich

Republican Governor of Ohio, Presidential candidate

"You know the way I conduct myself. Do you really believe I would say, '(John Kasich) is in charge of foreign and domestic policy and (Donald Trump) will focus on making America great again'? What am I, a meathead?"

TRUMP ON John Kerry

Secretary of State

"Kerry did not read the Art of the Deal or probably the Bible either."

"He's an incompetent negotiator."

"They have no respect for him. He falls off bicycles at age 73 in the middle of a negotiation."

TRUMP ON John McCain

Republican Senator Arizona and former Presidential candidate "has done nothing"

"I am no fan"

"All he does is go on television is talk, talk, talk"

"incapable of doing anything."

"has failed miserably"

"doing a lousy job in taking care of our Vets"

"let us down"

"dummy"

"graduated last in his class"

"should be defeated in the primaries"

"He's not a war hero. He was a war hero because he was captured. I like people who weren't captured."

TRUMP ON Jon Stewart

Former host, producer "The Daily Show"

"I promise you that I'm much smarter than Jonathan Leibowitz - I mean Jon Stewart @TheDailyShow. Who, by the way, is totally over rated."

"If Jon Stewart is so above it all and legit, why did he change his name from Jonathan Leibowitz? He should cherish his past-not run from it. He is a total phony."

"Amazing how the haters and losers keep tweeting the name (Clownstick). What's funny about the name "F**kface Von Clownstick? It was not coined by him. He stole it from some moron on twitter."

TRUMP ON Judge Gonzalo P. Curiel

District judge of the United States District Court for the Southern District of California

"very biased"

"unfair"

"Totally biased"

"I have had horrible rulings, I have been treated unfairly by this judge. Now this judge is of Mexican heritage, I'm building a wall."

"He's a member of a society, where you know, very pro-Mexico and that's fine, it's all fine.

But I think he could recuse himself."

TRUMP ON Justice Ruth Bader Ginsberg

U.S. Supreme Court Associate Justice

"I think it's highly inappropriate that a United States Supreme Court judge gets involved in a political campaign, frankly. I think it's a disgrace to the court, and I think she should apologize to the court. I couldn't believe it when I saw it."

"It's so beneath the court for her to be making statements like that. It only energizes my base even more. And I would hope that she would get off the court as soon as possible."

TRUMP ON Karl Rove

Former deputy White House chief of staff

"a failed Jeb Bushy"

"Never says anything good & never will"

"Shouldn't be on the air!"

"should be fired!"

"sick"

"loser"

"so biased"

"still thinks Romney won"

"unfair"

"dummy"

"no credibility"

"FoxNews should can him"

"dopey"

"pushing Republicans down the same old path of defeat"

"a loser"

"shouldn't be allowed to do [his] bias commentary"

"establishment flunky"

"dummy"

"should get a life"

"just totally bombed"

"a loser"

"has ZERO credibility"

"an establishment dope"

"has made so many mistakes"

"loser"

"dope"

"total fool"

"an all talk, no action dummy!"

"part of the Republican Establishment problem"

"purposely mischaracterized my statement"

"dopey"

"dummy"

"biased dope"

"moron"

"easy to beat!"

"dopey"

"spent $430 million and lost ALL races"

"dope"

"wasted $400 million"

"didn't win one race"

"total loser"

"a clown with zero credibility"

"irrelevant clown, sweats and shakes nervously"

"has zero cred"

"made fool of himself in '12"

"a Bush plant who called all races wrong"

TRUMP ON Khan family

"Mr. Khan, who does not know me, viciously attacked me from the stage of the DNC and is now all over T.V. doing the same - Nice!"

"I've sacrificed plenty by building buildings!"

TRUMP ON Kim Il Un

"He's a maniac and madman who is sick enough to use nuclear weapons."

"Kim deserves credit for how he took over his country at such a young age, at age 25 or 26 when his father died."

"He goes in, he takes over from these tough generals and all of a sudden, you know it's pretty amazing, he's the boss."

"Nobody talks to him other than of course Dennis Rodman. I would have no problem talking to him."

TRUMP ON Lindsey Graham

United States Republican Senator, Presidential candidate

"failed presidential candidate"

"no honor!"

"I ran him out of the race like a little boy"

"in the end he had no support"

"ALL TALK AND NO ACTION!"

"Failed presidential candidate"

"should respect me"

"nasty!"

"dumb mouthpiece"

"got zero against me- no cred!"

"had zero in his presidential run before dropping out in disgrace"

"embarrassed himself with his failed run for President"

"embarrasses himself with endorsement of Bush"

"so easy to beat!"

TRUMP ON Marco Rubio

United States Republican Senator, Florida

"bought and paid for by lobbyists!"

"worst voting record in the U.S. Senate in many years"

"will never MAKE AMERICA GREAT AGAIN!"

"Dishonest"

"dishonest lightweight"

"he is scamming Florida"

"fraud lightweight"

"big loser"

"failed presidential candidate"

"Rubio puts out ad that my pilot was a drug dealer- not true, not my pilot!"

"never even shows up to vote"

"worst record"

"a joke!"

"Interesting how my numbers have gone so far up since lightweight Marco Rubio has turned nasty. Love it!"

"Phony"

"treated America's ICE officers 'like absolute trash' in order to pass Obama's amnesty"

"gave amnesty to criminal aliens guilty of 'sex offenses.' DISGRACE!"

"just another Washington D.C. politician"

"all talk and no action"

"Little Marco"

"poor work ethic!"

"the lightweight no show Senator from Florida, just another Washington politician"

"set to be the 'puppet' of the special interest Koch brothers"

"not as smart as Cruz, and may be an even bigger liar"

"once a choker, always a choker!"

"looks like a little boy on stage"

"not presidential material!"

"Doesn't even show up for votes!"

"he is a choker, and once a choker, always a choker!"

"Mr. Meltdown"

"Lying"

"very weak on illegal immigration"

"a lightweight choker"

"couldn't even respond properly to President Obama's State of the Union Speech without pouring sweat & chugging water"

"a highly overrated politician"

"cannot be President"

"only won the debate in the minds of desperate people"

"lightweight"

"very disloyal to Jeb"

"VERY weak on illegal immigration"

"perfect little puppet"

"very disloyal"

"never made ten cents"

"totally controlled"

"worst voting record in Senate"

"lazy"

"all talk and no action"

"very weak on stopping illegal immigration"

"VERY weak on immigration"

"knows nothing about finance"

"incapable of making great trade deals"

"rarely there to vote on a bill"

"worst attendance record in Senate"

"weak on illegal immigration"

"will allow anyone into the country"

"just another all talk, no action, politician"

"truly doesn't have a clue!"

TRUMP ON Media (also see Megyn Kelly, Don Lemon, Trump around the world overseas media, editorials on Trump in this book)

"The media is all low-life."

ABC News Politics

News organization

"LIE"

Anderson Cooper "360"

CNN News program

"a waste"

The Associated Press

News organization

"false"

"has one of the worst reporters in the business"

"dishonest reporting"

"always looking for a hit to bring them back into relevancy—ain't working"

"Reuters is a far more professional operation"

"reporting is terrible & highly inaccurate"

"now irrelevant"

"they have lost their way and are no longer credible"

"should change their fraudulent story"

CNBC

News organization

"crazy"

"fictitious polling numbers"

"sad"

"continues to report fictious poll numbers"

"pushing the GOP around"

"ridiculous debate terms"

CNN

News organization (editor's note: They have 7 paid Trump spokesmen)

"all negative when it comes to me"

"Clinton News Network"

"losing all credibility"

"totally biased"

"so biased"

"Shows are predictable garbage!"

"one big lie!"

"Clinton News Network"

"getting more and more biased"

"so negative, getting even worse"

"Don't watch CNN!"

"I no longer watch"

"working hard to make me look as bad as possible"

"Very unprofessional"

"bad television!"

"so negative it is impossible to watch"

"Terrible panel"

"angry haters"

"really one-sided and unfair reporting"

"so sad"

"dishonest reporting"

"paid a fortune for an Iowa Poll, which shows me in first place over Cruz by 13%, 33% to 20% - then doesn't use it"

"When will @CNN get some real political talent"

"totally one-sided and biased against me that it is becoming boring"

"bad reporters"

"only says negative"

"just plain dumb!"

"ratings starved"

"does not cover me accurately"

"why can't they get it right"

The Daily Beast

News website

"failing"

"money losing"

The Des Moines Register

Newspaper

"failing"

"I think something's going on w/them"

"ultra liberal"

"seriously failing"

"they lie"

"has no power in Iowa"

Don Lemon, CNN (see CNN)

Forbes

Magazine

"failed magazine"

"circulation way down"

"failing"

Fortune

Magazine

"few people know that Fortune Magazine is still in business"

Fox News

News organization (also see Megyn Kelly)

"How many times can the same people ask the same question?"

"totally biased and disgusting reporting"

"clown announcers"

"in the bag!"

"so biased it is disgusting"

"only puts negative people on"

"Biased - a total joke!"

"the only network that does not even mention my very successful event last night"

"childishly written & taunting PR statement"

"The statement put out yesterday by @FoxNews was a disgrace to good broadcasting and journalism"

"pathetic"

"without me they'd have no ratings!"

"treats me so badly"

"not fair"

"why doesn't @FoxNews quote the new Iowa @CNN Poll where I have a 33% to 20% lead over Ted Cruz and all others"

"has been treating me very unfairly"

"other networks seem to treat me so much better than Fox News"

"only Fox News is consistantly fighting the Trump win"

"should be ashamed of yourself"

"not very good or professional"

The Huffington Post

News organization

"should change their fraudulent story"

"money-losing"

"they only write bad stories about me!"

The mainstream media

"so totally biased"

"dishonesty"

"one big lie!"

"totally biased"

"biased"

"phony"

"on a new phony kick about my management style"

"dishonest"

"disgusting"

"really on a witch-hunt against me"

"False reporting, and plenty of it"

"Crooked"

"pushing the false narrative that I want to raise taxes"

"unfair"

"has not covered my long-shot great finish in Iowa fairly"

"dishonest reporters!"

"able to so incorrectly define a word for the public"

"always tough when they falsify"

"won't report!"

"wants to surrender constitutional rights"

"they only want negatives"

"will not report the highly respected new national poll that just came out"

"how will the media put a negative spin on this one?"

"troublemakers"

"despite the[ir] best efforts, the people are speaking loudly and clearly"

"totally dishonest"

"So sad!"

"lies"

"Meet the Press"
Television show

"did a 1 hour hit job on me today"

"totally biased and mostly false"

"Dishonest"

"very dishonest"

"terrible ratings"

"ratings starved"

"Morning Joe"
Television show

"Nobody is watching"

"Gone off the deep end"

"bad ratings"

"Small audience"

"low ratings!"

"They misrepresent my positions!"

"rapidly fading"

"off the rails"

"waste of time"

"so off"

National Review
Magazine

"over"

"dying"

"losing for years"

"failing"

"dying"

"very few people read"

"failing"

"lost it's way"

"New Day"
CNN News program

"treats me very badly"

"not going to watch anymore"

The New Hampshire Union Leader

Newspaper

"won't survive"

"highly unethical"

"kicked out of the ABC news debate like a dog"

"has lost all credibility"

"circulation dropping to record lows"

"they aren't worthy of representing the great people of NH"

"endorsed a candidate who can't win"

"unethical record"

"failing"

"stupid"

"desperate"

"bad management"

"begged me for ads"

"dying"

"will be dead in 2 years"

"has been run into the ground"

"dying"

"in turmoil"

"dying"

"very unethical"

Don Fass

The New York Daily News

Newspaper

"failing"

"worthless"

"bleeding red ink"

"a total loser!"

"Worthless"

"nobody reads it"

"dying tabloid"

"it is dead"

The New York Times

Newspaper

"So totally dishonest!"

"failing"

"will always take a good story about me and make it bad"

"Every article is unfair and biased"

"Very sad!"

"a disgusting fraud"

"has become a joke!"

"false, malicious & libelous"

"totally dishonest"

"a fraud!"

"Wow, I have had so many calls from high ranking people laughing at the stupidity of the failing @nytimes piece"

"Everyone is laughing at the @nytimes for the lame hit piece they did on me and women"

"wrote yet another hit piece on me"

"A joke!"

"bad"

"the most inaccurate coverage constantly"

"Always trying to belittle"

"has lost its way!"

"a seriously failing paper"

"Becoming irrelevant!"

"covers me so inaccurately"

"truly one of the worst newspapers"

"They knowingly write lies"

"never even call to fact check"

"Really bad people!"

"allows dishonest writers to totally fabricate stories"

"change your false story"

"should focus on fair and balanced reporting"

"boring articles"

"big help will be needed fast"

"SAD!"

"made all bad decisions over the last decade"

"incompetent"

"dopes"

"poorly run and managed"

"should be focused on good reporting and the papers financial survival"

"The O'Reilly Factor"

Fox News program

"why don't you have some knowledgeable talking heads on your show for a change"

"Boring!"

Politico

News organization

"in total disarray"

"almost everybody quitting"

"bad, dishonest journlists"

"going out of business"

"Losing too much money. Great news!"

"Bad reporting- no money, no cred!"

"3rd rate $ losing"

"no credibility"

"If they were legit, they would be doing far better"

"some very untalented reporters"

"money losing"

"Losers!"

"considered by many in the world of politics to be the dumbest and most slanted of the political sites"

"a scam!"

"pure scum"

"dishonest"

"has no power"

"so dishonest!"

"clowns"

"serious haters"

"dishonest"

"failing"

"losing lots of money"

"really dishonest"

"not read or respected by many"

"covers me more inaccurately than any other media source"

"go out of their way to distort truth!"

RedState.com
Conservative web site

"small crowds"

"The Last Word With Lawrence O'Donnell"
Television show

"unwatchable"

"The View"
Television show

"A total disaster."

"failing so badly that it will soon be taken off thr air"

"close to death"

"dead T.V."

"put it to sleep"

Univision

Media organization

"doing really badly"

"too much debt and not enough viewers"

"need money fast"

"controlled by Mexican government?"

Vanity Fair

Magazine

"has lost almost all of it's former allure"

"failing"

The Wall Street Journal

Newspaper

"bad at math, nobody cares what they say in their editorials anymore, especially me!"

"failing"

"seldom has a paper been so wrong"

"reported 'Cruz momentum' but nothing about the fact that I easily won!"

"so dishonest"

"purposely mischaracterized my statement"

"failing"

"so totally wrong"

"dummies"

"so wrong, so often"

"loves to write badly about me"

"some of the dumbest people on television work for the Wall Street Journal"

"looks like a tabloid"

"ever-dwindling"

The Wall Street Journal editorial board

Opinion pages of the Wall Street Journal

"dummies"

The Washington Post

Newspaper

"dishonest"

"phony"

"tax scam"

"inaccurate"

"dishonest reporting"

"bad"

"big tax shelter"

"loses a fortune"

The Weekly Standard
Magazine

"small and slightly failing magazine"

"World News Tonight"
ABC News program

"bad reporting"

TRUMP ON Megyn Kelly (also see women)
Fox News anchor

''Trump made Megyn Kelly look really bad —- she was a mess with her anger and totally caught off guard. Blood was coming out of her eyes and whatever."

"I meant her nose. Only a deviant would think anything else."

"BAD"

"highly overrated"

"so average in so many ways!"

"crazy"

"Never worth watching"

"sick, & the most overrated person on tv"

"Highly overrated"

"crazy"

"is always complaining about Trump and yet she devotes her shows to me"

"Crazy"

"her bad show is a total hit piece on me"

"Crazy"

"Can't watch Crazy Megyn anymore"

"Without me her ratings would tank"

"Get a life Megyn!"

"lightweight reporter"

"I refuse to call Megyn Kelly a bimbo, because that would not be politically correct"

"so average in every way"

"dopey"

"lies"

"highly overrated"

"bad!"

"very bad at math"

"the most overrated anchor"

"really weird, she's being driven crazy"

"don't watch her show"

"had her two puppets say bad stuff"

"I don't watch"

"should take another eleven day 'unscheduled' vacation"

"highly overrated"

"really off her game"

"not very good or professional"

"really bombed tonight"

TRUMP ON Mexico, Mexicans (also see immigration, full immigration speech following this section, our Trump South of the Border page.)

"When Mexico sends its people, they're not sending their best. They're not sending you. They're not sending you. They're sending people that have lots of problems, and they're bringing those problems with us. They're bringing drugs. They're bringing crime. They're rapists. And some, I assume, are good people."

"But I speak to border guards and they tell us what we're getting. And it only makes common sense. It only makes common sense. They're sending us not the right people."

"We are taking hundreds of thousands of people. Some good people and some rapists and some killers and drug lords and everyone else and they are flowing through the southern border."

"I would build a wall like nobody can build a wall… Nobody can build a fence like me."

"They will pay for it because they have really ripped this country off. They have really taken advantage of us both economically and at the border. They will pay for that fence.(When the wall is built,) nobody comes in illegally anymore."

"totally corrupt government"

"we get the killers, drugs & crime, they get the money!"

"unbelievable corruption"

"not our friend"

"they're killing us"

"What they're doing, they're having a baby. And then all of a sudden, nobody knows ... the baby's here."

"So true. Jeb Bush is crazy, who cares that he speaks Mexican, this is America, English !!"

(To Hispanic commentator Jorge Ramos) "Go back to Univision."

'Sadly, the overwhelming amount of violent crime in our major cities is committed by blacks and hispanics-a tough subject-must be discussed.''

"We will impound all remittance payments derived from illegal wages; increase fees on all temporary visas issued to Mexican CEOs and diplomats (and if necessary cancel them); increase fees on all border crossing cards - of which we issue about 1 million to Mexican nationals each year (a major source of visa overstays); increase fees on all NAFTA worker visas from Mexico (another major source of overstays); and increase fees at ports of entry to the United States from Mexico [Tariffs and foreign aid cuts are also options]. We will not be taken advantage of anymore."

"We're going to keep the families together, but they (11 million Mexican undocumented immigrants) have to go."

"The cost of building a permanent border wall pales mightily in comparison to what American taxpayers spend every single year on dealing with the fallout of illegal immigration on their communities, schools and unemployment offices."

TRUMP ON Michael Bloomberg

Billionaire businessman, media mogul and former 3-term mayor, New York City

"Mike Bloomberg is doing a great job as Mayor of New York City." (2012)

"Bloomberg is a little man who never had the guts to run for president."

"'Little' Michael Bloomberg, who never had the guts to run for president, knows nothing about me. His last term as Mayor was a disaster."

"If Michael Bloomberg ran again for Mayor of New York, he wouldn't get 10% of the vote - they would run him out of town!"

TRUMP ON Mitch McConnell

Republican Majority Leader, U.S. Senate

"He's 100 percent wrong. Okay? He's 100 percent wrong (about NATO) if he said that... He's 100 percent wrong and frankly, it's sad"

"I 'm so surprised at Senate Majority Leader Mitch McConnell, you 'd think Senate Majority Leader Mitch McConnell 'd be very positive. I always thought I had a good relationship with Senate Majority Leader Mitch McConnell, but perhaps I don't."

TRUMP ON Mitt Romney

Former Massachusetts governor, Republican Presidential Candidate

"choked like a dog"

"a mixed up man who doesn't have a clue. No wonder he lost!"

"Failed"

"Failed presidential candidate"

"the man who 'choked' and let us all down"

"let us all down in the last presidential race"

"a disaster candidate who had no guts and choked"

"a total joke, and everyone knows it!"

"Why did Mitt Romney BEG me for my endorsement four years ago?"

"doesn't know how to win"

"desperate move by the man who should have easily beaten Barrack Obama"

"Failed Presidential Candidate"

"didn't show his tax return until SEPTEMBER 21, 2012, and then only after being humiliated by Harry R"

"bad messenger for estab!"

"failed"

"one of the dumbest and worst candidates in the history of Republican politics"

"so awkward and goofy"

"I don't need his angry advice"

"blew an election that should have never been lost"

"terrible 'choke' loss to Obama"

"he choked!"

"why would anybody listen to @MittRomney?"

"lost an election that should have easily been won"

TRUMP ON Muslims (also see immigration, Khan family)

"Donald J. Trump is calling for a total and complete shutdown of Muslims entering the United States until our country's representatives can figure out what is going on.

According to Pew Research, among others, there is great hatred towards Americans by large segments of the Muslim population."

Hillary Clinton, as president, would "be admitting hundreds of thousands of refugees

from the Middle East with no system to vet them, or to prevent the radicalization of their

children. We have to stop the tremendous flow of Syrian refugees into the United States,"

"I think Islam hates us We have to get to the bottom of it. There is an unbelievable hatred of us — anybody."

"Tens of thousands of people were entering America with cell phones with Isis flags on them...I don't think so. They're not coming to this country if I'm president. And if Obama has brought

some to this country they are leaving, they're going, they're gone."

"I'm talking about territories now," People don't want me to say Muslim. I prefer not saying it frankly, myself. So we're talking about territories."

"These people (Americans) are stupid people . I don't know. Our leaders, people that do this, they're stupid people. When you look at Germany, they had a knife wielder yesterday who killed two women and violently came from Syria. I don't know if you know this, but [Tim] Kaine signed a letter wanting to take in far more [refugees] than Obama."

"The U.S. must immediately suspend immigration from any nation that has been compromised by terrorism until such time it's proven that vetting mechanisms have been put in place."

TRUMP ON NATO

"The United States would only defend NATO states attacked by Russia if those nations "have fulfilled their obligations to us."

"(McConnell) is 100 percent wrong. Okay?" He's 100 percent wrong if he said that... He's 100 percent wrong and frankly, it's sad. We have NATO and we have many countries that aren't paying for what they are supposed to be paying, which is already too little but not paying anyway and we're giving them a free ride or a ride where they owe us tremendous amounts of money and have the money but they are not paying it."

"We have countries that aren't paying and this goes beyond NATO because we take care of Japan," We take care of Germany and South Korea, Saudi Arabia and lose on everything.

"Now, a country gets invaded. They haven't paid. Everyone said, 'Oh, but we have a treaty.' They have a treaty, too. They are supposed to be paying. We have countries within NATO taking advantage of us. With me, I believe they are going to pay and when they pay, I'm a big believer in NATO."

TRUMP ON Newt Gingrich

(On criticism about Trump's Judge Curiel comment) "I was surprised at Newt. I thought it was inappropriate what he said."

"(Gingrich) is such a great guy, such a great supporter."

TRUMP ON New York Times (see media)

TRUMP ON North Korea (see Kim Il Un)

TRUMP ON Nukes

"Using nuclear weapons should be the absolute last step." "Power of weaponry today is beyond anything ever thought of, or even, you know, it's unthinkable, the power,"It's a very scary nuclear world," "Biggest problem, to me, in the world, is nuclear, and proliferation."

"I don't want to rule out anything .I will be the last to use nuclear weapons. It's a horror to use nuclear weapons. I will not be a happy trigger like some people might be,But I will never, ever rule it out."

"Japan and South Korea might need to obtain their own nuclear arsenal to protect themselves from North Korea and China if the U.S. is unable to defend them. It's a position that we have to talk about. If the United States keeps on its path, its current path of weakness, they're going to want to have that anyway with or without me discussing it, because I don't think they feel very secure in what's going on with our country."

"At some point, we cannot be the policeman of the world. And unfortunately, we have a nuclear world now."

"You know, when we did these deals, we were a rich country. We're not a rich country. We were a rich country with a very strong military and tremendous capability in so many ways. We're not anymore.We have a military that's severely depleted. We have nuclear arsenals which are in very terrible shape. They don't even know if they work."

"Can I be honest are you? Maybe it's going to have to be time to change, because so many people, you have Pakistan has it, you have China has it. You have so many other countries are now having it. I don't want more nuclear weapons."

"I will have a military that's so strong and powerful, and so respected, we're not gonna have to nuke anybody"

"I am amazingly calm under pressure. It is highly unlikely that I would ever be using them."

TRUMP ON Obamacare/Affordable Healthcare Act (also see health)

"As far as Obamacare is concerned... it's a disaster. It is really kicking in... in 16. It is going to be a tremendous negative for the country. And here's the problem, it's terrible, the rates are going up through the roof. You look at every aspect of Obamacare, it's just not working. And there are a lot of people that still don't have insurance. But the people that had good insurance now have bad insurance. Their deductibles are through the roof. Their rates are through the roof. And I hear more and more complaints. Another thing that nobody talks about... is doctors. I know so many doctors that are going to retire, they don't want to do it. One of my friends whose a doctor said you know I have more accountants than I have nurses because of the complexity of it. So it really does have to be changed... And, ideally, repealed and replaced... I want healthcare for everyone... You can't let the people in this country that are poor people, the people without the money, without the resources, go without healthcare. I just can't even imagine that you're sick and you can't even go to a doctor."

"Obamacare kicks in in 2016. Really big league. It is going to be amazingly destructive. Doctors are quitting. I have a friend who's a doctor, and he said to me the other day, "Donald, I never saw anything like it. I have more accountants than I have nurses. It's a disaster. My patients are beside themselves. They had a plan that was good. They have no plan now."

We have to repeal Obamacare, and it can be -- and -- and it can be replaced with something much better for everybody. Let it be for everybody. But much better and much less expensive for people and for the government. And we can do it."

TRUMP ON Paul Ryan

Republican Congressman, Speaker of the House

"I was surprised by the rebuke from Mr. Ryan on Thursday. The party needs to come together.

I was really surprised. By the way, many other people were surprised by it, and some were really surprised by it, and not happy about it. You talk about unity, but what is this? With 'billions' of people coming into the party, obviously I'm saying the right thing."

TRUMP on Penn Jillette

Performer

"sad"

"worst show in Las Vegas"

"hokey garbage"

"goofball atheist"

"never had a chance"

"wrote letter to me begging for forgiveness"

"boring guy"

TRUMP ON Pope Francis

"My people came up to me, they said, 'Mr. Trump, the Pope just made a big statement about you.' And I said, 'good or bad?' They said, 'Not good.' I said, 'Oh, this is a disaster. "

"He actually was very, very nice the next day. The Pope was misled by Mexican surrogates during a visit to Mexico. Nobody explained to him about the crime, nobody explained to him about the drugs pouring across and the economy and he was actually very nice. You don't want to hear the day before the election that the Pope said something about you."

"You saw the Pope came out against me a little bit, but that was before he knew ... "

"It was the day before the election, right? And I said to myself, 'Oh no.' "

TRUMP ON Rand Paul

Republican U.S. Senator and Presidential candidate

"Rand Paul should not be on this stage. He polls less than 1%."

"He is lowly and very weird."

"I never attacked him or his looks, and believe me, there's plenty of subject matter right there."

TRUMP ON Rick Perry

Former Governor of Texas, Republican Presidential candidate

"Perry used to say the *worst things* about me but I always liked Perry."

"Politics is a dirty business. I've never seen people able to pivot like politicians."

You quickly get the idea that Perry is just another unprincipled politician who is willing to say anything to be on the winning side.

Of course then Trump praises Perry for seeing the light and endorsing him.

Now say what you will about Perry, because he really did pivot. Perhaps he was just following up on his pledge, or maybe he really did see the 'light.'

"Perry failed to secure the border in Texas."

"Perry was a good governor."

"He put on glasses so people think he's smart. People can see through the glasses."

TRUMP ON Rick Santorum

Former member of Congress, Republican Presidential candidate

"He's a loser."

"Well, but you're too conservative. You're just out there. You're just way conservative. You're too hard-core on pro-life, you're too hard-core on marriage. I don't know anyone who shares that opinion with you."

TRUMP ON Religion (see our separate page)

TRUMP ON Rosie O'Donnell (see women)

Comedienne and TV host

TRUMP ON Saddam Hussein

Former dictator, Iraq   (also see Iraq)

"Saddam Hussein was a bad guy. Right? He was a bad guy, really bad guy. But you know what he did well? He killed terrorists. He did that so good. They didn't read them the rights — they didn't talk, they were a terrorist, it was over. Today, Iraq is Harvard for terrorism. You want to be a terrorist, you go to Iraq. It's like Harvard. Okay? So sad."

"The world would be "100 percent" better if dictators like Hussein and Moammar Gaddafi were still in power."

TRUMP ON Scott Walker

Wisconsin Republican governor

"puppet"

"cratered"

"massive deficit, bad jobs forecast, a mess."

"not presidential material"

"not smart"

"your very dumb fundraiser hit me very hard--- not smart!"

TRUMP ON Second Amendment (see Hillary Clinton, guns, crime)

TRUMP ON sex life (see women)

TRUMP ON Syria (see immigration)

TRUMP ON taxes (see speeches, others on Trump's plans)

TRUMP on Ted Cruz

Don Fass

United States senator, chief rival for GOP nomination

"Lyin', he should drop out of the race-stop wasting time & money"

"really went wacko today"

"Made all sorts of crazy charges"

"Can't function under pressure"

"not very presidential"

"Sad!"

"has NO path to victory"

"weak"

"desperate"

"has to team up with a guy who openly can't stand him"

"mathematically dead and totally desperate"

"Drop out LYIN' Ted"

"all he can do is be a spoiler, never a nice thing to do"

"hates New York"

"can't win with the voters so he has to sell himself to the bosses"

"can't get votes (I am millions ahead of him)"

"has to get his delegates from the Republican bosses"

"will never be able to beat Hillary, " "Hillary would destroy him"

"Despite a rigged delegate system, I am hundreds of delegates ahead of him."

"attacked New Yorkers and New York values- we don't forget!"

"losing big"

"just another dishonest politician"

"Mormons don't like LIARS!"

"Who should star in a reboot of Liar Liar- Hillary Clinton or Ted Cruz? Let me know."

"a big problem!"

"desperate"

"his lying is getting worse"

"can't win!"

"bought and paid for by lobbyists!"

"he has accomplished absolutely nothing"

"another all talk, no action pol!"

"choker"

"a nasty guy"

"lies like a dog-over and over again!"

"does not have the right 'temperment' to be President"

"disloyal"

"biggest liar in politics!"

"a world class LIAR"

"a true lowlife pol!"

"holds the Bible high and then lies and misrepresents the facts!"

"Nasty"

"cheater"

"I have standing to sue him for not being a natural born citizen"

"lies so much and is so dishonest"

"His father was with Lee Harvey Oswald at the Kennedy Assassination"

"the worst liar, crazy or very dishonest"

"caught cold in lie"

"should be immediately disqualified in Iowa"

"just lied again"

"told thousands of caucusgoers (voters) that Trump was strongly in favor of ObamaCare and 'choice' - a total lie!"

"fraud"

"sent out a VOTER VIOLATION certificate to thousands of voters"

"didn't win Iowa, he illegally stole it"

"lying on so many levels"

"totally unelectable"

"dishonest"

"deceptive"

"can't even get a Senator like @BenSasse, who is easy, to endorse him"

"Not one Senator is endorsing Canada Ted!"

"will do anything to stay at the trough"

"dropping like a rock"

"a nervous wreck"

"not caring for the truth"

"reckless"

"in bed w/ Wall St."

"puppet!"

"people do not like Ted"

"a nervous wreck"

"falling in the polls"

"spending $millions on ads paid for by his N.Y. bosses"

"greatly dishonest"

"When will Ted Cruz give all the New York based campaign contributions back to the special interests that control him."

"why did he accept money from people who espouse gay marriage?"

"the ultimate hypocrite"

"says one thing for money, does another for votes"

"didn't list on his personal disclosure form personally guaranteed bank loans. They own him!"

"The Ted Cruz wise guy apology to the people of New York is a disgrace"

"Goldman Sachs owns him"

"not much of a reformer"

"not believable"

"not nice"

"would speak behind my back, get caught, and then deny it"

"should not make statements behind closed doors to his bosses"

"he will fall like all others"

TRUMP ON trade   (see his speeches, others on Trump)

TRUMP ON Trump

"I don't have thin skin I have very strong, very thick skin," Trump said. "I have a strong temperament. I have a temperament that's totally in control."

"I have a good brain. A very good brain."

"My best quality is my temperament. I have a great temperament."

TRUMP ON violence (see second amendment, Trump South of the Border, crime, guns, NRA)

TRUMP ON wealth see earlier separate section),

TRUMP on Whoopi Goldberg

Actress, producer, television personality

"now in total freefall"

"terrible"

"very sad!"

TRUMP ON Women (also see sex life, Carly Fiorina, Megan Kelly, abortion, Planned Parenthood)

"Arianna Huffington"is unattractive both inside and out. I fully understand why her former husband left her for a man—he made a good decision."

"It's a pretty picture of (former Playboy Playmate) Brande Roderick dropping to her knees."

"All of the women on *The Apprentice* flirted with me— consciously or unconsciously. That's to be expected."

"You know, it doesn't really matter what [the media] write as long as you've got a young and beautiful piece of [expletive]."

"Rosie O'Donnell is an animal, an extremely unattractive person and a slob."

"You could see (Megyn Kelly's) there was blood coming out of her eyes–blood coming out of her wherever."

"She's a bimbo and lightweight."

"I don't know why, but I seem to bring out either the best or worst in women."

"I'm not a crusader for feminism, and I'm not against it, either. I'm just oblivious to a person's gender when it comes to hiring people and handing out assignments."

"It's funny. My own mother was a housewife all her life. And yet it's turned out that I've hired a lot of women for top jobs, and they've been among my best people. Often, in fact, they are far more effective than the men around them."

"The [1997 Miss Universe] pageant in Miami Beach, my first as owner, was a huge success. We'd sold out the house; it was a mob scene. From my position offstage, I was able to glance up to the greenroom occasionally. I could just see Alicia Machado, the current Miss Universe, sitting there plumply. God, what problems I had with this woman. First, she wins. Second, she gains fifty pounds. Third, I urge the committee *not* to fire her. Fourth, I go to the gym *with* her, in a show of support. Final act: She trashes me in *The Washington Post* — after I stood by her the entire time. What's wrong with this picture? Anyway, the best part about the evening was the knowledge that next year, she would no longer be Miss Universe."

"I grew up in a very normal family. I was always of the opinion that aggression, sex drive, and everything that goes along with it was on the man's part of the table, not the woman's. As I grew older and witnessed life firsthand from a front-row seat at the great clubs, social events, and parties of the world — I have seen just about everything — I began to realize that women are far stronger than men. Their sex drive makes us look like babies. Some women try to portray themselves as being of the weaker sex, but don't believe it for a minute."

"Women have one of the great acts of all time. The smart ones act very feminine and needy, but inside they are real killers. The person who came up with the expression 'the weaker sex' was either very naive or had to be kidding. I have seen women manipulate men with just a twitch of their eye — or perhaps another body part."

"There's nothing I love more than women, but they're really a lot different than portrayed. They are far worse than men, far more aggressive, and boy, can they be smart. "

"If I told the real stories of my experiences with women, often seemingly very happily married and important women, this book would be a guaranteed best-seller (which it will be anyway!). I'd love to tell all, using names and places, but I just don't think it's right."

"I've never had any trouble in bed, but if I'd had affairs with half the starlets and female athletes the newspapers linked me with, I'd have no time to breathe."

"I was especially carefree [in the early-mid 1970s]. I was out four or five nights a week, usually with a different woman each time, and I was enjoying myself immensely."

"One of the first things I did was join Le Club, which at the time was the hottest club in the city and perhaps the most exclusive — It turned out to be a great move for me, socially and professionally. I met a lot of beautiful young single women, and I went out almost every night.. These were beautiful women, but many of them couldn't carry on a normal conversation. Some were vain, some were crazy, some were wild, and many of them were phonies. For example, I quickly found out that I couldn't take these girls back to my apartment, because by their standards, what I had was a disaster, and in their world appearances were everything."

"Part of the problem I've had with women has been in having to compare them to my incredible mother, Mary Trump. My mother is smart as hell."

"I knew from the start that Ivana was different from just about all of the other women I'd been spending time with. Good looks had been my top — and sometimes, to be honest, my only — priority in my man-about-town days. Ivana was gorgeous, but she was also ambitious and intelligent. I also stayed with Ivana because, as in most marriages, there was pressure to keep things intact. . . . There's nothing wrong, of course, with worrying about the effects of divorce on your children and the other people around you. I even thought, briefly, about approaching Ivana with the idea of an 'open marriage.' But I realized there was something hypocritical and tawdry about such an arrangement that neither of us could live with — especially Ivana. She's too much of a lady. My big mistake with Ivana was taking her out of the role of wife and allowing her to run one of my casinos in Atlantic City, then the Plaza Hotel. The problem was, work was all she wanted to talk about. When I got home at night, rather than talking about the softer subjects of life, she wanted to tell me how well the Plaza was doing, or what a great day the casino had. It was just too much. . . I will never again give a wife responsibility within my business. "

"My marriage to Marla lasted three and a half years. Sadly, like so many couples these days, we. wanted different things. Marla was content when it was just her, [their daughter] Tiffany, and me. I, on the other hand, realized that business needed to be taken care of constantly. You don't mind traveling around in beautiful helicopters and airplanes, and you don't mind living at the top of Trump Tower, or at Mar-a-Lago, or traveling to the best hotels, or shopping in the best stores and never having to worry about money, do you? Why would you want to take something that I enjoy and change it?" I always viewed her whys as being very selfish."

"For a man to be successful he needs support at home, just like my father had from my mother, not someone who is always griping and bitching. When a man has to endure a woman who is not supportive and complains constantly about his not being home enough or not being attentive enough, he will not be very successful unless he is able to cut the cord. One thing I have learned: There is high maintenance. There is low maintenance. I want no maintenance."

"The calculating woman refuses to sign the prenuptial agreement because she is expecting to take advantage of the poor, unsuspecting sucker she's got in her grasp. There is also the woman who will openly and quickly sign a prenuptial agreement in order to make a quick hit and take the money given to her."

"'Donald,' she said. 'I don't care. I have to have you, and I have to have you now.' I told her that I'd call her, but that she had to stop the behavior immediately. She made me promise, and I did. When I called I just called to say hello, and that was the end of that.

But the level of aggression was unbelievable. This is not infrequent, it happens all the time."

"I only have one regret in the women department — that I never had the opportunity to court Lady Diana Spencer. I met her on a number of occasions. I couldn't help but notice how she moved people. She lit up the room with her charm, her presence. She was a genuine princess — a dream lady."

To a contestant on Celebrity Apprentice: "That must be a pretty picture, you dropping to your knees,"

"Rosie O'Donnell had a fat, ugly face."

To an overweight female exec who oversaw construction of his NYC headquarters, "You like your candy."

Ladies' Man: TRUMP

Trump in the New York Military Academy's 1964 yearbook.

Regarding his beauty contests, "I don't care if she's sweet,". "Is she hot?" …

THE OCTOBER SURPRISES!

October hadn't quite begun. Yet, just 5 weeks before the election, lots of surprises were still happening…. primarily against Trump and many of them his own doing..

His first Presidential debate with Hillary Clinton at Hofstra University, watched by an estimated 84 million people (not counting streaming and social media) was a worse disaster for Trump than many would bet it would be. Trump apparently hadn't really prepared at all for his biggest and most important campaign event in 16 months. All polls and most pundits clearly gave Secretary Clinton the victory…except for Sean Hannity's easy-to-sway and unimportant call-in polls, which even Fox News reprimanded Hannity for using.

At the debate, Trump got caught going down numerous rabbit holes, many of which he constructed, while constantly sniffling loudly (but which he later said never happened). Numerous others speculated that he was 'on' something, Dr. Howard Dean even speculating it might be cocaine. A tweeter wrote that it was 'Trump being allergic to his own crap. Trump also drank a lot of water, reminding many of his making fun of Marco Rubio during the primary for doing the same.

NBC moderator Lester Holt did do fact-checking, even calling out Trump predictably for having really been for the Iraq war before it began and until 2 years after we invaded. Holt also caught Trump on not releasing any of his tax returns as every other candidate since Nixon had done and having been a birther for 5 years after President Obama produced his birth certificate. On all these, Trump just sputtered.

David Gergen, pundit, advisor to several administrations and professor at Harvard's Kennedy School, said that Hillary Clinton "crushed Trump."   Gergen went on to say that "Mrs. Clinton carefully marshaled her arguments and facts and then sent them into battle with a smile. She rolled out a long list of indictments against Donald Trump, often damaging. By contrast, he came in unprepared, had nothing fresh to say, and increasingly gave way to rants. As the evening ended, the media buried him in criticisms."

Many shared Gergen's opinion of the debate. They also were of the view that Secretary Clinton did a good job dismantling Trump's business record. She hit him on well-reported incidents, turning his claim to fame against him, bringing up his handful of bankruptcies, allegations that he's stiffed workers, his liking the housing meltdown for his own financial benefit and his aversion to releasing his perpetually under-audit tax returns. "It must be something really important, even terrible, that he's trying to hide," Clinton said.

Trump all but acknowledged he doesn't pay income taxes, saying "they would be wasted," and that it makes him "really smart." One pundit pointed out that it made Trump "seem more like an abusive one-percenter than a man of the people." His birther explanation made no sense, and his claim that Hillary has been "fighting ISIS your entire life," was as ridiculous as his notion of stealing Iraq's oil. His denial of the well-established fact that he supported the Iraq war was an awkward dance.

Much talked about after the debate was the bait Clinton gave Trump about his shaming a Miss Universe winner, Alicia Machado. Trump took it and made it worse with his remarks. For days, Trump kept that subject alive, unable to let go, further denigrating Machado and even falsely accusing her of making a porn video.

The well-behaved Hofstra audience laughed at Trump when he said that his 'temperament was his biggest asset,' clearly disagreeing with his assessment of himself. And throughout, the split screen showing Clinton's facial reactions to much of what Trump said did him damage even further.

THE SPLIT SCREEN

By the time it was over, many observers felt that, despite Trump interrupting her dozens of times talking loud and often angry, Clinton unmasked Trump as a con man (over his failure to release tax returns, penchant for not paying his workers, loving the housing crisis for his own benefit and more).

A CNN commentator said that "Clinton consistently appeared poised and attacked with methodical precision. The most effective part of Clinton's attacks was to connect him to a kind of trickle-down economics and raise questions about his business record and his consistant pattern of racism. Clinton's best moments also came when she attacked him on birtherism. In the final half hour, Trump was mired deep in his Trumpian statements about women's looks and more."

Another commentator reminded that, near the end of Monday night's debate, "Hillary Clinton looked straight into the camera to address America's allies. She wanted our friends and partners in NATO, and allies like Japan, South Korea, and others to know that we meant to honor our obligations. In that moment, Donald Trump entirely disappeared, and Clinton no longer looked like a candidate for President. She sounded like she was already President."

"Donald criticized me for preparing for this debate," Clinton said. "You know what else I prepared for? To be President."

The grin on Clinton's face near the end of the debate was evidence that she was aware that she had had a great night. "Once you've traveled the world, negotiated treaties, and testified before Congress for 11 hours," she said to Trump with a hint of mockery, then "you can talk to me about stamina." Mic drop. Game over.

THE AFTER GLOW---NON STOP!

Afterward, Trump first said the debate had been rigged and then that it was the fault of a bad microphone, then said he won the debate and then once again, blamed moderator Lester Holt, the microphone and everything else for the debate not turning out as he wanted. He denied any sniffles.

Trump would go on to say that the 'cards were stacked against him' but that polls proved he had won. (Untrue. No scientific poll or focus group, not even on Fox, had concluded that Trump had won the debate)

After the debate, Trump kept alive the controversy over his treatment of the Miss Universe for nearly a week, relentlessly putting her down even more and making up that she had appeared in a porn video. *(Ironically, it was later uncovered that it was Trump who had done a cameo in a Playboy soft porn.)*

But things would get much worse for Trump the week after the first debate and his continuing Miss Universe attacks and as Clinton got a poll bounce from her debate performance..

Trump, who has very much favored the Cuban embargo, was found to have violated it, trying to do prohibited business in Cuba under that embargo.

Numerous staunch Republican daily newspapers, none of which had ever backed a Democrat in 80 years or ever, came out with editorials against electing Trump. One distinguished member of The Wall Street Journal's editorial board did the same. USA Today, which in its nearly four decade history had never endorsed a Presidential candidate did endorse one, Hillary Clinton and add a side editorial warning of a Trump presidency.

Stories came out of how Trump has been using his charitable foundation to buy paintings of himself and pay business debts in obvious violation of the law. Then a bigger shoe dropped when New York State found that the Trump Foundation never registered to receive money donations from others and issued a 'cease and desist' order shutting the Trump Foundation down.

Another story indicated that Trump hadn't donated to that foundation or likely made other charitable donations in at least 8 years.

A number of workers and contestants on Trump's Apprentice show released statements of how much he either sexually harassed them or repeatedly made sexual and sexist statements to or about them.

More people who worked for or contracted with Trump came forward to say that he stiffed them too on salaries or contracted payments.

Another story came out that accused Trump of doing business with an Iranian bank under embargo, like he was accused of doing with Cubans.

But still worse—much worse---The New York Times received from someone at Trump Tower they later verified with a Trump attorney in Florida, then released several pages of one Trump tax return from the 90's which showed Trump taking an almost *billion* dollar loss. It was speculated then that Trump could have used that loss to keep from paying any income tax at all for as many as the next 18 years.

Trump again bragged that paying no income tax made him 'smart.' Others including Mrs. Clinton and her many high-profile surrogates questioned how successful a businessman was who lost nearly one billion dollars in one year. But it later appeared that Trump had still another, second giant loss beside that one!

And all this was happening just a month before the election!

Don Fass

TRUMP'S FULL SPEECH ON IMMIGRATION

The state that has a very, very special place in my heart. I love people of Arizona and together we are going to win the White House in November.

(APPLAUSE)

Now, you know this is where it all began for me. Remember that massive crowd also? So, I said let's go and have some fun tonight. We're going to Arizona, O.K.?

This will be a little bit different. This won't be a rally speech, per se. Instead, I'm going to deliver a detailed policy address on one of the greatest challenges facing our country today, illegal immigration.

I've just landed having returned from a very important and special meeting with the president of Mexico, a man I like and respect very much. And a man who truly loves his country, Mexico.

And, by the way, just like I am a man who loves my country, the United States.

(APPLAUSE)

We agree on the importance of ending the illegal flow of drugs, cash, guns, and people across our border, and to put the cartels out of business.

(APPLAUSE)

We also discussed the great contributions of Mexican-American citizens to our two countries, my love for the people of Mexico, and the leadership and friendship between Mexico and the United States. It was a thoughtful and substantive conversation and it will go on for awhile. And, in the end we're all going to win. Both countries, we're all going to win.

This is the first of what I expect will be many, many conversations. And in a Trump administration we're going to go about creating a new relationship between our two countries, but it's going to be a fair relationship. We want fairness.

But to fix our immigration system, we must change our leadership in Washington and we must change it quickly. Sadly, sadly there is no other way. The truth is our immigration system is worse than anybody ever realized. But the facts aren't known because the media won't report on them. The politicians won't talk about them and the special interests spend a lot of money trying to cover them up because they are making an absolute fortune. That's the way it is.

Today, on a very complicated and very difficult subject, you will get the truth. The fundamental problem with the immigration system in our country is that it serves the needs of wealthy donors, political activists and powerful, powerful politicians. It's all you can do. Thank you. Thank you.

(APPLAUSE)

Let me tell you who it does not serve. It does not serve you the American people. Doesn't serve you. When politicians talk about immigration reform, they usually mean the following: amnesty, open borders, lower wages. Immigration reform should mean something else entirely. It should mean improvements to our laws and policies to make life better for American citizens.

But if we're going to make our immigration system work, then we have to be prepared to talk honestly and without fear about these important and very sensitive issues. For instance, we have to listen to the concerns that working people, our forgotten working people, have over the record pace of immigration and it's impact on their jobs, wages, housing, schools, tax bills and general living conditions.

These are valid concerns expressed by decent and patriotic citizens from all backgrounds, all over. We also have to be honest about the fact that not everyone who seeks to join our country will be able to successfully assimilate. Sometimes it's just not going to work out. It's our right, as a sovereign nation, to chose immigrants that we think are the likeliest to thrive and flourish and love us.

Then there is the issue of security. Countless innocent American lives have been stolen because our politicians have failed in their duty to secure our borders and enforce our laws like they have to be enforced. I have met with many of the great parents who lost their children to sanctuary cities and open borders. So many people, so many, many people. So sad. They will be joining me on this stage in a little while and I look forward to introducing, these are amazing, amazing people.

Countless Americans who have died in recent years would be alive today if not for the open border policies of this administration and the administration that causes this horrible, horrible thought process, called Hillary Clinton.

This includes incredible Americans like 21-year-old Sarah Root. The man who killed her arrived at the border, entered federal custody and then was released into the U.S., think of it, into the U.S. community under the policies of the White House Barack Obama and Hillary Clinton. Weak, weak policies. Weak and foolish policies.

He was released again after the crime, and now he's out there at large. Sarah had graduated from college with a 4.0, top student in her class one day before her death.

Also among the victims of the Obama-Clinton open-border policy was Grant Ronnebeck, a 21-year-old convenience store clerk and a really good guy from Mesa, Arizona. A lot of you have known about Grant.

He was murdered by an illegal immigrant gang member previously convicted of burglary, who had also been released from federal custody, and they knew it was going to happen again.

Another victim is Kate Steinle. Gunned down in the sanctuary city of San Francisco, by an illegal immigrant, deported five previous times. And they knew he was no good.

Then there is the case of 90-year-old Earl Olander, who was brutally beaten and left to bleed to death in his home, 90 years old and defenseless. The perpetrators were illegal immigrants with criminal records a mile long, who did not meet Obama administration standards for removal. And they knew it was going to happen.

In California, a 64-year-old Air Force veteran, a great woman, according to everybody that knew her, Marilyn Pharis, was sexually assaulted and beaten to death with a hammer. Her killer had been arrested on multiple occasions but was never, ever deported, despite the fact that everybody wanted him out.

A 2011 report from the Government Accountability Office found that illegal immigrants and other non-citizens, in our prisons and jails together, had around 25,000 homicide arrests to their names, 25,000.

On top of that, illegal immigration costs our country more than $113 billion a year. And this is what we get. For the money we are going to spend on illegal immigration over the next 10 years, we could provide one million at-risk students with a school voucher, which so many people are wanting.

While there are many illegal immigrants in our country who are good people, many, many, this doesn't change the fact that most illegal immigrants are lower skilled workers with less education, who compete directly against vulnerable American workers, and that these illegal workers draw much more out from the system than they can ever possibly pay back.

And they're hurting a lot of our people that cannot get jobs under any circumstances.

But these facts are never reported. Instead, the media and my opponent discuss one thing and only one thing, the needs of people living here illegally. In many cases, by the way, they're treated better than our vets.

Not going to happen anymore, folks. November 8th. Not going to happen anymore.

AUDIENCE: Trump! Trump! Trump!

The truth is, the central issue is not the needs of the 11 million illegal immigrants or however many there may be — and honestly we've been hearing that number for years. It's always 11 million. Our government has no idea. It could be three million. It could be 30 million. They have no idea what the number is. Frankly our government has no idea what they're doing on many, many fronts, folks.

But whatever the number, that's never really been the central issue. It will never be a central issue. It doesn't matter from that standpoint. Anyone who tells you that the core issue is the needs of those living here illegally has simply spent too much time in Washington.

Only the out of touch media elites think the biggest problems facing America — you know this, this is what they talk about, facing American society today is that there are 11 million illegal immigrants who don't have legal status. And, they also think the biggest thing, and you know this, it's not nuclear, and it's not ISIS, it's not Russia, it's not China, it's global warming.

To all the politicians, donors, and special interests, hear these words from me and all of you today. There is only one core issue in the immigration debate, and that issue is the well being of the American people.

(APPLAUSE)

Nothing even comes a close second. Hillary Clinton, for instance, talks constantly about her fears that families will be separated, but she's not talking about the American families who have been permanently separated from their loved ones because of a preventable homicide, because of a preventable death, because of murder.

No, she's only talking about families who come here in violation of the law. We will treat everyone living or residing in our country with great dignity. So important.

We will be fair, just, and compassionate to all, but our greatest compassion must be for our American citizens.

President Obama and Hillary Clinton have engaged in gross dereliction of duty by surrendering the safety of the American people to open borders, and you know it better than anybody right here in Arizona. You know it.

President Obama and Hillary Clinton support sanctuary cities. They support catch and release on the border. They support visa overstays. They support the release of dangerous, dangerous, dangerous, criminals from detention. And they support unconstitutional executive amnesty.

Hillary Clinton has pledged amnesty in her first 100 days, and her plan will provide Obamacare, Social Security, and Medicare for illegal immigrants, breaking the federal budget.

On top of that she promises uncontrolled, low-skilled immigration that continues to reduce jobs and wages for American workers, and especially for African-American and Hispanic workers within our country. Our citizens.

Most incredibly, because to me this is unbelievable, we have no idea who these people are, where they come from. I always say

Trojan horse. Watch what's going to happen, folks. It's not going to be pretty.

This includes her plan to bring in 620,000 new refugees from Syria and that region over a short period of time. And even yesterday, when you were watching the news, you saw thousands and thousands of people coming in from Syria. What is wrong with our politicians, our leaders if we can call them that. What the hell are we doing?

Hard to believe. Hard to believe. Now that you've heard about Hillary Clinton's plan, about which she has not answered a single question, let me tell you about my plan. And do you notice...

And do you notice all the time for weeks and weeks of debating my plan, debating, talking about it, what about this, what about that. They never even mentioned her plan on immigration because she doesn't want to get into the quagmire. It's a tough one, she doesn't know what she's doing except open borders and let everybody come in and destroy our country by the way.

While Hillary Clinton meets only with donors and lobbyists, my plan was crafted with the input from Federal Immigration offices, very great people. Among the top immigration experts anywhere in this country, who represent workers, not corporations, very important to us.

I also worked with lawmakers, who've led on this issue on behalf of American citizens for many years. And most importantly I've met with the people directly impacted by these policies. So important.

Number one, are you ready? Are you ready?

(APPLAUSE)

We will build a great wall along the southern border.

(APPLAUSE)

AUDIENCE: Build the wall! Build the wall! Build the wall!

And Mexico will pay for the wall.

One hundred percent. They don't know it yet, but they're going to pay for it. And they're great people and great leaders but they're going to pay for the wall.

On day one, we will begin working on an impenetrable, physical, tall, power, beautiful southern border wall.

(APPLAUSE)

We will use the best technology, including above and below ground sensors that's the tunnels. Remember that, above and below.

Above and below ground sensors. Towers, aerial surveillance and manpower to supplement the wall, find and dislocate tunnels and keep out criminal cartels and Mexico you know that, will work with us. I really believe it. Mexico will work with us. I absolutely believe it. And especially after meeting with their wonderful, wonderful president today. I really believe they want to solve this problem along with us, and I'm sure they will.

Number two, we are going to end catch and release. We catch them, oh go ahead. We catch them, go ahead.

Under my administration, anyone who illegally crosses the border will be detained until they are removed out of our country and back to the country from which they came.

And they'll be brought great distances. We're not dropping them right across. They learned that. President Eisenhower. They'd drop them across, right across, and they'd come back. And across.

Then when they flew them to a long distance, all of a sudden that was the end. We will take them great distances. But we will take them to the country where they came from, O.K.?

Number three. Number three, this is the one, I think it's so great. It's hard to believe, people don't even talk about it. Zero tolerance for criminal aliens. Zero. Zero.

(APPLAUSE)

Zero. They don't come in here. They don't come in here.

According to federal data, there are at least two million, two million, think of it, criminal aliens now inside of our country, two million people criminal aliens. We will begin moving them out day one. As soon as I take office. Day one. In joint operation with local, state, and federal law enforcement.

Now, just so you understand, the police, who we all respect — say hello to the police. Boy, they don't get the credit they deserve. I can tell you. They're great people. But the police and law enforcement, they know who these people are.

They live with these people. They get mocked by these people. They can't do anything about these people, and they want to. They know who these people are. Day one, my first hour in office, those people are gone.

And you can call it deported if you want. The press doesn't like that term. You can call it whatever the hell you want. They're gone.

Beyond the two million, and there are vast numbers of additional criminal illegal immigrants who have fled, but their days have run out in this country. The crime will stop. They're going to be gone. It will be over.

(APPLAUSE)

They're going out. They're going out fast.

Moving forward. We will issue detainers for illegal immigrants who are arrested for any crime whatsoever, and they will be placed into immediate removal proceedings if we even have to do that.

We will terminate the Obama administration's deadly, and it is deadly, non-enforcement policies that allow thousands of criminal aliens to freely roam our streets, walk around, do whatever they want to do, crime all over the place.

That's over. That's over, folks. That's over.

Since 2013 alone, the Obama administration has allowed 300,000 criminal aliens to return back into United States communities. These are individuals encountered or identified by ICE, but who were not detained or processed for deportation because it wouldn't have been politically correct.

My plan also includes cooperating closely with local jurisdictions to remove criminal aliens immediately. We will restore the highly successful Secure Communities Program. Good program. We will expand and revitalize the popular 287(g) partnerships, which will help to identify hundreds of thousands of deportable aliens in local jails that we don't even know about.

Both of these programs have been recklessly gutted by this administration. And those were programs that worked.

This is yet one more area where we are headed in a totally opposite direction. There's no common sense, there's no brain power in our administration by our leader, or our leaders. None, none, none.

On my first day in office I am also going to ask Congress to pass Kate's Law, named for Kate Steinle...

... to ensure that criminal aliens convicted of illegal reentry receive strong mandatory minimum sentences. Strong. And then we get them out.

Another reform I'm proposing is the passage of legislation named for Detective Michael Davis and Deputy Sheriff Danny Oliver, two law enforcement officers recently killed by a previously deported illegal immigrant.

The Davis-Oliver bill will enhance cooperation with state and local authorities to ensure that criminal immigrants and terrorists are swiftly, really swiftly, identified and removed. And they will go face, believe me. They're going to go.

We're going to triple the number of ICE deportation officers. Within ICE I am going to create a new special deportation task force focused on identifying and quickly removing the most dangerous criminal illegal immigrants in America who have evaded justice just like Hillary Clinton has evaded justice, O.K.?

Maybe they'll be able to deport her.

(APPLAUSE)

The local police who know every one of these criminals, and they know each and every one by name, by crime, where they live, they will work so fast. And our local police will be so happy that they don't have to be abused by these thugs anymore.

There's no great mystery to it, they've put up with it for years, and now finally we will turn the tables and law enforcement and our police will be allowed to clear up this dangerous and threatening mess.

We're also going to hire 5,000 more Border Patrol agents. Who gave me their endorsement, 16,500 gave me their endorsement.

And put more of them on the border instead of behind desks which is good. We will expand the number of border patrol stations significantly.

I've had a chance to spend time with these incredible law enforcement officers, and I want to take a moment to thank them. What they do is incredible.

And getting their endorsement means so much to me. More to me really than I can say. Means so much. First time they've ever endorsed a presidential candidate.

Number four, block funding for sanctuary cities. We block the funding. No more funds.

We will end the sanctuary cities that have resulted in so many needless deaths. Cities that refuse to cooperate with federal authorities will not receive taxpayer dollars, and we will work with Congress to pass legislation to protect those jurisdictions that do assist federal authorities. Number five, cancel unconstitutional executive orders and enforce all immigration laws.

(APPLAUSE)

We will immediately terminate President Obama's two illegal executive amnesties in which he defied federal law and the Constitution to give amnesty to approximately five million illegal immigrants, five million.

(BOOING)

And how about all the millions that are waiting on line, going through the process legally? So unfair.

Hillary Clinton has pledged to keep both of these illegal amnesty programs, including the 2014 amnesty which has been blocked by the United States Supreme Court. Great. Clinton has also pledged to add a third executive amnesty. And by the way, folks, she will be a disaster for our country, a disaster in so many other ways.

And don't forget the Supreme Court of the United States. Don't forget that when you go to vote on November 8. And don't forget your Second Amendment. And don't forget the repeal and replacement of Obamacare.

And don't forget building up our depleted military. And don't forget taking care of our vets. Don't forget our vets. They have been forgotten.

Clinton's plan would trigger a constitutional crisis unlike almost anything we have ever seen before. In effect, she would be abolishing the lawmaking powers of Congress in order to write her own laws from the Oval Office. And you see what bad judgment she has. She has seriously bad judgment.

(BOOING)

Can you imagine? In a Trump administration all immigration laws will be enforced, will be enforced. As with any law enforcement activity, we will set priorities. But unlike this administration, no one will be immune or exempt from enforcement. And ICE and Border Patrol officers will be allowed to do their jobs the way their jobs are supposed to be done.

Anyone who has entered the United States illegally is subject to deportation. That is what it means to have laws and to have a country. Otherwise we don't have a country.

Our enforcement priorities will include removing criminals, gang members, security threats, visa overstays, public charges. That is those relying on public welfare or straining the safety net along with millions of recent illegal arrivals and overstays who've come here under this current corrupt administration.

Number six, we are going to suspend the issuance of visas to any place where adequate screening cannot occur.

(APPLAUSE)

According to data provided by the Senate Subcommittee on Immigration, and the national interest between 9/11 and the end of 2014, at least 380 foreign born individuals were convicted in terror cases inside the United States. And even right now the largest number of people are under investigation for exactly this that we've ever had in the history of our country.

Our country is a mess. We don't even know what to look for anymore, folks. Our country has to straighten out. And we have to straighten out fast.

The number is likely higher. But the administration refuses to provide this information, even to Congress. As soon as I enter office I am going to ask the Department of State, which has been brutalized by Hillary Clinton, brutalized.

(BOOING)

Homeland Security and the Department of Justice to begin a comprehensive review of these cases in order to develop a list of regions and countries from which immigration must be suspended until proven and effective vetting mechanisms can be put in place.

I call it extreme vetting right? Extreme vetting. I want extreme. It's going to be so tough, and if somebody comes in that's fine but they're going to be good. It's extreme.

And if people don't like it, we've got have a country folks. Got to have a country. Countries in which immigration will be suspended would include places like Syria and Libya. And we are going to stop the tens of thousands of people coming in from Syria. We have no idea who they are, where they come from. There's no documentation. There's no paperwork. It's going to end badly folks. It's going to end very, very badly.

For the price of resettling one refugee in the United States, 12 could be resettled in a safe zone in their home region. Which I agree with 100 percent. We have to build safe zones and we'll get the money from Gulf states. We don't want to put up the money. We owe almost $20 trillion. Doubled since Obama took office, our national debt.

But we will get the money from Gulf states and others. We'll supervise it. We'll build safe zones which is something that I think all of us want to see.

Another reform involves new screening tests for all applicants that include, and this is so important, especially if you get the right people. And we will get the right people. An ideological certification to make sure that those we are admitting to our country share our values and love our people.

(APPLAUSE)

Thank you. We're very proud of our country. Aren't we? Really? With all it's going through, we're very proud of our country. For instance, in the last five years, we've admitted nearly 100,000 immigrants from Iraq and Afghanistan. And these two countries according to Pew Research, a majority of residents say that the barbaric practice of honor killings against women are often or sometimes justified. That's what they say.

That's what they say. They're justified. Right? And we're admitting them to our country. Applicants will be asked their views about honor killings, about respect for women and gays and minorities. Attitudes on radical Islam, which our president refuses to say and many other topics as part of this vetting procedure. And if we have the right people doing it, believe me, very, very few will slip through the cracks. Hopefully, none.

(APPLAUSE)

Number seven, we will insure that other countries take their people back when they order them deported.

There are at least 23 countries that refuse to take their people back after they've been ordered to leave the United States. Including large numbers of violent criminals, they won't take them back. So we say, O.K., we'll keep them. Not going to happen with me, not going to happen with me.

Due to a Supreme Court decision, if these violent offenders cannot be sent home, our law enforcement officers have to release them into your communities.

And by the way, the results are horrific, horrific. There are often terrible consequences, such as Casey Chadwick's tragic death in Connecticut just last year. Yet despite the existence of a law that commands the secretary of state to stop issuing visas to these countries.

Secretary Hillary Clinton ignored this law and refused to use this powerful tool to bring nations into compliance. And, they would comply if we would act properly.

In other words, if we had leaders that knew what they were doing, which we don't.

The result of her misconduct was the release of thousands and thousands of dangerous criminal aliens who should have been sent home to their countries. Instead we have them all over the place. Probably a couple in this room as a matter of fact, but I hope not.

According to a report for the Boston Globe from the year 2008 to 2014 nearly 13,000 criminal aliens were released back into U.S. communities because their home countries would not, under any circumstances, take them back. Hard to believe with the power we have. Hard to believe.

We're like the big bully that keeps getting beat up. You ever see that? The big bully that keeps getting beat up.

These 13,000 releases occurred on Hillary Clinton's watch. She had the power and the duty to stop it cold, and she decided she would not do it.

(BOOING)

And Arizona knows better than most exactly what I'm talking about.

Those released include individuals convicted of killings, sexual assaults, and some of the most heinous crimes imaginable.

The Boston Globe writes that a Globe review of 323 criminals released in New England from 2008 to 2012 found that as many as 30 percent committed new offenses, including rape, attempted murder, and child molestation. We take them, we take them.

(BOOING)

Number eight, we will finally complete the biometric entry-exit visa tracking system which we need desperately.

For years Congress has required biometric entry-exit visa tracking systems, but it has never been completed. The politicians are all talk, no action, never happens. Never happens.

Hillary Clinton, all talk. Unfortunately when there is action it's always the wrong decision. You ever notice?

In my administration we will ensure that this system is in place. And, I will tell you, it will be on land, it will be on sea, it will be in air. We will have a proper tracking system.

Approximately half of new illegal immigrants came on temporary visas and then never, ever left. Why should they? Nobody's telling them to leave. Stay as long as you want, we'll take care of you.

Beyond violating our laws, visa overstays pose — and they really are a big problem — pose a substantial threat to national security. The 9/11 Commission said that this tracking system should be a high priority and would have assisted law enforcement and intelligence officials in August and September 2001 in conducting a search for two of the 9/11 hijackers that were in the United States on expired visas.

And you know what that would have meant, what that could have meant. Wouldn't that have been wonderful, right? What that could have meant.

Last year alone nearly half a million individuals overstayed their temporary visas. Removing these overstays will be a top priority of my administration.

If people around the world believe they can just come on a temporary visa and never, ever leave, the Obama-Clinton policy, that's what it is, then we have a completely open border, and we no longer have a country.

We must send a message that visa expiration dates will be strongly enforced.

Number nine, we will turn off the jobs and benefits magnet.

(APPLAUSE)

We will ensure that E-Verify is used to the fullest extent possible under existing law, and we will work with Congress to strengthen and expand its use across the country.

Immigration law doesn't exist for the purpose of keeping criminals out. It exists to protect all aspects of American life. The work site, the welfare office, the education system, and everything else.

That is why immigration limits are established in the first place. If we only enforced the laws against crime, then we have an open border to the entire world. We will enforce all of our immigration laws.

And the same goes for government benefits. The Center for Immigration Studies estimates that 62 percent of households headed by illegal immigrants use some form of cash or non-cash welfare programs like food stamps or housing assistance.

Tremendous costs, by the way, to our country. Tremendous costs. This directly violates the federal public charge law designed to protect the United States Treasury. Those who abuse our welfare system will be priorities for immediate removal.

Number 10, we will reform legal immigration to serve the best interests of America and its workers, the forgotten people. Workers. We're going to take care of our workers.

And by the way, and by the way, we're going to make great trade deals. We're going to renegotiate trade deals. We're going to bring our jobs back home. We're going to bring our jobs back home.

We have the most incompetently worked trade deals ever negotiated probably in the history of the world, and that starts with Nafta. And now they want to go TPP, one of the great disasters.

We're going to bring our jobs back home. And if companies want to leave Arizona and if they want to leave other states, there's going to be a lot of trouble for them. It's not going to be so easy. There will be consequence. Remember that. There will be consequence. They're not going to be leaving, go to another country, make the product, sell it into the United States, and all we end up with is no taxes and total unemployment. It's not going to happen. There will be consequences.

We've admitted 59 million immigrants to the United States between 1965 and 2015. Many of these arrivals have greatly enriched our country. So true. But we now have an obligation to them and to their children to control future immigration as we are following, if you think, previous immigration waves.

We've had some big waves. And tremendously positive things have happened. Incredible things have happened. To ensure assimilation we want to ensure that it works. Assimilation, an important word. Integration and upward mobility.

Within just a few years immigration as a share of national population is set to break all historical records. The time has come for a new immigration commission to develop a new set of reforms to our legal immigration system in order to achieve the following goals.

To keep immigration levels measured by population share within historical norms. To select immigrants based on their likelihood of success in U.S. society and their ability to be financially self-sufficient.

We take anybody. Come on in, anybody. Just come on in. Not anymore.

You know, folks, it's called a two-way street. It is a two-way street, right? We need a system that serves our needs, not the needs of others. Remember, under a Trump administration it's called America first. Remember that.

(APPLAUSE)

To choose immigrants based on merit. Merit, skill, and proficiency. Doesn't that sound nice? And to establish new immigration controls to boost wages and to ensure that open jobs are offered to American workers first. And that in particular African-American and Latino workers who are being shut out in this process so unfairly.

And Hillary Clinton is going to do nothing for the African-American worker, the Latino worker. She's going to do nothing. Give me your vote, she says, on November 8th. And then she'll say, so long, see you in four years. That's what it is.

She is going to do nothing. And just look at the past. She's done nothing. She's been there for 35 years. She's done nothing. And I say what do you have to lose? Choose me. Watch how good we're going to do together. Watch.

You watch. We want people to come into our country, but they have to come into our country legally and properly vetted, and in a manner that serves the national interest. We've been living under outdated immigration rules from decades ago. They're decades and decades old.

To avoid this happening in the future, I believe we should sunset our visa laws so that Congress is forced to periodically revise and revisit them to bring them up to date. They're archaic. They're ancient. We wouldn't put our entire federal budget on auto pilot for decades, so why should we do the same for the very, very complex subject of immigration?

So let's now talk about the big picture. These 10 steps, if rigorously followed and enforced, will accomplish more in a matter of months than our politicians have accomplished on this issue in the last 50 years. It's going to happen, folks. Because I am proudly not a politician, because I am not behold to any special interest, I've spent a lot of money on my campaign, I'll tell you. I write those checks. Nobody owns Trump.

I will get this done for you and for your family. We'll do it right. You'll be proud of our country again. We'll do it right. We will accomplish all of the steps outlined above. And, when we do, peace and law and justice and prosperity will prevail. Crime will go down. Border crossings will plummet. Gangs will disappear.

And the gangs are all over the place. And welfare use will decrease. We will have a peace dividend to spend on rebuilding America, beginning with our American inner cities. We're going to rebuild them, for once and for all.

For those here illegally today, who are seeking legal status, they will have one route and one route only. To return home and apply for reentry like everybody else, under the rules of the new legal immigration system that I have outlined above. Those who have left to seek entry —

Thank you. Thank you. Those who have left to seek entry under this new system — and it will be an efficient system — will not be awarded surplus visas, but will have to apply for entry under the immigration caps or limits that will be established in the future.TRUMP: We will break the cycle of amnesty and illegal immigration. We will break the cycle. There will be no amnesty.

Our message to the world will be this. You cannot obtain legal status or become a citizen of the United States by illegally entering our country. Can't do it.

This declaration alone will help stop the crisis of illegal crossings and illegal overstays, very importantly. People will know that you can't just smuggle in, hunker down and wait to be legalized. It's not going to work that way. Those days are over. Importantly, in several years when we have accomplished all of our enforcement and deportation goals and truly ended illegal immigration for good, including the construction of a great wall, which we will have built in record time. And at a reasonable   cost, which you never hear from the government.

And the establishment of our new lawful immigration system then and only then will we be in a position to consider the appropriate disposition of those individuals who remain.

That discussion can take place only in an atmosphere in which illegal immigration is a memory of the past, no longer with us, allowing us to weigh the different options available based on the new circumstances at the time.

Right now, however, we're in the middle of a jobs crisis, a border crisis and a terrorism crisis like never before. All energies of the federal government and the legislative process must now be focused on immigration security. That is the only conversation we should be having at this time, immigration security. Cut it off.

Whether it's dangerous materials being smuggled across the border, terrorists entering on visas or Americans losing their jobs to foreign workers, these are the problems we must now focus on fixing. And the media needs to begin demanding to hear Hillary Clinton's answer on how her policies will affect Americans and their security.

These are matters of life and death for our country and its people, and we deserve answers from Hillary Clinton. And do you notice, she doesn't answer.

She didn't go to Louisiana. She didn't go to Mexico. She was invited.

She doesn't have the strength or the stamina to make America great again. Believe me.

(APPLAUSE)

What we do know, despite the lack of media curiosity, is that Hillary Clinton promises a radical amnesty combined with a radical reduction in immigration enforcement. Just ask the Border Patrol about Hillary Clinton. You won't like what you're hearing.

The result will be millions more illegal immigrants; thousands of more violent, horrible crimes; and total chaos and lawlessness. That's what's going to happen, as sure as you're standing there.

This election, and I believe this, is our last chance to secure the border, stop illegal immigration and reform our laws to make your life better. I really believe this is it. This is our last time. November 8. November 8. You got to get out and vote on November 8.

It's our last chance. It's our last chance. And that includes Supreme Court justices and Second Amendment. Remember that. So I want to remind everyone what we're fighting for and who we are fighting for.

I am going to ask — these are really special people that I've gotten to know. I'm going to ask all of the "Angel Moms" to come join me on the stage right now.

These are amazing women.

AUDIENCE: USA! USA! USA!

These are amazing people, and I am not asking for their endorsement, believe me that. I just think I've gotten to know so many of them, and many more, from our group. But they are incredible people and what they're going through is incredible, and there's just no reason for it. Let's give them a really tremendous hand.

(APPLAUSE)

That's tough stuff, I will tell you. That is tough stuff. Incredible people.

So, now is the time for these voices to be heard. Now is the time for the media to begin asking questions on their behalf. Now is the time for all of us as one country, Democrat, Republican, liberal, conservative to band together to deliver justice, and safety, and security for all Americans.

Let's fix this horrible, horrible problem. It can be fixed quickly. Let's our secure our border.

(APPLAUSE)

Let's stop the drugs and the crime from pouring into our country. Let's protect our social security and Medicare. Let's get unemployed Americans off the welfare and back to work in their own country.

This has been an incredible evening. We're going to remember this evening. November 8, we have to get everybody. This is such an important state. November 8 we have to get everybody to go out and vote.

We're going to bring — thank you, thank you. We're going to take our country back, folks. This is a movement. We're going to take our country back.

Thank you.

This is an incredible movement. The world is talking about it. The world is talking about it and by the way, if you haven't been looking to what's been happening at the polls over the last three or four days I think you should start looking. You should start looking.

(APPLAUSE)

Together we can save American lives, American jobs, and American futures. Together we can save America itself. Join me in this mission, we're going to make America great again.

Don Fass

We haven't made a voting recommendation in 34 years. For this election, we made an exception.

The Editorial Board has never taken sides in the presidential race. We're doing it now.

In the 34-year history of USA TODAY, the Editorial Board has never taken sides in the presidential race. Instead, we've expressed opinions about the major issues and haven't presumed to tell our readers, who have a variety of priorities and values, which choice is best for them. Because every presidential race is different, we revisit our no-endorsement policy every four years. We've never seen reason to alter our approach. Until now.

This year, the choice isn't between two capable major party nominees who happen to have significant ideological differences. This year, one of the candidates — Republican nominee Donald Trump — is, by unanimous consensus of the Editorial Board, unfit for the presidency.

From the day he declared his candidacy 15 months ago through this week's first presidential debate, Trump has demonstrated repeatedly that he lacks the temperament, knowledge, steadiness and honesty that America needs from its presidents.

Whether through indifference or ignorance, Trump has betrayed fundamental commitments made by all presidents since the end of World War II. These commitments include unwavering support for NATO allies, steadfast opposition to Russian aggression, and the absolute certainty that the United States will make good on its debts. He has expressed troubling admiration for authoritarian leaders and scant regard for constitutional protections.

We've been highly critical of the GOP nominee in a number of previous editorials. With early voting already underway in several states and polls showing a close race, now is the time to spell out, in one place, the reasons Trump should not be president:

He is erratic. Trump has been on so many sides of so many issues that attempting to assess his policy positions is like shooting at a moving target. A list prepared by NBC details 124 shifts by Trump on 20 major issues since shortly before he entered the race. He simply spouts slogans and outcomes (he'd replace Obamacare with "something terrific") without any credible explanations of how he'd achieve them.

He is ill-equipped to be commander in chief. Trump's foreign policy pronouncements typically range from uninformed to incoherent. It's not just Democrats who say this. Scores of Republican national security leaders have signed an extraordinary open letter calling Trump's foreign policy vision "wildly inconsistent and unmoored in principle." In a *Wall Street Journal* column this month, Robert Gates, the highly respected former Defense secretary who served presidents of both parties over a half-century, described Trump as "beyond repair."

He traffics in prejudice. From the very beginning, Trump has built his campaign on appeals to bigotry and xenophobia, whipping up resentment against Mexicans, Muslims and migrants. His proposals for mass deportations and religious tests are unworkable and contrary to America's ideals.

Trump has stirred racist sentiments in ways that can't be erased by his belated and clumsy outreach to African Americans. His attacks on an Indiana-born federal judge of Mexican heritage fit "the textbook definition of a racist comment," according to House Speaker Paul Ryan, the highest-ranking elected official in the Republican Party. And for five years, Trump fanned the absurd "birther" movement that falsely questioned the legitimacy of the nation's first black president.

His business career is checkered. Trump has built his candidacy on his achievements as a real estate developer and entrepreneur. It's a shaky scaffold, starting with a 1973 Justice Department suit against Trump and his father for systematically discriminating against blacks in housing rentals. (The Trumps fought the suit but later settled on terms that were viewed as a government victory.) Trump's companies have had some spectacular financial successes, but this track record is marred by six bankruptcy filings, apparent misuse of the family's charitable foundation, and allegations by Trump University customers of fraud. A series of investigative articles published by the USA TODAY Network found that Trump has been involved in thousands of lawsuits over the past three decades, including at least 60 that involved small businesses and contract employees who said they were stiffed. So much for being a champion of the little guy.

He isn't leveling with the American people. Is Trump as rich as he says? No one knows, in part because, alone among major party presidential candidates for the past four decades, he refuses to release his tax returns. Nor do we know whether he has paid his fair share of taxes, or the extent of his foreign financial entanglements.

He speaks recklessly. In the days after the Republican convention, Trump invited Russian hackers to interfere with an American election by releasing Hillary Clinton's emails, and he raised the prospect of "Second Amendment people" preventing the

Democratic nominee from appointing liberal justices. It's hard to imagine two more irresponsible statements from one presidential candidate.

He has coarsened the national dialogue. Did you ever imagine that a presidential candidate would discuss the size of his genitalia during a nationally televised Republican debate? Neither did we. Did you ever imagine a presidential candidate, one who avoided service in the military, would criticize Gold Star parents who lost a son in Iraq? Neither did we. Did you ever imagine you'd see a presidential candidate mock a disabled reporter? Neither did we. Trump's inability or unwillingness to ignore criticism raises the specter of a president who, like Richard Nixon, would create enemies' lists and be consumed with getting even with his critics.

He's a serial liar. Although polls show that Clinton is considered less honest and trustworthy than Trump, it's not even a close contest. Trump is in a league of his own when it comes to the quality and quantity of his misstatements. When confronted with a falsehood, such as his assertion that he was always against the Iraq War, Trump's reaction is to use the Big Lie technique of repeating it so often that people begin to believe it.

We are not unmindful of the issues that Trump's campaign has exploited: the disappearance of working-class jobs; excessive political correctness; the direction of the Supreme Court; urban unrest and street violence; the rise of the Islamic State terrorist group; gridlock in Washington and the influence of moneyed interests. All are legitimate sources of concern.

Nor does this editorial represent unqualified support for Hillary Clinton, who has her own flaws (though hers are far less likely to threaten national security or lead to a constitutional crisis). The Editorial Board does not have a consensus for a Clinton endorsement.

Some of us look at her command of the issues, resilience and long record of public service — as first lady, U.S. senator and secretary of State — and believe she'd serve the nation ably as its president.

Other board members have serious reservations about Clinton's sense of entitlement, her lack of candor and her extreme carelessness in handling classified information.

Where does that leave us? Our bottom-line advice for voters is this: Stay true to your convictions. That might mean a vote for Clinton, the most plausible alternative to keep Trump out of the White House. Or it might mean a third-party candidate. Or a write-in. Or a focus on down-ballot candidates who will serve the nation honestly, try to heal its divisions, and work to solve its problems.

Whatever you do, however, resist the siren song of a dangerous demagogue. By all means vote, just not for Donald Trump.

USA TODAY's editorial opinions are decided by its Editorial Board, separate from the news staff.

WHAT OTHERS SAY *ABOUT* TRUMP

Alex Jones   conspiracy theorist, head of Infowars

"Trump is riding high in the polls. But this is not an indication he will remain there. He will not get anywhere near the White House. However, Trump is the best candidate. Why? Because a Trump presidency will bring gridlock to the state.

Mark Capra, writing for Mofo, notes a number of truisms about government based in part on the philosophy of Thomas Jefferson. Capra bullet points: The less a President does, the better. The more Congress is gridlocked, the better. The fewer lobbyist-written laws are passed by corrupt Washington politicians, the safer our liberty. Capra notes that all the candidates — unfortunately including Rand Paul — plan to steamroll legislation through Congress.

More troubling, *every* major candidate (if not now, then by the general election) are funded by the same incestuous group of transnational conglomerates,' he writes. Thus Trump, with his "divisiveness, high unfavorability ratings, and unrealistic policy proposals" is the best we can hope for "in the age of statism and the low-information voter."

Trump: A Dangerous Authoritarian

Former Congressman Ron Paul — the only truly libertarian candidate to have run for president — disagrees. While Paul admits Trump's presence in the election is highly disruptive of the establishment's dog and pony show that invariably selects statists who faithfully carry out the agenda of the elite, he notices an authoritarian streak in the man.

"I think he's is a dangerous person, and a lot of people find him sort of funny, and love him, even Libertarian types. They like him because he's so disruptive to the party system, and I enjoy that too."

Paul worries that if Trump makes it to the White House and the economic house of cards collapses, he will become a ruthless dictator.

"He's an authoritarian and that's the way he claims he made all his money. So I see that as dangerous," Paul said.

Trump plans to spend a billion dollars on his campaign, but this will not ensure he will win. Well before the election the American voter will reject Trump and the other outsider, Bernie Sanders."Trump is not going to be president. Bernie Sanders is also not going to be president," writes Megan McArdle for The Chicago Tribune. "Their appeal to their supporters is precisely the reason they are not going to be president. Every few years, a large number of Americans need to learn the same lesson: The reason you don't hear the solutions that you want coming from the boring, scripted, mainstream politicians who get elected is that the solutions that you want do not appeal to the majority of your fellow countrymen."

In other words, while many of us enjoy the fireworks of a Trump campaign and revel in the anger and frustration of the party elite in response to it, come November, 2016 most of us will vote for whatever candidate the Democrats and Republicans nominate.

Enjoy the disruptive antics of Donald Trump and the blue sky bromides of the socialist Bernie Sanders while they last. Neither candidate will make it out of the Iowa and New Hampshire caucuses come February, 2016. The caucuses are events controlled by the establishment parties and more or less determined by rigged straw polls. Recall how the Diebold machines were rigged against Ron Paul in Iowa.

Donald Trump will be but a faint whisper in July of 2016 in Cleveland when the Republicans hold their convention and the Sanderites will be tamed and corralled the following week in Philadelphia at the Democratic national convention. The party elite will guarantee it."

Barbara Bush

" Trump is like a "comedian or something."

"What about women? I don't know how women could vote for someone who said what he said about Megyn Kelly. It's terrible! And we knew what he meant too."

"Don't you get in his firing line."

Bassem Youssef (the Jon Stewart of Egypt)

"It is ironic (Trump's xenophobia) in a country built by immigrants as is Trump's appalling attitude toward refugees escaping Syria."

"This kind of rhetoric — spreading fear and suspicion against the other — is not something new. We're used to it in the Middle East. You always need something to hold on to, an enemy to direct your hatred to, to cover up your incompetence and cover up your failure."

"I can't even being to express my sorrow and sadness towards those people. Leaving their countries is not a luxury thing for them. This is out of necessity, out of survival. It is this systematic dehumanization of the other is why we have a negative outlook on refugees."

Ben Carson

Surgeon and GOP Presidential candidate

"Trump's attack on my character is completely gratuitous. It's not the kind of dialogue that I would ever engage in. I'm hopeful that maybe [Trump's] advisers will help him understand the word 'pathological,' and recognize that it does not denote 'incurable.' Pathological describes something that is highly abnormal – something that fortunately, I've been able to be delivered from for over half a century."

"I don't believe Trump called me a child molester. I always find it a little amusing what people in the press like to say."

Benjamin 'Bibi' Netanyahu   Prime Minister, Israel

"The prime minister rejects the recent comments by Donald Trump with regard to Muslims. Israel respects all religions and diligently guards the rights of all its citizens."

"This policy does not reflect support for the candidates or for their platforms, rather, it expresses the importance that the prime minister ascribes to the strong alliance between Israel and the United States."

Bernie Sanders Tweets

Democratic U.S. Senator Vermont and Presidential candidate

"Those who voted for me will not support Trump who has made bigotry and divisiveness the cornerstone of his campaign."

"Trump is wrong. The real cause of instability in the Middle East was the Bush-Cheney invasion of Iraq. By the way, where is President Bush?"

"What a hypocrite! If Trump wants to "fix" trade he can start by making his products in the US, not low-wage countries abroad. "

"Trump: "I alone can fix this." Is this guy running for president or dictator? "

"As is the case virtually every day, Donald Trump is showing the American people that he is a pathological liar. Obviously, while I appreciate that we had supporters at Trump's rally in Chicago, our campaign did not organize the protests."

"What caused the protests at Trump's rally is a candidate that has promoted hatred and division against Latinos, Muslims, women, and people with disabilities, and his birther attacks against the legitimacy of President Obama."

"What caused the violence at Trump's rally is a campaign whose words and actions have encouraged it on the part of his supporters. He recently said of a protester, 'I want to punch him in the face.' Another time Trump yearned for the old days when the protester would have been punched and "carried out on a stretcher.' Then just a few days ago a female reporter apparently was assaulted by his campaign manager. "When that is what the Trump campaign is doing, we should not be surprised that there is a response."

"What Donald Trump must do now is stop provoking violence and make it clear to his supporters that people who attend his rallies or protest should not be assaulted, should not be punched, should not be kicked. In America people have a right to attend a political rally without fear of physical harm."

Bernie Sanders Democratic Convention speech (excerpts)

"Together, my friends, we have begun a political revolution to transform America and that revolution – Our Revolution – continues. Election days come and go. But the struggle of the people to create a government which represents all of us and not just the 1 percent – a government based on the principles of economic, social, racial and environmental justice – that struggle continues. And I look forward to being part of that struggle with you.

Let me be as clear as I can be. This election is not about, and has never been about, Hillary Clinton, or Donald Trump, or Bernie Sanders or any of the other candidates who sought the presidency. This election is not about political gossip. It's not about polls. It's not about campaign strategy. It's not about fundraising. It's not about all the things the media spends so much time discussing.

This election is about – and must be about – the needs of the American people and the kind of future we create for our children and grandchildren.

This election is about ending the 40-year decline of our middle class the reality that 47 million men, women and children live in poverty. It is about understanding that if we do not transform our economy, our younger generation will likely have a lower standard of living then their parents.

This election is about ending the grotesque level of income and wealth inequality that we currently experience, the worst it has been since 1928. It is not moral, not acceptable and not sustainable that the top one-tenth of one percent now own almost as much wealth as the bottom 90 percent, or that the top 1 percent in recent years has earned 85 percent of all new income. That is unacceptable. That must change.

This election is about remembering where we were 7 1/2 years ago when President Obama came into office after eight years of Republican trickle-down economics.

The Republicans want us to forget that as a result of the greed, recklessness and illegal behavior on Wall Street, our economy was in the worst economic downturn since the Great Depression. Some 800,000 people a month were losing their jobs. We were running up a record-breaking deficit of $1.4 trillion and the world's financial system was on the verge of collapse.

We have come a long way in the last 7 1/2 years, and I thank President Obama and Vice President Biden for their leadership in pulling us out of that terrible recession. Yes, we have made progress, but I think we can all agree that much, much more needs to be done.

This election is about which candidate understands the real problems facing this country and has offered real solutions – not just bombast, fear-mongering, name-calling and divisiveness.

We need leadership in this country which will improve the lives of working families, the children, the elderly, the sick and the poor. We need leadership which brings our people together and makes us stronger – not leadership which insults Latinos, Muslims, women, African-Americans and veterans – and divides us up.

By these measures, any objective observer will conclude that – based on her ideas and her leadership – Hillary Clinton must become the next president of the United States. The choice is not even close.

This election is about a single mom I saw in Nevada who, with tears in her eyes, told me that she was scared to death about the future because she and her young daughter were not making it on the $10.45 an hour she was earning. This election is about that woman and the millions of other workers in this country who are struggling to survive on totally inadequate wages.

Hillary Clinton understands that if someone in America works 40 hours a week, that person should not be living in poverty. She understands that we must raise the minimum wage to a living wage. And she is determined to create millions of new jobs by rebuilding our crumbling infrastructure – our roads, bridges, water systems and wastewater plants.

But her opponent – Donald Trump – well, he has a very different view. He does not support raising the federal minimum wage of $7.25 an hour – a starvation wage. While Donald Trump believes in huge tax breaks for billionaires, he believes that states should actually have the right to lower the minimum wage below $7.25. What an outrage!

This election is about overturning Citizens United, one of the worst Supreme Court decisions in the history of our country. That decision allows the wealthiest people in America, like the billionaire Koch brothers, to spend hundreds of millions of dollars buying elections and, in the process, undermine American democracy.

Hillary Clinton will nominate justices to the Supreme Court who are prepared to overturn Citizens United and end the movement toward oligarchy in this country. Her Supreme Court appointments will also defend a woman's right to choose, workers' rights, the rights of the LGBT community, the needs of minorities and immigrants and the government's ability to protect the environment.

If you don't believe this election is important, if you think you can sit it out, take a moment to think about the Supreme Court justices that Donald Trump would nominate and what that would mean to civil liberties, equal rights and the future of our country.

This election is about the thousands of young people I have met who have left college deeply in debt, and the many others who cannot afford to go to college. During the primary campaign, Secretary Clinton and I both focused on this issue but with different approaches. Recently, however, we have come together on a proposal that will revolutionize higher education in America. It will guarantee that the children of any family this country with an annual income of $125,000 a year or less – 83 percent of our population – will be able to go to a public college or university tuition free. That proposal also substantially reduces student debt.

This election is about climate change, the greatest environmental crisis facing our planet, and the need to leave this world in a way that is healthy and habitable for our kids and future generations. Hillary Clinton is listening to the scientists who tell us that – unless we act boldly and transform our energy system in the very near future – there will be more drought, more floods, more acidification of the oceans, more rising sea levels. She understands that when we do that we can create hundreds of thousands of good-paying jobs.

Donald Trump? Well, like most Republicans, he chooses to reject science. He believes that climate change is a "hoax," no need to address it. Hillary Clinton understands that a president's job is to worry about future generations, not the short-term profits of the fossil fuel industry.

This campaign is about moving the United States toward universal health care and reducing the number of people who are uninsured or under-insured. Hillary Clinton wants to see that all Americans have the right to choose a public option in their health care exchange. She believes that anyone 55 years or older should be able to opt in to Medicare and she wants to see millions more Americans gain access to primary health care, dental care, mental health counseling and low-cost prescription drugs through a major expansion of community health centers.

And What is Donald Trump's position on health care? No surprise there. Same old, same old Republican contempt for working families. He wants to abolish the Affordable Care Act, throw 20 million people off of the health insurance they currently have and cut Medicaid for lower-income Americans.

Hillary Clinton also understands that millions of seniors, disabled vets and others are struggling with the outrageously high cost of prescription drugs and the fact that Americans pay the highest prices in the world for their medicine. She knows that Medicare must negotiate drug prices with the pharmaceutical industry and that drug companies should not be making billions in profits while one in five Americans are unable to afford the medicine they need. The greed of the drug companies must end.

This election is about the leadership we need to pass comprehensive immigration reform and repair a broken criminal justice system. It's about making sure that young people in this country are in good schools and at good jobs, not in jail cells. Hillary Clinton understands that we have to invest in education and jobs for our young people, not more jails or incarceration.

In these stressful times for our country, this election must be about bringing our people together, not dividing us up. While Donald Trump is busy insulting one group after another, Hillary Clinton understands that our diversity is one of our greatest strengths. Yes.

We become stronger when black and white, Latino, Asian-American, Native American – all of us – stand together. Yes. We become stronger when men and women, young and old, gay and straight, native born and immigrant fight to create the kind of country we all know we can become.

It is no secret that Hillary Clinton and I disagree on a number of issues. That's what this campaign has been about. That's what democracy is about. But I am happy to tell you that at the Democratic Platform Committee there was a significant coming together between the two campaigns and we produced, by far, the most progressive platform in the history of the Democratic Party. Among many other strong provisions, the Democratic Party now calls for breaking up the major financial institutions on Wall Street and the passage of a 21st Century Glass-Steagall Act. It also calls for strong opposition to job-killing free trade agreements like the Trans-Pacific Partnership.

Our job now is to see that platform implemented by a Democratic Senate, a Democratic House and a Hillary Clinton presidency – and I am going to do everything I can to make that happen.

I have known Hillary Clinton for 25 years. I remember her as a great first lady who broke precedent in terms of the role that a first lady was supposed to play as she helped lead the fight for universal health care. I served with her in the United States Senate and know her as a fierce advocate for the rights of children. Hillary Clinton will make an outstanding president and I am proud to stand with her here tonight."

Bill Kristol   Iconic Neo con and Editor, Weekly Standard

"I will leave the Republican Party in support of a third party bid if Trump becomes the Republican presidential nominee. I doubt I'd support Donald. I doubt I'd support the Democrat. I think I'd support getting someone good on the ballot as a third party candidate."

"Donald Trump would make a terrible nominee and a terrible president — I would rather have Hillary Clinton in the White House than the Republican front-runner."

"I gather Donald Trump said I'm a loser. I've won some and I've lost some, but one thing I've always tried not to be is a roaring jackass."

"The whole controversy (about the Khan family) is so horrifying, in terms of what it reveals about Trump's character. But the most revealing thing was the initial statement, where it didn't occur to him when he was asked about it, as a matter of graciousness and decency to thank the Khan family for their son's heroism, to, say, express gratitude for what he did. It doesn't even occur to Trump, because he is such a narcissist, and he's so, honestly unfit to be president of the United States. He is unstable, I mean I really think so. And I do think he is unstable, and he is so narcissistic, that you couldn't trust his judgment about anything."

Bill Gates   billionaire, former co-founder Microsoft, major philanthropist

"Donald hasn't been known for his philanthropy. He's been known for other things."

Bono   philanthropist, rock star, activist

"America is like the best idea the world ever came up with, but Donald Trump is potentially the worst idea that ever happened to America. He could destroy it.

Trump's rise to prominence within the GOP is really dangerous. I think he's hijacked the party, and I think he's trying to hijack the idea of America and I think it's bigger than all of us. This is really dangerous. Whatever voters decide will have global implications."

Bruce Springsteen   mega rock star, songwriter, activist, philanthropist

"Well, you know, the republic is under siege by a moron, basically. The whole thing is tragic.

Without overstating it, it's a tragedy for our democracy. When you start talking about elections being rigged, you're pushing people beyond democratic governance. And it's a very, very dangerous thing to do. Once you let those genies out of the bottle, they don't go back in so easy, if they go back in at all. The ideas he's moving to the mainstream are all very dangerous ideas – white nationalism and the alt-right movement.

The outrageous things that he's done – not immediately disavowing David Duke? These are things that are obviously beyond the pale for any previous political candidate. It would sink your candidacy immediately.

I believe that there's a price being paid for not addressing the real cost of the deindustrialization and globalization that has occurred in the United States for the past 35, 40 years and how it's deeply affected people's lives and deeply hurt people to where they want someone who says they have a solution. And Trump's thing is simple answers to very complex problems. Fallacious answers to very complex problems. And that can be very appealing.

I think you have a limited amount of impact as an entertainer, performer or musician. I feel what I've done was certainly worth doing. And I did it at the time because I felt the country was in crisis, which it certainly is right now."

Charles Blow

Op-Ed Columnist New York Times, writer Huffington Post, broadcast commentator

Enough Is Enough August 27, 2015

When Donald Trump's security escorted the Univision anchor Jorge Ramos out of a news conference on Tuesday, I decided that I was officially done.

Maybe I should have been long before that.

Maybe I should have been done the one and only time I ever met Trump and his first words to me were a soliloquy about how black people loved him, and he was *the most popular white man among black people.*

Maybe I should have been done when Trump demanded to see the president's birth certificate.

Maybe I should have been done any number of times over the years when Trump made any number of racist, sexist comments.

Earlier this month, Politico rounded up 199 of his greatest — and vilest — hits. Here are just a few from the magazine:

9. "I have black guys counting my money. ... I hate it. The only guys I want counting my money are short guys that wear yarmulkes all day." (USA Today, May 20, 1991)

23. "Oftentimes when I was sleeping with one of the top women in the world I would say to myself, thinking about me as a boy from

Queens, 'Can you believe what I am getting?' " ("Think Big: Make it Happen in Business and Life," 2008)

32. "… she does have a very nice figure. I've said if Ivanka weren't my daughter, perhaps I'd be dating her." (ABC's "The View," March 6, 2006)

35. "If Hillary Clinton can't satisfy her husband what makes her think she can satisfy America?" (Twitter, April 16, 2015)

117. "Rosie's a person that's very lucky to have her girlfriend. And she better be careful or I'll send one of my friends over to pick up her girlfriend. Why would she stay with Rosie if she had another choice?" ("Entertainment Tonight," Dec. 21, 2006)

121. Arianna Huffington is "a dog." (Twitter, April 6, 2015)

Need I go on? (Thanks, Politico!)

Maybe I should have been done when Trump announced his candidacy this year with an attack on Mexican immigrants, saying:

"When Mexico sends its people, they're not sending their best — they're not sending you. They're not sending you. They're sending people that have lots of problems, and they're bringing those problems … drugs … crime … rapists. And some, I assume, are good people."

The Ramos episode wasn't worse than these; it was just the last straw. A member of the media who dared to raise a truly substantive issue, even out of turn, was dismissed and removed. And yet the band played on. The live coverage continued. In that moment, I was disgusted at Trump's contempt and the press's complicity in the shallow farce that is his candidacy. Trump is addicted to press, but the press is also addicted to him, and the entire spectacle is wide and shallow.

(Ramos was allowed back in and permitted to ask his question. I had to see this later, because when he was ejected, I stopped watching.)

Yes, the Republican Party created this Frankenstein of hatred, hubris, narcissism and nativism, but the media is giving it life.

The never-ending, exhaustive, even breathless coverage of every outrage that issues forth from this man's mouth is not news. Every offense and attack is not news.

Every morning that Trump rolls out of bed and calls in to a news show is not news.

Covering a political phenomenon as news is one thing. See the coverage of Bernie Sanders. Creating a political phenomenon and calling it news is quite another.

I reasoned in a 2010 column that Sarah Palin was no longer an elected official and wasn't seeking elected office, and was therefore not worthy of constant attacks. But more important, the attacks were elevating her profile, not diminishing it. As I wrote:

"This is it. This is the last time I'm going to write the name Sarah Palin until she does something truly newsworthy, like declare herself a candidate for the presidency. Until then, I will no longer take part in the left's obsessive-compulsive fascination with her, which is both unhealthy and counterproductive."

I kept that promise. The only other time she appeared by name in one of my columns was in a passing reference to her speaking at the Conservative Political Action Conference in 2013. This column is only the second reference.

The same is true of Trump. The constant harping on him only helps him.

He is different from Palin in 2010, however. He is not only running for office, he's leading in the polls among Republican candidates. He can't be ignored. But coverage is not the same as drooling over the daily shenanigans of a demagogue.

I will cover Trump as he addresses issues with specific policy prescriptions and details, like answers to the question Ramos asked.

Until then, this man is not worthy of the attention he's garnering. We in the media have to own our part in this. We can't say he's not serious and then cover him in a way that actually demonstrates that *we* are not serious.

Is he an easy target for righteous criticism? Of course he is. But is he aware that criticism from the mainstream media is invaluable among certain segments of the political right? Of course he is. Is he also aware that he's getting more free publicity for being outrageous than he would ever be willing to buy? Of course he is.

The media is being trolled on a massive scale and we look naïve and silly to have fallen for it, even if he draws readers and viewers. When people refer to the press as the fourth estate, it shouldn't be confused with a Trump property.

Allow me to share one more of Trump's quotes from Politico:

89. "My brand became more famous as I became more famous, and more opportunities presented themselves." (Amazon.com, 2007)

About the 'Basket of Deplorables' (September, 2016)

"Let's get straight to it: Hillary Clinton's comments Friday at a fund-raiser that half of Donald Trump's supporters could be put in a "basket of deplorables" wasn't a smart political play.

Candidates do themselves a tremendous disservice when they attack voters rather than campaigns. Whatever advantage is procured through the rallying of one's own base is outweighed by what will be read as divisiveness and disdain.

Here is Clinton's full quote:

"You know, to just be grossly generalistic, you could put half of Trump's supporters into what I call the basket of deplorables. Right? The racist, sexist, homophobic, xenophobic, Islamophobic — you name it. And unfortunately there are people like that. And he has lifted them up. He has given voice to their websites that used to only have 11,000 people — now 11 million. He tweets and retweets their offensive, hateful, mean-spirited rhetoric. Now some of those folks — they are irredeemable, but thankfully they are not America."

Then, she continued: "But the other basket — and I know this because I see friends from all over America here — I see friends from Florida and Georgia and South Carolina and Texas — as well as, you know, New York and California — but that other basket of people are people who feel that the government has let them down, the economy has let them down, nobody cares about them, nobody worries about what happens to their lives and their futures, and they're just desperate for change. It doesn't really even matter where it comes from. They don't buy everything he says, but he seems to hold out some hope that their lives will be different. They won't wake up and see their jobs disappear, lose a kid to heroin, feel like they're in a dead end. Those are people we have to understand and empathize with as well."

That second basket got too little attention. Context doesn't provide the sizzle on which shock media subsists. Noted.

What Clinton said was impolitic, but it was not incorrect. There are things a politician cannot say. Luckily, I'm not a politician.

Donald Trump is a deplorable candidate — to put it charitably — and anyone who helps him advance his racial, religious and ethnic bigotry is part of that bigotry. Period. Anyone who elevates a sexist is part of that sexism. The same goes for xenophobia. You can't conveniently separate yourself from the detestable part of him because you sense in him the promise of cultural or economic advantage. That hair cannot be split.

Furthermore, one doesn't have to actively hate to contribute to a culture that allows hate to flourish.

It doesn't matter how lovely your family, how honorable your work or service, how devout your faith — if you place ideological adherence or economic self interest above the moral imperative to condemn and denounce a demagogue, then you are deplorable.

And there is some evidence that Trump's supporters don't simply have a passive, tacit acceptance of an undesirable platform, but instead have an active set of beliefs that support what is deplorable in Trump.

In state after state that Trump won during the primaries, he won a majority or near majority of voters who supported a temporary ban on Muslims entering this country and who supported deporting immigrants who are in this country illegally.

In June a Reuters/Ipsos poll found: "Nearly half of Trump's supporters described African-Americans as more 'violent' than whites. The same proportion described African-Americans as more 'criminal' than whites, while 40 percent described them as more 'lazy' than whites."

A Pew poll released in February found that 65 percent of Republicans believe the next president should "speak bluntly even if critical of Islam as a whole" when talking about Islamic extremists.

Another Reuters/Ipsos online poll in July found that 58 percent of Trump supporters have a "somewhat unfavorable" view of Islam and 78 percent believe Islam was more likely to encourage acts of terrorism.

A February Public Policy Polling survey found "Trump's support in South Carolina is built on a base of voters among whom religious and racial intolerance pervades." What the poll found about those South Carolina supporters' beliefs was truly shocking:

- Eighty percent of likely Trump primary voters supported Trump's proposed ban on Muslims.
- Sixty-two percent supported creating a national database of Muslims and 40 percent supported shutting down mosques in the United States.

- Thirty-eight percent wished the South had won the Civil War.
- Thirty-three percent thought the practice of Islam should be illegal in this country.
- Thirty-two percent supported the policy of Japanese internment during World War II.
- Thirty-one percent would support a ban on homosexuals entering the country.

On Saturday, Clinton issued a statement pointing out that "I regret saying 'half' — that was wrong." Place the percentage where you will — or don't — but the fact is indisputable.

I understand that people recoil at the notion that they are part of a pejorative basket. I understand the reflexive resistance to having your negative beliefs disrobed and your sense of self dressed down.

I understand your outrage, but I'm unmoved by it. If the basket fits …"

Charlie Sykes

Wisconsin Conservative talk show host, member of Never Trump movement

(To a listener) "You're comparing American citizens, Muslims, to rabid dogs."

"Were these people that we actually thought were our allies?"

"Did "the faux outrage machine" of Breitbart.com and other right-wing outlets foment the noxious opinions that Trump has stoked so effectively on the trail?"

"When I would deny that there was a significant racist component in some of the politics on our side, it was because the people I hung out with were certainly not. When suddenly, this rock is turned over, there is this—'Oh shit, did I not see that?'

"I kind of had that reaction this morning, with that woman: Did we ignore this? There's got to be some serious introspection, because of the things that we either didn't see, or that we ignored, or that we enabled."

(To Trump) "Before you called into my show, did you know that I'm a #NeverTrump guy?" "We're not on a playground. We're running for president of the United States."

"I am dealing with the daily flood of emails on how we're never going to listen to you anymore," Sykes says. Longtime listeners write to say conservative talk radio should criticize Hillary Clinton and not Trump. If I lose listeners, that's a price I've just got to pay. I'd rather say what I really think than fall in line with other broadcasters' embrace of Trump. I feel dumber every time I listen to Sean Hannity. I don't want to be that guy."

Chris Christie   Republican Governor N.J. and Presidential candidate in primaries

"Trump acts like a teenager instead of a leader who was ready for the White House.

" Trump's fight with Fox News symbolized what kind of president he would be. "

"I don't answer it (talking about Trump) anymore."

"That's my position. I don't comment on his comments. It's just not worth the time. I'm happy to stand by my record and what I've done in New Jersey and how our particular brand of being blunt and direct and telling the truth actually works toward getting things done."

Christie Todd Whitman   Former Republican
Governor, N.J.

"I'm planning to vote for Hillary Clinton if Trump gets the nod.

"You'll see a lot of Republicans do that. We don't want to. But I know I won't vote for Trump."

"I am ashamed that Chris Christie would endorse anyone who has employed the kind of hate mongering and racism that Trump has. I would have thought being from a diverse state would have given him more awareness and compassion."

Colin Powell

Former Chairman Joint Chiefs of Staff and Secretary of State

"Benghazi was a witch hunt."

"Trump embraced a "racist" movement when he questioned the validity of President Obama's birth certificate. Yup, the whole birther movement was racist. That's what the 99% believe. When Trump couldn't keep that up he said he also wanted to see if the certificate noted that he was a Muslim. As I have said before, 'What if he was?' Muslims are born as Americans everyday."

"Trump is a national disgrace and an international pariah."

Cory Booker   Democratic U.S. Senator, N.J.

"Trump will not become the country's next president."

"I thought that Donald Trump's ascendancy would end when he attacked John McCain, saying he's not a war hero. I found that shocking, for him to say that. But I've been wrong on everything about Trump, I've been wrong about everything on the Republican side of the ledger but allow me — with that caveat — to made the prediction that Donald Trump will not be the president of the United States. It just will not happen."

"His approval ratings are below water on a lot of very important metrics in this country."

"I know Donald Trump, I've met him, I know his family. I have love, and friendship, and affection for his family members. But I'm going to work very hard to ensure that he is not our president."

"I won't answer his hate with hate. I'm not going to answer his darkness with darkness. I thank him for including me along with all the others he's demeaned. I hope (he) finds some kindness in his heart. ..and that he's not going to be somebody who only spews out insults and his kind of mean-spirited hate. It doesn't even belong in a playground. I just don't want him to have the White House to be spewing out that."

Dan Rather   former CBS News anchor, commentator on AXS TV

"I felt a shudder down my spine yesterday watching Donald Trump's fusilade against the press. This is not a moment to be trifled with. It wasn't his first tirade and it won't be his last. There will be "violence" if Trump is left unchecked."

"I know what it is like to sit in those seats and feel the scorn and even wrath of politicians of all political persuasions. Attacking the press for unfair coverage has long been a bipartisan pursuit. Sometimes it works. I am happy to say that more often it doesn't. But Trump's brand of vituperation is particularly personal and vicious. It carries with it the drumbeats of threatening violence. It cannot be left unanswered."

"This is not about politics or policy. It's about protecting our most cherished principles. The relationship between the press and the powerful they cover is by its very definition confrontational. That is how the Founding Fathers envisioned it, with noble clauses of protection enshrined in our Constitution."

"Good journalism — the kind that matters — requires reporters who won't back up, back down, back away or turn around when faced with efforts to intimidate them. It also requires owners and other bosses with guts, who stand by and for their reporters when the heat is on."

for Moyers and Company:

"Um. Wow. If anybody thought that Donald Trump would deliver a moderated speech on immigration, that ended pretty much in the first moments he walked onto the stage in Phoenix. He claimed it would be a detailed policy address, and yet from the start his tone was a seething, angry attack on what he described as a world of dangerous murderers and rapists who seem to be roaming "sanctuary cities." Focusing on a few isolated and already well-documented tragedies, he painted the entire undocumented world with the casual brush of violence. This approach was punctuated by family members of those who have died, paraded at the end. The crowd — nearly all white from the looks of the cutaway shots — ate it up with a hostility that seems in keeping with those who have flocked to Trump's angry march through this campaign season. There was of course no mention of the de facto integration of millions of immigrants already entwined in the fabric of our daily lives and economy.

I expected a law-and-order theme, but not this level of searing rhetoric. Of course, I shouldn't have been surprised. Trump feeds off his crowds and they were giving it right back. It was ultimate in the "us versus them" mentality. Real Americans versus others. I frankly saw echoes of the George Wallace speeches from the 1968 campaign.

The applause lines seemed like ready red meat for this crowd and I am sure for those who regularly watch Fox News. They were names and anecdotes that frankly will be unknown to most Americans. That's because Donald Trump's America does not comport with what many voters see in their own lives. It was an attack on "thugs" and those on "welfare." I suppose there was a structure to this speech. He would say "and 3," "and 4" as if it were a detailed list of proposals, but any sense of order was swamped by a tsunami of rhetoric and tone.

Going in, there was a question, after a confusing and contradictory trip to Mexico earlier in the day, about the status of Trump's wall. Trump said he would, without equivocation, "build the wall." The crowd again went wild. And of course Mexico will pay for the wall — "100 percent. They don't know it yet." But by that point, even this news item seemed like an afterthought consumed by the overall tone.

Trump and Clinton are not running for the president of the same country.

Along the way he slammed climate change, suggested that Hillary Clinton could be deported and told African-Americans they should vote for him because "what do they have to lose?"

But any details are beside the point. With a raspy roar, leaning over the podium, Trump delivered his message with glee. This is our country and we are being overwhelmed by hordes not fit to be in our country. He suggested that "these people" are well known to law enforcement and could be rounded up with ease. It was a line that seemed more in keeping with the culture of the old East

Germany than the United States. "We have got to have a county folks" he summed it up. "Under a Trump administration it's called America first!"

You could try to fact check this speech, but that is a fool's errand. Trump and Clinton are not running for the president of the same country. The one who wins will be the one whose vision of America most conforms with reality.

Make no mistake, this was a toxic mix of jingoism, nativism and chauvinism. Many of you would like to think, not in America, not in our country could this type of rhetoric gain currency. But in other countries, and in other times in history, we have seen the impossible become possible to horrific effect. Trump is betting his political future on this idea — that there is a deep, tribal and dark sea of the molten lava of hate and aggrievement. This volcano from below appeals to dangerous instincts — can it yield a path to the presidency and power?"

David Cameron   former British Prime Minister

"I think his remarks are divisive, stupid and wrong and I think if he came to visit our country I think it'd unite us all against him."

David Duke   former Ku Klux Klan Grand Wizard, candidate for Senator, Louisiana

"The climate of this country has moved in my direction."

"I'm 100 percent behind Trump's agenda. As a United States senator, nobody will be more supportive of his legislative agenda, his Supreme Court agenda, than I will."

"Trump's attacks on Muslims and illegal immigration have brought my own beliefs into the mainstream."

"I think that those Republicans, or those so-called conservatives (those not supporting Trump) are betraying the principles of the Republican Party and certainly conservatism. Donald Trump is not a racist. And the truth is in this country if you simply defend the heritage of European American people then you're automatically a racist."

"There is massive racist, racial discrimination against European-Americans and a very vicious anti-white narrative" in the media. Hollywood, is not controlled by European-Americans. Well they're from the Middle East, that's not European. That's not European, is it? That's Middle Eastern. And they have a particular orientation for their positions and their programs. Europeans built America."

"Donald Trump has to run his own campaign; I have to run my own campaign. I don't know if he's with me or not but I would hope that he and others would realize that the same lies they make about him is what they say about me. I've always said that I'm for equal rights for all people, but I also believe that European-Americans shouldn't be facing discrimination either."

"Trump voters are my voters. Of course they are! Because I represent the ideas of preserving this country and the heritage of this country, and I think Trump represents that as well."

David Letterman   former host, The Late Show With David Letterman

'He's Repugnant to People'

"There's nothing illegal going on. It's just that he's despicable"

"I understand that he's repugnant to people. But you tell me: The men putting together the Constitution, witnessing this election, wouldn't they have just said, 'That's part of the way we set it up. Good luck'?"

"While many teachers attempt to inspire their students by saying "the great thing about America is anybody can grow up to be President," that thought is also terrifying. Oh, jeez,I guess that might be true!"

Elizabeth Warren   Democratic U.S. Senator Massachusetts

"Trump is a "racist bully and a "small insecure money-grubber."

"I'm right where I want to be, @realDonaldTrump: Calling you out & holding you responsible for your reckless vision for America."

"Trump's entire campaign is just one more late-night Trump infomercial. Hand over your money, your jobs, your children's future, and The Great Trump Hot Air Machine will reveal all the answers, And, for one low, low price, he'll even throw in a goofy hat."

Elizabeth Warren's DNC speech:

"Thank you, Joe, and thank you to Massachusetts for the great honor of serving as your Senator. Wow! What a night. Michelle Obama. Cory Booker. And we still have Bernie coming up. Bernie reminds us what Democrats fight for every day! Thank you, Bernie!

We are here tonight because America faces a choice, the choice of a new president.

On one side is a man who inherited a fortune from his father and kept it going by cheating people and skipping out on debts. A man who has never sacrificed anything for anyone. A man who cares only for himself — every minute of every day.

On the other side is one of the smartest, toughest, most tenacious people on the planet — a woman who fights for children, for women, for health care, for human rights, a woman who fights for all of us, and who is strong enough to win those fights.

We're here today because our choice is Hillary Clinton! I'm with Hillary!

For me, this choice is personal. It's about who we are as a people. It's about what kind of country we want to be.

I grew up in Oklahoma. My daddy ended up as a maintenance man, and my mom worked for minimum wage at Sears. My three brothers served in the military. The oldest was career, 288 combat missions in Vietnam. The second worked construction. The third started his own business. Me? I got married at 19 and graduated from a commuter college in Texas that cost $50 a semester. The way I see it, I'm a janitor's daughter who became a public school teacher, a professor, and a United States Senator. America is truly a country of opportunity!

I'm deeply grateful to that America. I believe in that America. But I'm worried. Worried that my story is locked in the past. Worried that opportunity is slipping away for people who work hard and play by the rules.

Look around. Americans bust their tails, some working two or three jobs, but wages stay flat. Meanwhile, the basic costs of making it from month to month keep going up. Housing, health care, child care — costs are out of sight. Young people are getting crushed by student loans. Working people are in debt. Seniors can't stretch a Social Security check to cover the basics.

And even families who are OK today worry that it could all fall apart tomorrow. This. Is. Not. Right!

Here's the thing: America isn't going broke. The stock market is breaking records. Corporate profits are at all-time highs. CEOs make tens of millions of dollars. There's lots of wealth in America, but it isn't trickling down to hard-working families like yours.

Does anyone here have a problem with that? Well, I do too.

People get it: the system is rigged.

So-called experts claim America is in trouble because both political parties in Washington refuse to compromise. Gridlock!

That is just flat wrong. Washington works great for those at the top.

When giant companies wanted more tax loopholes, Washington got it done. When huge energy companies wanted to tear up our environment, Washington got it done. When enormous Wall Street banks wanted new regulatory loopholes, Washington got it done. No gridlock there!

But try to do something, anything, for working people, and you'll have a fight on your hands.

Democrats have taken on those fights. Democrats fought to get health insurance for more Americans. Democrats fought for a strong consumer agency so big banks can't cheat people. We fought, we won, and we improved the lives of millions of people — thank you, President Obama!

Yes, we won, but Republicans and lobbyists battled us every step of the way. Five years later, that consumer agency has returned $11 billion to families who were cheated. And Republicans? They're still trying to kill it.

I'm not someone who thinks Republicans are always wrong and Democrats are always right. There's enough blame to go around.

But there is a huge difference between the people fighting for a level playing field, and the people keeping the system rigged.

Look at Congress since the Republicans took over. Democrats proposed refinancing student loans. And Republicans? They said no! Democrats proposed ending tax breaks for corporations that ship jobs overseas. And Republicans? They said no! Democrats proposed raising the minimum wage. And Republicans? They said no!

To every Republican in Congress who said no: this November, the American people are coming for you!

And where was Donald Trump? In all these fights, not once did he lift a finger to help working people. Why would he? His whole life has been about taking advantage of that rigged system. Time after time he preyed on working people, people in debt, people who had fallen on hard times. He's conned them, he's defrauded them, and he's ripped them off.

Look at his history. Donald Trump said he was "excited" for the 2008 housing crash that devastated millions of American families because he thought it would help him scoop up more real estate on the cheap. Donald Trump set up a fake university to make money while cheating people and taking their life savings.

Donald Trump goes on, and on, and on, about being a successful businessman, but he filed business bankruptcies six times, always to protect his own money and stick his investors and contractors with the bill. Donald Trump hired plumbers and painters and construction workers to do hard labor for his businesses, then told them to take only a fraction of what he owed or fight his lawyers in court for years.

What kind of a man acts like this? What kind of a man roots for the economic crash that cost millions of people their jobs? Their homes? Their life savings? What kind of a man cheats students, cheats investors, cheats workers?

I'll tell you what kind of man. A man who must NEVER be President of the United States! And we've got the leaders to make it happen: Hillary Clinton and Tim Kaine!

Donald Trump knows that the American people are angry — a fact so obvious he can see it from the top of Trump Tower. So now he's insisting that he, and he alone, can fix the rigged system.

Last week Donald Trump spoke for more than an hour on the biggest stage he's ever had. But other than talking about building a stupid wall, which will NEVER get built, really, did you hear any actual ideas? Did you hear even one solid proposal from Trump for increasing incomes, or improving your kids' education, or creating even one single good-paying job?

Donald Trump has no real plans for jobs or for college kids or for seniors, no plans to make ANYTHING great for ANYONE except rich guys like Donald Trump. Just look at his ideas. Donald Trump wants to get rid of the federal minimum wage. Donald Trump wants to roll back financial regulations and turn Wall Street loose to wreck our economy again.

And Donald Trump has a tax plan to give multi-millionaires and billionaires like himself an average tax cut of $1.3 million — a year. You're struggling to put your kids through college, and Donald Trump thinks HE needs a million-dollar tax break!

Trump's entire campaign is just one more late-night Trump infomercial. Hand over your money, your jobs, your children's future, and The Great Trump Hot Air Machine will reveal all the answers. And, for one low, low price, he'll even throw in a goofy hat.

And here's the really ugly underside to his pitch. Trump thinks he can win votes by fanning the flames of fear and hatred. By turning neighbor against neighbor. By persuading you that the real problem in America is your fellow Americans — people who don't look like you, or don't talk like you, or don't worship like you. He even picked a vice president famous for trying to make it legal to openly discriminate against gays and lesbians.

That's Donald Trump's America. An America of fear and hate. An America where we all break apart. Whites against blacks and Latinos. Christians against Muslims and Jews. Straight against gay. Everyone against immigrants. Race, religion, heritage, gender, the more factions the better. But ask yourself this. When white workers in Ohio are pitted against black workers in North Carolina, or Latino workers in Florida, who really benefits?

"Divide and Conquer" is an old story in America. Dr. Martin Luther King knew it. After his march from Selma to Montgomery, he spoke of how segregation was created to keep people divided. Instead of higher wages for workers, Dr. King described how poor whites in the South were fed Jim Crow, which told a poor white worker that, "No matter how bad off he was, at least he was a white man, better than the black man." Racial hatred was part of keeping the powerful on top.

And now Trump and his campaign have embraced it all. Racial hatred. Religious bigotry. Attacks on immigrants, on women, on gays. A deceitful and ugly blame game that says, whatever worries you, the answer is to blame that other group, and don't put any energy into making real change.

When we turn on each other, bankers can run our economy for Wall Street, oil companies can fight off clean energy, and giant corporations can ship the last good jobs overseas.

When we turn on each other, rich guys like Trump can push through more tax breaks for themselves and then we'll never have enough money to support our schools, or rebuild our highways, or invest in our kids' future.

When we turn on each other, we can't unite to fight back against a rigged system.

Well, I've got news for Donald Trump. The American people are not falling for it! We've seen this ugliness before, and we're not going to be Donald Trump's hate-filled America. Not now, not ever!

I come to you as the daughter of a janitor, a daughter who believes in an America of opportunity. The hand of history is on our shoulders. We know how to build a future, a future that works not just for some of our children, but for all of our children. We know, and we must have the courage to make it happen.

This is about our values, our shared values with our candidates Hillary Clinton and Tim Kaine!

We believe that no matter who you are, no matter where you're from, no matter who you love, equal means equal. Hillary will fight to make sure discrimination has no place in America. And we're with her!

We believe that no one, no one, who works full time should live in poverty. Hillary will fight for raising the minimum wage, fair scheduling, paid family and medical leave! And we're with her!

We believe every kid in America should have a chance for a great education without getting crushed by debt. Hillary will fight for refinancing student loans and debt-free college. And we're with her!

We believe that after a lifetime of hard work, seniors should be able to retire with dignity. Hillary will fight to expand Social Security, strengthen Medicare, and protect retirement accounts. And we're with her!

We believe that oil companies shouldn't call the shots in Washington, that science matters, that climate change is real. Hillary will fight to preserve this earth for our children and grandchildren. And we're with her!

We believe – and I can't believe I have to say this in 2016 – in equal pay for equal work and a woman's right to control over her own body! Hillary will fight for women. And we're with her!

We believe we don't need WEAKER rules on Wall Street, we need stronger rules, and when big banks get too risky, break 'em up. Hillary will fight to hold big banks accountable. And we're with her!

We believe that the United States should never, never, sign trade deals that help giant corporations but leave working people in the dirt! Hillary will fight for American workers. And we're with her!

And just one more. We believe we must get big money out of politics and root out corruption. Hillary will fight to overturn Citizens United and return this government to the people! And we're with her!

If you believe that America must work for all of us, not just the rich and powerful, if you believe we must reject the politics of fear and division, if you believe we are stronger together, then let's work our hearts out to make Hillary Clinton the next President of the United States!"

Erich Schneiderman   NY State Attorney General

"Trump ran a thoroughly fraudulent enterprise. In New York, we have laws against business fraud, we have laws against consumer fraud. We have laws against running an illegal unlicensed university. This never was a university. The fraud started with the name of the organization, and you can't just go around saying this is the (so-and-so) Law Firm/Hospital/University without actually qualifying and registering, so it was really a fraud from beginning to end."

"He doesn't have immunity from civil fraud trials."

"Well, if it was a philanthropic venture, he certainly made out well from the philanthropic venture. The initial estimates are that he personally pocketed $5 million from this. We're going to get more information when we get to the damages phase of the trial, but we're confident that he didn't do this for free."

"The charges are not politically motivated. Not at all. The case was brought in August of 2013 after over a year of investigation and extensive negotiations with Trump. If I had come on your show and said in August 2013 he would be the Republican nominee for president, you probably never would have invited me again. This is not a political case. It's a straight-up fraud case."

"Donald Trump is a 2-Year-Old. It's time for the press to treat him like one."

"We were bringing cases against different for-profit colleges. This one stuck out like a sore thumb because it really was remarkable. The New York State Department of Education was chasing them around, saying you can't hold yourself out as a university. They kept saying they would change their name or move out of New York. This was just a scam."

"It's fraud. This is just straight up fraud. It's like selling people something you say is a Mercedes and it turns out to be a Volkswagen and even if some people say, 'Well I actually kind of like the Volkswagen, it's still fraud, 'cause it's not a Mercedes. This is not a university. And in New York, we are a little sensitive. We can use the evidence that we've gathered. We're not here to have fun."

"We have now also started an investigation into the practices of the Trump Foundation."

Eugene Robinson   Pulitzer-prize winning columnist, The
Washington Post

Is Donald Trump just plain crazy?

"During the primary season, as Donald Trump's bizarre outbursts helped him crush the competition, I thought he was being crazy like a fox. Now I am increasingly convinced that he's just plain crazy.

I'm serious about that. Leave aside for the moment Trump's policies, which in my opinion range from the unconstitutional to the un-American to the potentially catastrophic. At this point, it would be irresponsible to ignore the fact that Trump's grasp on reality appears to be tenuous at best.

Begin with the fact that he lies the way other people breathe. Telling a self-serving lie — no matter how transparent, no matter how easily disproved — seems to be a reflex for him. Look at the things he has said in just the past week.

On Wednesday, at a news conference in Florida, Trump said he has never met Russian President Vladimir Putin. "I never met Putin, I don't know who Putin is," he said.

Last November, he claimed that he "got to know [Putin] very well because we were both on '60 Minutes.' " That made no sense; while the two men were featured the same evening on the CBS newsmagazine show, they were interviewed in different cities and would have had no interaction. But there's more: In 2014, speaking at the National Press Club, Trump said, "I was in Moscow recently and I spoke, indirectly and directly, with President Putin, who could not have been nicer, and we had a tremendous success."

Republican presidential nominee Donald Trump said the United States gets "no respect" from Russian President Vladimir Putin during a town hall event in Scranton, Pa., July 27. (The Washington Post)

So was he lying last week, when he was trying to deflect criticism of his admiring words for the Russian strongman? Or was he lying two years ago, when he was trying to convince everyone what a big shot he was?

Also within the week, Trump lied in complaining about the presidential debate schedule and its conflicts with professional football. He told ABC News's George Stephanopoulos, "I got a letter from the NFL saying, 'This is ridiculous. Why are the debates against — ' because the NFL doesn't want to go against the debates."

The National Football League responded: "We did not send a letter."

Trump also lied about his interactions with the conservative billionaire Koch brothers. "I turned down a meeting with Charles and David Koch. Much better for them to meet with the puppets of politics, they will do much better!" Trump proclaimed Saturday on Twitter.

A spokesman for the Koch organization said no meeting with Trump was requested.

It is theoretically possible, I suppose, that Trump is telling the truth and everyone else is lying — although in the case of the Putin relationship, it's Trump's word against Trump's. Or perhaps the lies about the NFL and the Koch brothers are little things. But he also lies about big things — claiming, for example, that he opposed the Iraq War and the Libya intervention all along, when the record shows that initially he supported both. No, Trump is clearly a liar.

Also, he's alarmingly thin-skinned. Referring to critics who spoke at the Democratic National Convention, Trump said Thursday that he wanted to "hit a number of those speakers so hard, their heads would spin." And: "I was going to hit one guy in particular, a very little guy." Trump made clear Friday on Twitter that he was talking about " 'Little' Michael Bloomberg, who never had the guts to run for president."

Bloomberg, a far wealthier New York billionaire, had belittled Trump's supposed strength — his business acumen. In a tantrum of tweets, Trump charged that Bloomberg's last term as mayor of New York was a "disaster." Back during Bloomberg's final year, however, Trump called Bloomberg a "great" mayor. Which is it, I wonder?

Finally, there's ample evidence that Trump is the worst kind of bully. Look at the way he reacted to the powerful Democratic convention speech by Khizr Khan, the father of a Muslim American soldier who was killed in the Iraq War.

Trump initially did not have the courage to respond directly to Khan. Instead he smarmily attacked Khan's wife, Ghazala, who had stood silently on the stage. "She was standing there. She had nothing to say. She probably, maybe she wasn't allowed to have anything to say. You tell me."

There's no need for me to defend Ghazala Khan, who spoke eloquently for herself in a Post op-ed. But tell me: What kind of man has so little empathy for a grieving mother's loss? Is that normal? Is it healthy?

The presidency comes with far-reaching powers. Not everyone should be allowed to wield them."

Fareed Zakaria   CNN commentator, Washington Post opinion writer

"It's not just Trump: The GOP is not serious on the economy

In recent days, I have had a dream: that America has a real Republican Party, a party offering a serious right-of-center alternative to the Democrats. Such a contest of ideas would improve the public debate and offer Americans a real choice, not the cartoon campaign we have today.

Donald Trump had the opportunity to reset his campaign this week and managed to derail it. But forget the detour for a moment. Trump's much-heralded speech laying out his economic policies was a mishmash of populism, hypocrisy and pandering. It promised protectionism, trade wars and tax cuts for the rich and proposed no changes to the United States' fast-growing entitlement programs. It was ideologically incoherent and fiscally irresponsible.

When did this Republican intellectual decay begin? According to conservative writer David Frum in his brilliant book "Dead Right," it started in the Ronald Reagan years. Historically, the Republican Party was all about fiscal discipline. Reagan had viciously attacked Jimmy Carter for racking up deficits and debt. In fact, by the end of Reagan's two terms, the national debt had tripled.

Republicans came to recognize that, whatever it might say, the public in fact didn't want cuts in government programs. The country was, in George F. Will's phrase, "ideologically conservative but operationally liberal." This was the Republicans' moment of truth, Frum argued, and they blinked.

Since then, most Republican presidential candidates have promised the public huge tax cuts without any real spending restraint to pay for them. The result, of course, has been massive deficits. The only Republican who tried to adhere to some notion of fiscal conservatism, George H.W. Bush, was attacked and destroyed for this sin by conservatives led by Newt Gingrich.

Republican economic plans nowadays are simply not serious. In the primaries, the three main candidates of "the party of fiscal discipline" — Marco Rubio, Ted Cruz and Donald Trump — presented plans that added $8 trillion, $10 trillion or $11 trillion in debt over the next decade (according to the nonpartisan Tax Policy Center). Even the much-respected Paul Ryan proposed a plan with a $2.4 trillion hole in it. These vast gaps are papered over with magical assumptions of higher growth and the usual vague calls to end waste, fraud and abuse. (Whether you like or dislike Hillary Clinton's economic plan, its numbers add up.)

Trump's plans are a replay of these dishonest techniques. He proposes large tax cuts but of course doesn't pay for them, assuming the usual bogus growth numbers to make them look better on paper. He promises to cut regulations, saying at a rally this week that he might reduce them by 70 or 75 percent, which is so absurd that I don't think even he believes it. His added twist is protectionism, but even here the technique is the same. He makes wild promises that he would never be able to fulfill.

Imagine, instead of all this, a Republican Party that believed firmly in limited government — and proposed policies that were true to these beliefs. It could present a serious plan that rationalized America's unwieldy and corrupt tax code, simplifying the structure, even cutting rates — but only to the extent these were actually paid for by increased revenues from closing loopholes, deductions and credits.

Imagine a Republican Party that focused less on tax cuts for the rich and more on improved access to the market for the poor and middle class. For example, a party that proposed not to eliminate Obamacare but to reform it using stronger market mechanisms, allowing greater competition and transparency in prices and services.

Imagine a party that presented specific plans to cut regulations that hamper the formation and growth of small businesses and encouraged large companies to hire more workers and make new investments (rather than engaging in financial engineering and stock buybacks). A party that encouraged states to get rid of the ever-expanding licensing requirements put into place to keep out the competition. (In the 1950s, less than 5 percent of jobs required a license to do the work. Today 29 percent do, at a cost of nearly 3 million jobs, according to University of Minnesota professor Morris Kleiner, who has studied the topic extensively.) As the Kauffman Foundation has discovered in surveying small businesses, they care far more about too many regulations than they do about their tax rates.

Political systems need debate and choices. But for these to be useful, both sides have to accept certain informal rules — that their proposals will be serious and coherent and that their numbers will add up. The United States would benefit greatly if the Republican Party were to focus on its core ideas, and be a substantive, market oriented, right-of-center party."

Trump and the politics of cultural despair

For some of us, the puzzle of this election is not why Donald Trump is doing so badly but why he is doing so well. Given his obvious lack of qualifications, his absurd proposals, his hypocrisy, his obnoxious rhetoric, his sheer incompetence as a candidate, why is he not down 10 points in every state?

In other words, who are Trump's voters and why do they stick with him? Sometimes a good writer with a keen eye can provide more insight than a dozen polls. J.D. Vance has done just that in his lovely book "Hillbilly Elegy: A Memoir of a Family and Culture in Crisis." The book has rocketed up the best-seller lists — deservedly so. But it has some interesting and important gaps.

We all now know that Trump's rise has been fueled by the alienation and anger of the country's white working class. That cohort has seen its incomes stagnate, cities crumble and dreams vanish. But Vance gets underneath the data and shows us what these impersonal forces mean to actual people. He describes the abandoned children, the poor work habits, the drug abuse, the violence, the rage. But he does it with sympathy and love. They are his family, after all.

For Vance, the problem is ultimately cultural, one of values, attitudes and mores. "We hillbillies must wake the hell up," he writes, and "stop blaming Obama or Bush or faceless companies and ask ourselves what can we do to make things better." His own life story — coming from low expectations, dysfunctional relationships and persistent poverty to end up a graduate of Yale Law School and a Silicon Valley executive — demonstrates that grit can conquer all.

But Vance got some help along the way. He tells us that his public schools were decent enough and, when he got motivated, his teachers helped him succeed. He notes that his trajectory changed when he was admitted to Ohio State University, which he was able to attend because of generous federal loans and grants. And the turning point in the book and his life takes place when he decides to enlist in the Marine Corps. He describes how the armed forces taught him discipline, hard work, high expectations and good values. (When he was contemplating buying a car, an older Marine steered him away from his choice of a flashy BMW and toward a Honda.)

This is federal bureaucracy engaged in shaping mores and morals, the ultimate example of government as nanny. When so much of what government does is under siege, it is odd that Vance seems to minimize the role that government can play in providing opportunities for others like him.

The other, larger gap in Vance's book is race. He speaks about the causes of the anxiety and pain of the white working class, but he describes the causes almost entirely in economic terms. Their jobs have disappeared, their wages have stagnated, their lives have become more unstable. But there is surely something else at work here — the sense that people who look and sound very different are rising up. Surveys, polls and other research confirm that racial identity and anxiety are at the heart of support for Trump.

Vance touches on this sideways, when speaking about the almost pathological suspicion his "hillbillies" have for Barack Obama. Vance explains that it is because of the president's accent — "clean, perfect, neutral" — his urban background, his success in the meritocracy, his reliability as a father. "And," one wants to whisper to Vance, "because he's black ." After all, over the years the white working class has voted for plenty of Republican and

Democratic candidates with fancy degrees and neutral accents. That's not what makes Obama different.

The white working class has always derived some of its status because there was a minority underclass below it. In his seminal work, "American Slavery, American Freedom," Edmund Morgan argues that even before the revolution, the introduction of slavery helped dampen class conflict within the white population. No matter how poor you were, there was security in knowing there was someone beneath you.

The rage that is fueling the Trump phenomenon is not just about stagnant wages. It is about a way of life under siege, and it risks producing a "politics of cultural despair." That phrase was coined by Fritz Stern to describe Germany a century ago. The key to avoiding that fate is not a series of public policies — whether tariffs or tax credits — but enlightened politics, meaning leadership that does not prey on people's fears and phobias."

The unbearable stench of Trump's B.S.

"A few days ago, I was asked on CNN to make sense of one more case in which Donald Trump had said something demonstrably false and then explained it away with a caustic tweet and an indignant interview. I replied that there was a pattern here and a term for a person who did this kind of thing: a "bullshit artist." I got cheers and boos for the comment from partisans on both sides, but I was not using that label casually. Trump is many things, some of them dark and dangerous, but at his core, he is a B.S. artist.

Harry Frankfurt, an eminent moral philosopher and former professor at Princeton, wrote a brilliant essay in 1986 called "On Bullshit." (Frankfurt himself wrote about Trump in this vein, as have Jeet Heer and Eldar Sarajlic.) In the essay, Frankfurt distinguishes crucially between lies and B.S.: "Telling a lie is an act with a sharp focus. It is designed to insert a particular falsehood at a specific point. . . . In order to invent a lie at all, [the teller of a lie] must think he knows what is true."

But someone engaging in B.S., Frankfurt says, "is neither on the side of the true nor on the side of the false. His eye is not on the facts at all . . . except insofar as they may be pertinent to his interest in getting away with what he says." Frankfurt writes that the B.S.-er's "focus is panoramic rather than particular" and that he has "more spacious opportunities for improvisation, color, and imaginative play. This is less a matter of craft than of art. Hence the familiar notion of the 'bullshit artist.' "

This has been Trump's mode all his life. He boasts — and boasts and boasts — about his business, his buildings, his books, his wives. Much of it is a concoction of hyperbole and falsehoods. And when he's found out, he's like that guy we have all met at a bar who makes wild claims but when confronted with the truth, quickly responds, "I knew that!"

Take, for instance, the most extraordinary example, his non-relationship with Vladimir Putin. In May 2014, addressing the National Press Club, Trump said, "I was in Russia, I was in Moscow recently and I spoke, indirectly and directly, with President Putin, who could not have been nicer." In November 2015, at a Fox Business debate, he said of Putin, "I got to know him very well because we were both on '60 Minutes.' "

Did Trump really believe that you could say something like that on live TV and no one would check? Did he think that no one would notice that the "60 Minutes" show consisted of two separate prerecorded interviews, with Putin in Moscow and Trump in New York? (By that logic, I have gotten to know Franklin Roosevelt very well because I have run some clips of him on my television show.)

In fact, Trump was bullshitting. He sees himself as important, a global celebrity, the kind of man who should or could have met Putin. Why does it matter that they did not actually meet?

Or look at the issue that fueled his political rise, birtherism. Trump said in 2011 that he had sent investigators to Hawaii and that "they cannot believe what they're finding." For weeks, he continued to imply that there were huge findings to be released. He hinted to George Stephanopoulos, "We're going to see what happens." That was five years ago, in April 2011. Nothing happened.

In fact, it appears highly unlikely that Trump ever sent any investigators to Hawaii. In 2011, Salon asked Trump attorney Michael Cohen for details about the investigators. Cohen said that it was all very secret, naturally. Trump has said the same about his plan to defeat the Islamic State, which he can't reveal. He has boasted that he has a strategy to win solidly Democratic states this fall, but he won't reveal which ones. (Even by Trump's standards, this one is a head-scratcher. Won't we notice when he campaigns in these places? Or will it be so secret that even the voters won't know?) Of course, these are not secret strategies. It's just B.S.

Harry Frankfurt concludes that liars and truth-tellers are both acutely aware of facts and truths. They are just choosing to play on opposite sides of the same game to serve their own ends. The B.S. artist, however, has lost all connection with reality. He pays no attention to the truth. "By virtue of this," Frankfurt writes, "bullshit is a greater enemy of truth than lies are."

We see the consequences. As the crazy talk continues, standard rules of fact, truth and reality have disappeared in this campaign. Donald Trump has piled such vast quantities of his trademark product into the political arena that the stench is now overwhelming and unbearable."

.It is the most famous ducktail in America today, the hairdo of wayward youth of a bygone era, and it's astonishing to imagine it under the spotlight in Cleveland, being cheered by Republican dignitaries. The class hood, the bully and braggart, the guy revving his pink Chevy to make the pipes rumble, presiding over the student council. This is the C-minus guy who sat behind you in history and poked you with his pencil and smirked when you asked him to stop. That smirk is now on every front page in America. It is not what anybody — left, right or center — looks for in a president. There's no philosophy here, just an attitude. He is a little old for a ducktail. By the age of 70, most ducks have moved on, but not Donald. He is apparently still fond of the sidewalls and the duck's ass in back and he is proud as can be of his great feat, the first punk candidate to get this close to the White House. He says that the country is run by a bunch of clowns and that he is going to make things great again and beat up on the outsiders who are coming into our neighborhood. His followers don't necessarily believe that — what they love about him is what kids loved about Johnny Rotten and Sid Vicious, the fact that he horrifies the powers that be and when you are pro-duck you are giving the finger to Congress, the press, clergy, lawyers, teachers, cake-eaters, big muckety-mucks, VIPs, all those people who think they're better than you — you have the power to scare the pants off them, and that's what this candidate does better than anybody else.

After the worst mass shooting in American history on Sunday, 50 persons dead in Orlando, the bodies still being carted from the building, the faces of horror-stricken cops and EMTs on TV, the gentleman issued a statement on Twitter thanking his followers for their congratulations, that the tragedy showed that he had been "right" in calling for America to get "tough."

Anyone else would have expressed sorrow. The gentleman expressed what was in his heart, which was personal pride.

We had a dozen or so ducktails in my high school class and they were all about looks. The hooded eyes, the sculpted swoop of the hair, the curled lip. They emulated Elvis but only the look, not the talent. Their sole ambition was to make an impression, to slouch gracefully and exhale in an artful manner. In the natural course of things, they struggled after graduation, some tried law enforcement for the prestige of it, others became barflies. If they were drafted, the Army got them shaped up in a month or two. Eventually, they all calmed down, got hitched up to a mortgage, worried about their blood pressure, lost the chippiness, let their hair down. But if your dad was rich and if he was born before you were, then the ducktail could inherit enough wealth to be practically impervious to public opinion. This has happened in New York City. A man who could never be elected city comptroller is running for president.

The dreamers in the Republican Party imagine that success will steady him and he will accept wise counsel and come into the gravitational field of reality but it isn't happening. The Orlando tweets show it: The man does not have a heart. How, in a few weeks, should Mr. Ryan and Mr. McConnell teach him basic humanity? The bigot and braggart they see today is the same man that New Yorkers have been observing for 40 years. A man obsessed with marble walls and gold-plated doorknobs, who has the sensibility of a giant sea tortoise.

His response to the Orlando tragedy is one more clue that this election is different from any other. If Mitt Romney or John McCain had been elected president, you might be disappointed but you wouldn't fear for the fate of the Republic. This time, the Republican Party is nominating a man who resides in the dark depths. He is a thug and he doesn't bother to hide it. The only greatness he knows about is himself.

So the country is put to a historic test. If the man is not defeated, then we are not the country we imagine we are. All of the trillions spent on education was a waste. The churches should close up shop. The nation that elects this man president is not a civilized society. The gentleman is not airing out his fingernail polish, he is not showing off his wedding ring; he is making an obscene gesture. Ignore it at your peril."

Garrison Keillor,   host, A Prairie Home Companion.

"The cap does not look good on you. It's your (Trump's) last bid for the respect of Manhattan."

"What the fans don't know is that it's not much fun being a billionaire. You own a lot of big houses and you wander around in them, followed by a waiter, a bartender, a masseuse, three housekeepers, and a concierge, and they probably gossip about you behind your back. Just like nine-tenths of your campaign staff. You're losing and they know it and they're telling mean stories about you to everybody and his brother. When this is over, I will have nothing that I want."

Trump calls for ideological screenings tests of immigrants DonaldRunning for president is your last bid for the respect of Manhattan. If you were to win election, they couldn't ridicule you anymore. They could be horrified, but there is nothing ridiculous about being Leader of the Free World. You have B-52 bombers at your command. When you go places, a battalion of security guys comb the environs. You attract really really good speechwriters who give you Churchillian cadences and toss in quotes from Emerson and Aeschylus and Ecclesiastes.

Labor Day and it is not going well. You had a very bad month. You tossed out those wisecracks on Twitter and the Earth shook and your ratings among white suburban women with French cookware declined. The teleprompter is not your friend. You are in the old tradition of locker room ranting and big honkers in the steam room, sitting naked, talking man talk, griping about the goons and ginks and lousy workmanship and the uppity broads and the great lays and how you vanquished your enemies at the bank. Profanity is your natural language and vulgar words so as not to offend the Christers but the fans can still hear it and that's something they love about you. You are their guy. You are losing and so are they but they love you for it.

So what do you do this winter? Hang around one of your mansions? Hit some golf balls? Hire a ghostwriter to do a new autobiography?

What the fans don't know is that it's not much fun being a billionaire. You own a lot of big houses and you wander around in them, followed by a waiter, a bartender, a masseuse, three housekeepers, and a concierge, and they probably gossip about you behind your back. Just like nine-tenths of your campaign staff. You're losing and they know it and they're telling mean stories about you to everybody and his brother."

George Will national columnist and commentator, Conservative icon

Trump's shallowness runs deep

"In the 1870s, when Boss Tweed's Tammany Hall controlled New York City, and in the 1950s and 1960s, when Chicago's Democratic machine was especially rampant, there was a phenomenon that can be called immunity through profusion: Fresh scandals arrived with metronomic regularity, so there was no time to concentrate on any of them. The public, bewildered by blitzkriegs of bad behavior, was enervated.

What Winston Churchill said about an adversary — "He spoke without a note, and almost without a point" — can be said of Donald Trump, but this might be unfair to him. His speeches are, of course, syntactical train wrecks, but there might be method to his madness. He rarely finishes a sentence ("Believe me!" does not count), but perhaps he is not the scatterbrain he has so successfully contrived to appear. Maybe he actually is a sly rascal, cunningly in pursuit of immunity through profusion.

He seems to understand that if you produce a steady stream of sufficiently stupefying statements, there will be no time to dwell on any one of them, and the net effect on the public will be numbness and ennui. So, for example, while the nation has been considering his interesting decision to try to expand his appeal by attacking Gold Star parents, little attention has been paid to this: Vladimir Putin's occupation of Crimea has escaped Trump's notice.

It is, surely, somewhat noteworthy that someone aspiring to be this nation's commander in chief has somehow not noticed the fact that for two years now a sovereign European nation has been being dismembered. But a thoroughly jaded American public, bemused by the depths of Trump's shallowness, might have missed the following from Trump's appearance Sunday on ABC's "This Week."

When host George Stephanopoulos asked, "Why did you soften the GOP platform on Ukraine?" — removing the call for providing lethal weapons for Ukraine to defend itself — Trump said: "[Putin's] not going into Ukraine, okay? Just so you understand. He's not going to go into Ukraine, all right? You can mark it down and you can put it down, you can take it anywhere you want."

Donald Trump says the U.S. gets 'no respect' from Vladimir Putin

"Trump said the United States gets "no respect" from Russian President Vladimir Putin during a town hall event in Scranton, Pa., July 27. (The Washington Post)

"Okay, well, he's there in the Ukraine) in a certain way, but I'm not there yet. You have [President] Obama there. And frankly, that whole part of the world is a mess under Obama, with all the strength that you're talking about and all of the power of NATO and all of this, in the meantime, he's going where — he takes — takes Crimea, he's sort of — I mean . . . From what I've heard" the people of Crimea "would rather be with Russia than where they were."

Before the interview ended, Trump expressed his displeasure with the schedule for presidential debates, two of which are on nights with nationally televised NFL games. (There are such games three nights each autumn week.) "I got a letter from the NFL," Trump claimed, "saying this is ridiculous." The NFL says it sent no such letter. But before this Trump fib/figment of his imagination/hallucination can be properly savored, it will be washed away by a riptide of others. Immunity through profusion.

The nation, however, is not immune to the lasting damage that is being done to it by Trump's success in normalizing post-factual politics. It is being poisoned by the injection into its bloodstream of the cynicism required of those Republicans who persist in pretending that although Trump lies constantly and knows nothing, these blemishes do not disqualify him from being president.

As when, last week, Mike Pence reproved Obama for deploring, obviously with Trump in mind, "homegrown demagogues." Pence, doing his well-practiced imitation of a country vicar saddened by the discovery of sin in his parish, said with sorrowful solemnity: "I don't think name-calling has any place in public life." As in "Lyin' Ted" Cruz and "Little Marco" Rubio and "Crooked Hillary" Clinton?

Pence is just the most recent example of how the rubble of ruined reputations will become deeper before Nov. 8. It has been well said that "sooner or later, we all sit down to a banquet of consequences." The Republican Party's multicourse banquet has begun."

Glenn Beck   TV commentator, CEO The Blaze

"Trump is a "dangerous man. We all look at Adolf Hitler in 1940. We should look at Adolf Hitler in 1929.He was a kind of a funny kind of character that said the things people were thinking. Where Donald Trump takes it, I have absolutely no idea. But Donald Trump is a dangerous man with the things that he has been saying."

"Donald Trump is the face of the GOP. Well, that makes us crony capitalists. It makes us wafflers. It makes us pretty racist," Beck said. "It makes us big government guys. Just, you name it — it makes us that."

"There's Trump's high unfavorable ratings among Hispanics — 77% in a recent Gallup poll — as one demographic shift that will halt Trump and enable a victory by Democratic front-runner Hillary Clinton this November. Because Donald Trump is the GOP candidate, and I believe Hillary Clinton is going to win because of this, you will never elect another GOP person to high office every again."

"Because what's going to happen is you are now going to have Hillary Clinton legalize as many voters as you can, the GOP is going to be completely racist – whether it's true or not – because of Donald Trump. You will never have another Republican president ever again."

"I don't think that the left could have planned a better candidate to blow up the right than Donald Trump. I blame Donald Trump for being the worst candidate for either party the country has ever seen. If Donald Trump loses, it's going to be Donald Trump's fault. If Donald Trump wins, it will be Donald Trump's fault."

"But it's the media for allowing the Trump phenomenon to grow. Look at what the media did: Instead of taking him seriously from the very beginning and actually holding him responsible for some of the things that he said, a lot people just looked at him as a circus show — 'This will drive up numbers and he will burn himself out. It was a huge mistake. "By last August, we were taking him very seriously, [yet] still thought he would blow himself up, but I don't think so. It's not Donald Trump. It's us."

Harry Reid   U.S. Senate Minority Leader and Democratic Senator, Nevada

Donald Trump one of 'the most unbelievably immoral people I've ever heard."

"Trump is a human leech and a spoiled brat who has used his money only to make more money."

Hillary Clinton   Former U.S. Senator New York, First Lady and Secretary of State, Democratic nominee for President

The Alt-Right

Thank you, Reno! It's great to be back in Nevada...

My original plan for this visit was to focus on our agenda to help small businesses and entrepreneurs.

This week we proposed new steps to cut red tape and taxes, and make it easier for small businesses to get the credit they need to grow and hire.

Because I believe that in America, if you can dream it, you should be able to build it.

We'll be talking a lot more about our economic plans in the days and weeks ahead.

But today, I want to address something I hear from Americans all over our country.

Everywhere I go, people tell me how concerned they are by the divisive rhetoric coming from my opponent in this election.

It's like nothing we've heard before from a nominee for President of the United States.

From the start, Donald Trump has built his campaign on prejudice and paranoia.

He's taking hate groups mainstream and helping a radical fringe take over one of America's two major political parties.

His disregard for the values that make our country great is profoundly dangerous.

In just the past week, under the guise of "outreach" to African Americans, Trump has stood up in front of largely white audiences and described black communities in insulting and ignorant terms:

"Poverty. Rejection. Horrible education. No housing. No homes. No ownership. Crime at levels nobody has seen… Right now, you walk down the street, you get shot."

Those are his words.

Donald Trump misses so much.

He doesn't see the success of black leaders in every field…

The vibrancy of black-owned businesses…Or the strength of the black church…

He doesn't see the excellence of historically black colleges and universities or the pride of black parents watching their children thrive…And he certainly doesn't have any solutions to take on the reality of systemic racism and create more equity and opportunity in communities of color.

It takes a lot of nerve to ask people he's ignored and mistreated for decades, "What do you have to lose?" The answer is everything!

Trump's lack of knowledge or experience or solutions would be bad enough. But what he's doing here is more sinister.

Trump is reinforcing harmful stereotypes and offering a dog whistle to his most hateful supporters.

It's a disturbing preview of what kind of President he'd be.

This is what I want to make clear today:

A man with a long history of racial discrimination, who traffics in dark conspiracy theories drawn from the pages of supermarket tabloids and the far reaches of the internet, should never run our government or command our military.

If he doesn't respect all Americans, how can he serve all Americans?

Now, I know some people still want to give Trump the benefit of the   doubt.
They hope that he will eventually reinvent himself – that there's a kinder, gentler, more responsible Donald Trump waiting in the wings somewhere.

After all, it's hard to believe anyone – let alone a nominee for President of the United States – could really believe all the things he says.

But the hard truth is, there's no other Donald Trump. This is it.

Maya Angelou once said: "When someone shows you who they are, believe them the first time."

Well, throughout his career and this campaign, Donald Trump has shown us exactly who he is. We should believe him.

When Trump was getting his start in business, he was sued by the Justice Department for refusing to rent apartments to black and Latino tenants.

Their applications would be marked with a "C" – "C" for "colored" – and then rejected.

Three years later, the Justice Department took Trump back to court because he hadn't changed.

The pattern continued through the decades.

State regulators fined one of Trump's casinos for repeatedly removing black dealers from the floor. No wonder the turn-over rate for his minority employees was way above average.

And let's not forget Trump first gained political prominence leading the charge for the so-called "Birthers."

He promoted the racist lie that President Obama isn't really an American citizen – part of a sustained effort to delegitimize America's first black President.

In 2015, Trump launched his own campaign for President with another racist lie. He described Mexican immigrants as rapists and criminals.

And he accused the Mexican government of actively sending them across the border. None of that is true.

Oh, and by the way, Mexico's not paying for his wall either. If it ever gets built, you can be sure that American taxpayers will be stuck with the bill.

Since then, there's been a steady stream of bigotry.

We all remember when Trump said a distinguished federal judge born in Indiana couldn't be trusted to do his job because, quote, "He's a Mexican."

Think about that.

The man who today is the standard bearer of the Republican Party said a federal judge was incapable of doing his job solely because of his heritage.

Even the Republican Speaker of the House, Paul Ryan, described that as "the textbook definition of a racist comment."

To this day, he's never apologized to Judge Curiel.

But for Trump, that's just par for the course.

This is someone who retweets white supremacists online, like the user who goes by the name "white-genocide-TM." Trump took this fringe bigot with a few dozen followers and spread his message to 11 million people.

His campaign famously posted an anti-Semitic image – a Star of David imposed over a sea of dollar bills – that first appeared on a white supremacist website.

The Trump campaign also selected a prominent white nationalist leader as a delegate in California. They only dropped him under pressure.

When asked in a nationally televised interview whether he would disavow the support of David Duke, a former leader of the Ku Klux Klan, Trump wouldn't do it. Only later, again under mounting pressure, did he backtrack.

And when Trump was asked about anti-Semitic slurs and death threats coming from his supporters, he refused to condemn them.

Through it all, he has continued pushing discredited conspiracy theories with racist undertones.

Trump said thousands of American Muslims in New Jersey cheered the 9/11 attacks. They didn't.

He suggested that Ted Cruz's father was involved in the Kennedy assassination. Perhaps in Trump's mind, because he was a Cuban immigrant, he must have had something to do with it. Of course there's absolutely no evidence of that.

Just recently, Trump claimed President Obama founded ISIS. And then he repeated that nonsense over and over.

His latest paranoid fever dream is about my health. All I can say is, Donald, dream on.

This is what happens when you treat the National Enquirer like Gospel.

It's what happens when you listen to the radio host Alex Jones, who claims that 9/11 and the Oklahoma City bombings were inside jobs. He said the victims of the Sandy Hook massacre were child actors and no one was actually killed there.

Trump didn't challenge those lies. He went on Jones' show and said: "Your reputation is amazing. I will not let you down."

This man wants to be President of the United States.

I've stood by President Obama's side as he made the toughest decisions a Commander-in-Chief ever has to make.

In times of crisis, our country depends on steady leadership... clear thinking... and calm judgment... because one wrong move can mean the difference between life and death.

The last thing we need in the Situation Room is a loose cannon who can't tell the difference between fact and fiction, and who buys so easily into racially-tinged rumors.

Someone detached from reality should never be in charge of making decisions that are as real as they come.

It's another reason why Donald Trump is simply temperamentally unfit to be President of the United States.

Now, some people will say that his bluster and bigotry is just over-heated campaign rhetoric – an outrageous person saying outrageous things for attention.

But look at the policies Trump has proposed. They would put prejudice into practice.

And don't be distracted by his latest attempts to muddy the waters.

He may have some new people putting new words in his mouth... but we know where he stands.

He would form a deportation force to round up millions of immigrants and kick them out of the country.

He'd abolish the bedrock constitutional principle that says if you're born in the United States, you're an American citizen. He says that children born in America to undocumented parents are, quote, "anchor babies" and should be deported. Millions of them.

And he'd ban Muslims around the world – 1.5 billion men, women, and children –from entering our country just because of their religion.

Think about that for a minute. How would it actually work? People landing in U.S. airports would line up to get their passports stamped, just like they do now. But in Trump's America, when they step up to the counter, the immigration officer would ask every single person, "What is your religion?"

And then what?

What if someone says, "I'm a Christian," but the agent doesn't believe them. Do they have to prove it? How would they do that?

Ever since the Pilgrims landed on Plymouth Rock, America has distinguished itself as a haven for people fleeing religious persecution.

Under Donald Trump, America would distinguish itself as the only country in the world to impose a religious test at the border.

Come to think of it, there actually may be one place that does that. It's the so-called Islamic State. The territory ISIS controls. It would be a cruel irony if America followed its lead.

Don't worry, some will say, as President, Trump will be surrounded by smart advisors who will rein in his worst impulses.

So when a tweet gets under his skin and he wants to retaliate with a cruise missile, maybe cooler heads will be there to convince him not to.

Maybe.

But look at who he's put in charge of his campaign.

Trump likes to say he only hires the "best people." But he's had to fire so many campaign managers it's like an episode of the Apprentice.

The latest shake-up was designed to – quote – "Let Trump be Trump." To do that, he hired Stephen Bannon, the head of a right-wing website called Breitbart.com, as campaign CEO.

To give you a flavor of his work, here are a few headlines they've published:

"Birth Control Makes Women Unattractive and Crazy."

"Would You Rather Your Child Had Feminism or Cancer?"

"Gabby Giffords: The Gun Control Movement's Human Shield"

"Hoist It High And Proud: The Confederate Flag Proclaims A Glorious Heritage."

That one came shortly after the Charleston massacre, when Democrats and Republicans alike were doing everything they could to heal racial divides. Breitbart tried to enflame them further.

Just imagine – Donald Trump reading that and thinking: "this is what I need more of in my campaign."

Bannon has nasty things to say about pretty much everyone.

This spring, he railed against Paul Ryan for, quote "rubbing his social-justice Catholicism in my nose every second."

No wonder he's gone to work for Trump – the only Presidential candidate ever to get into a public feud with the Pope.

According to the Southern Poverty Law Center, which tracks hate groups, Breitbart embraces "ideas on the extremist fringe of the conservative right.

Racist ideas.

Race-baiting ideas.

Anti-Muslim and anti-Immigrant ideas — all key tenets making up an emerging racist ideology known as the 'Alt-Right.'"

Alt-Right is short for "Alternative Right."

The Wall Street Journal describes it as a loosely organized movement, mostly online, that "rejects mainstream conservatism, promotes nationalism and views immigration and multiculturalism as threats to white identity."

The de facto merger between Breitbart and the Trump Campaign represents a landmark achievement for the "Alt-Right." A fringe element has effectively taken over the Republican Party.

This is part of a broader story — the rising tide of hardline, right-wing nationalism around the world.

Just yesterday, one of Britain's most prominent right-wing leaders, Nigel Farage, who stoked anti-immigrant sentiments to win the referendum on leaving the European Union, campaigned with Donald Trump in Mississippi.

Farage has called for a ban on the children of legal immigrants from public schools and health services, has said women are quote "worth less" than men, and supports scrapping laws that prevent employers from discriminating based on race — that's who Trump wants by his side.

The godfather of this global brand of extreme nationalism is Russian President Vladimir Putin.

In fact, Farage has appeared regularly on Russian propaganda programs. Now he's standing on the same stage as the Republican nominee.

Trump himself heaps praise on Putin and embrace pro-Russian policies. He talks casually of abandoning our NATO allies, recognizing Russia's annexation of Crimea, and of giving the Kremlin a free hand in Eastern Europe more generally.

American presidents from Truman to Reagan have rejected the kind of approach Trump is taking on Russia. We should, too.

All of this adds up to something we've never seen before.

Of course there's always been a paranoid fringe in our politics, steeped in racial resentment. But it's never had the nominee of a major party stoking it, encouraging it, and giving it a national megaphone. Until now.

On David Duke's radio show the other day, the mood was jubilant.

"We appear to have taken over the Republican Party," one white supremacist said.

Duke laughed. There's still more work to do, he said.

No one should have any illusions about what's really going on here. The names may have changed... Racists now call themselves "racialists." White supremacists now call themselves "white nationalists." The paranoid fringe now calls itself "alt-right." But the hate burns just as bright.

And now Trump is trying to rebrand himself as well. Don't be fooled.

There's an old Mexican proverb that says "Tell me with whom you walk, and I will tell you who you are."

We know who Trump is. A few words on a teleprompter won't change that.

He says he wants to "make America great again," but his real message remains "Make America hate again."

This isn't just about one election. It's about who we are as a nation.
It's about the kind of example we want to set for our children and grandchildren.

Next time you watch Donald Trump rant on television, think about all the kids listening across our country. They hear a lot more than we think.

Parents and teachers are already worried about what they're calling the "Trump Effect."

Bullying and harassment are on the rise in our schools, especially targeting students of color, Muslims, and immigrants.

At a recent high school basketball game in Indiana, white students held up Trump signs and taunted Latino players on the opposing team with chants of "Build the wall!" and "Speak English."

After a similar incident in Iowa, one frustrated school principal said, "They see it in a presidential campaign and now it's OK for everyone to say this."

We wouldn't tolerate that kind of behavior in our own homes. How can we stand for it from a candidate for president?

This is a moment of reckoning for every Republican dismayed that the Party of Lincoln has become the Party of Trump. It's a moment of reckoning for all of us who love our country and believe that America is better than this.

Twenty years ago, when Bob Dole accepted the Republican nomination, he pointed to the exits and told any racists in the Party to get out.

The week after 9/11, George W. Bush went to a mosque and declared for everyone to hear that Muslims "love America just as much as I do."

In 2008, John McCain told his own supporters they were wrong about the man he was trying to defeat. Senator McCain made sure they knew – Barack Obama is an American citizen and "a decent person."

We need that kind of leadership again.

Every day, more Americans are standing up and saying "enough is enough" – including a lot of Republicans. I'm honored to have their support.

And I promise you this: with your help, I will be a President for Democrats, Republicans, and Independents. For those who vote for me and those who don't.

For all Americans.

Because I believe we are stronger together.

It's a vision for the future rooted in our values and reflected in a rising generation of young people who are the most open, diverse, and connected we've ever seen.

Just look at our fabulous Olympic team.

Like Ibtihaj Muhammad, an African-American Muslim from New Jersey who won the bronze medal in fencing with grace and skill. Would she even have a place in Donald Trump's America?

When I was growing up, Simone Manuel wouldn't have been allowed to swim in the same public pool as Katie Ledecky. Now they're winning Olympic medals as teammates.

So let's keep moving forward together.

Let's stand up against prejudice and paranoia.

Let's prove once again, that America is great because is America is good."

HUFFINGTON POST after every Trump story

"Editor's note: Donald Trump regularly incites political violence and is a serial liar, rampant xenophobe, racist, misogynist and birther who has repeatedly pledged to ban all Muslims — 1.6 billion members of an entire religion — from entering the U.S."

Jeb Bush   Former Republican Governor Florida, GOP Presidential candidate

"All the things that Donald Trump railed against, he seems to be morphing into." "What to believe about a guy who doesn't believe in things, His views will change based on the feedback he gets from a crowd or what he thinks he has to do. Life is too complex."

"For me I couldn't do that. I have to believe what I believe, and if it's popular, great, if it's not, I try to get better at presenting my views. Shifting my views because it's political to do it? That's what politicians do in this country, that's what Trump is trying to do right now. I find it abhorrent."

"Trump has capitalized on legitimate frustrations with American politics."

"They have given rise to the success of a candidate who continues to grotesquely manipulate the deeply felt anger of many Americans. He harkens back to an 1850s political party. Trump's abrasive, Know Nothing-like nativist rhetoric has blocked out sober discourse about how to tackle America's big challenges."

"I am imploring Republicans to protect their control of Congress and reintroduce civility, ideas and optimism back into politics. Let's find ways to campaign and govern inclusively. Let's find ways to ease the angst and fear of people, without cynically feeding it."

Jerry Falwell Jr.   President, Liberty University *(also see our religion page about Trump earlier in this book)*

"Donald Trump is a successful executive and entrepreneur, a wonderful father and a man who I believe can lead our country to greatness again."

"Trump reminds me so much of my father. In my opinion, Donald Trump lives a life of loving and helping others as Jesus taught in the great commandment."

"He cannot be bought, he's not a puppet on a string like many other candidates ... who have wealthy donors as their puppet masters."

Joe Biden   Vice-President of the United States

"Trump, even as a candidate, has elevated the dangers confronting American allies and military personnel overseas. I am compelled to reassure allies that the United States would honor its commitment to NATO, given Mr. Trump's comments saying he would reassess the arrangement if elected. Because they're worried.

"If my (late) son Beau was still serving in Iraq, I would advise him that the danger had increased a couple clicks because of Trump's remarks, which have included the suggestion that President Obama was the "founder" of the Islamic State. Trump is so reckless that if Beau had planned to enlist in a Trump administration, I would have thrown my body in front of him."

"This guy's shame has no limits."

"Trump had demonstrated a fondness for brutal leaders like Saddam Hussein — He would have loved Stalin."

"He is trying to tell us he cares about the middle class. Give me a break. That's a bunch of malarkey."

"Trump is a populist fraud. Trump is no populist. Ladies and gentlemen, to state the obvious — and I'm not trying to be a wise guy here, I really mean it — that's not Donald Trump's story."

"His cynicism is unbounded. His lack of empathy and compassion can be summed up in a phrase I suspect he's most proud of having made famous: 'You're fired.' I'm not joking; think about that. This guy doesn't have a clue about the middle class — not a clue."

"He has no clue about what makes America great. Actually, he has no clue."

"No major-party nominee in the history of this nation has ever known less or has been less prepared to deal with our national security."

John Kasich   Republican Governor of Ohio, GOP
Presidential Candidate

"You know, it's painful. It's painful. You know, people even get divorces, you know? I mean, sometimes, things come out that, look, I'm sorry that this has happened. We'll see where it ends up. I'm not making any final decision yet, but at this point, I just can't do it."

"You know politics. They (Ryan and McConnell) don't care what I think. I would say that I think Paul Ryan is definitely torn. I mean, he's also the leader of the House. There's this thing called Republican loyalty. I've been a Republican all my life, how do you think I feel about this?

I'm the Republican governor of Ohio. It's difficult. I know as governor of Ohio, with some people who pound on me, I said I'm not prepared to do it and he's going to have to change."

"Nobody would have thought that Saul would change and so might Trump, but, unless it changes, you know, I'm not going to be able to get there. So, I'll watch."

"Trump's proposed temporary immigration ban on Muslims is bad and one of many things that gives me pause. Well, the list is getting tall. It's getting bigger. Or you imply that maybe somehow the president is sympathetic to an act of terrorism. I mean, those are outrageous things. It's trending all the wrong way."

"I had to list five things that continue to prove that Donald Trump is clearly not prepared to be President of the United States, commander in chief, leader of the free world.

-- As a commander in chief and leader of the free world, you don't get do-overs. You need to be able to get it right the first time.

-- We know about his comments on abortion, which would put women in a very difficult position. And we know that he has since moved to correct those in one way or another.

-- He actually talked about the use of nuclear weapons both in the Middle East and Europe. You wonder about his hand or his thumb getting any closer to the critical button that presidents are in charge of.

-- He says we should basically abolish the Geneva Convention, which was created to make sure that we had fair treatment for anybody who could be captured in war and that somehow we ought to abolish the Geneva Conventions and engage in, I guess, more torture, which doesn't sit well with any of the people who have served our country so honorably, like (Arizona senator and former prisoner-of-war) John McCain.

-- He's called on NATO to basically be abolished although I can't figure out what his position is today. I happen to believe that NATO needs to be strengthened and turned from basically solely a military organization into an intelligence and policing organization that can work across borders."

John McCain   GOP U.S. Senator, Arizona and 2008
Republican Presidential candidate

"No, I don't think so (Trump owing him an apology for saying McCain wasn't a hero). But I think he may owe an apology to the families of those who have sacrificed in conflict and those who have undergone the prison experience in serving their country."

"Trump's remarks were "totally inappropriate. To denigrate their service is offensive to most of our veterans. The best thing to do is put it behind us and move forward."

(Re Trump on the Khans) "While our party has bestowed upon Trump the nomination, it is not accompanied by unfettered license to defame those who are the best among us."

Jon Stewart   former host/producer The Daily Show, Comedy Central on the Stephen Colbert show

"Either Lumpy (Sean Hannity) and his friends are lying about being bothered by thin-skinned authoritarian less-than-Christian readers of prompter being president, or they don't care, as long as it's their thin-skinned prompter authoritarian tyrant narcissist. You just want that person to give you your country back because you feel that you're this country's rightful owners. The only problem with that, this country isn't yours!

You don't own it! It never was! There is no real America! You don't own it! You don't own patriotism, you don't own Christianity, you sure as hell don't own respect for the brave and sacrifice of military, police and firefighters! Trust me!"

"The people demanding equal rights aren't the divisive ones, the people keeping them from getting those equal rights are."

"The Republicans appear to have a very clear plan for America. One, jail your political opponent. Two, inject Rudy Giuliani with a speedball-and-Red Bull enema, and, three, spend the rest of the time scaring the holy bejesus out of everybody."

"I want to focus on the "contortions many conservatives will have to do to embrace Donald J. Trump, a man who clearly embodies all the things that they have said for years that they have hated about Barack Obama." "A 'thin-skinned narcissist' with 'no government experience?'

"While Hannity thought Obama was "the most divisive president in American history," he has no problem with Trump calling Mexican immigrants "rapists.", "I'm not an expert on racial unity, but I do believe that some of our more vaunted historical leaders in that area did re-tweet white supremacists less than Trump."

"Hannity likes to call Trump a "blue-collar billionaire. That's not a thing."

"Either Lumpy (Hannity) and friends are lying about being bothered by thin-skinned, authoritarian, less-than-Christian readers-of-prompter being president, or they don't care, as long as it's *their* thin-skinned prompter authoritarian tyrant narcissist. You just want that person to give you your country back, because you feel that you are this country's rightful owner. The only problem with that: This country isn't yours. You don't own it. It never was. There is no 'real' America. You don't own it. You don't own patriotism. You don't own Christianity. You sure as hell don't own respect for the bravery and sacrifice for military, police, and firefighters. Trust me!"

"I saw a lot of people on the convention floor with their 'Blue Lives Matter' rhetoric who either remained silent or actively fought against the 9/11 first responders' bill reauthorization," he continued. "So I see you, and I see your bullshit."

"Those fighting to be included in the ideal of equality are not being divisive. Those fighting to keep those people out are. So, Lumpy, you and your friends have embraced Donald Trump. Clearly the 'c' next to your names don't stand for constitutional or conservative, but cravenly convenient—"

Justice Ruth Bader Ginsburg   Associate Justice, U.S.
Supreme Court

"Trump is a faker. He has no consistency about him. He says whatever comes into his head at the moment. He really has an ego. ... How has he gotten away with not turning over his tax returns? The press seems to be very gentle with him on that."

"I can't imagine what this place would be -- I can't imagine what the country would be -- with Donald Trump as our president. To think that there's a possibility that he could be president ... ".

"I think he has gotten so much free publicity. There is tougher media treatment of Democratic candidate Hillary Clinton. And every other presidential candidate has turned over tax returns."

Keith Olbermann   TV news and sports anchor, columnist,
podcaster GQ

(In his new *GQ* web show, The Closer), "Here are the most outrageous of Donald Trump's offenses in what is now his 15-month assault on American democracy."

"Every few generations we Americans are called upon to defend our country. To defend it not so much from foreign dictators or war or terrorism, but from those here who have no commitment to progress or Democracy or representative government, no commitment to anything except their own out-of-control minds and the bottomless pits of their egos.

We have always thrown them out and now our generation has its own. The most dangerous individual ever nominated by a major party for the highest office in this country."

Our society has thrown up these people before: Joseph McCarthy. George Wallace. Father Coughlin. Jefferson Davis. Aaron Burr. The Know-Nothings. The Blacklisters. The America-Firsters. And we have always thrown them out.

And now our generation has its own: the most dangerous individual ever nominated by a major party for the highest office in this country.

His base wants few details and fewer facts; they just want to burn it down and blame their failures on the collective other. And Donald John Trump is their demonic messiah in Oompa Loompa's clothing.

We must stop him.

It is not pleasant.

It is not fair that we have to do this.

But it is our turn.

The Emperor's New Clothes quality to the Trump campaign has survived these 15 months because, as we react to each outrage, our shock and revulsion have been refracted like light through a prism.

But these outrages are not separate events, not even a pattern.

They are, simply, Donald Trump.

Seen all at once, they—and he—are horrifying.

You must see them all at once.

The Republican party has actually nominated for president a man who attacked the Pope.

Who attacked <u>John McCain</u> for being captured by the North Vietnamese.

(Watch the video online for the rest of Olbermann's 176 reasons at GQ's *The Closer with Keith Olbermann*.)

Khizr Khan   Muslim-American lawyer, Gold Star family speaking at Democratic Convention

"First, our thoughts and prayers are with our veterans and those who serve today. Tonight, we are honored to stand here as the parents of Capt. Humayun Khan, and as patriotic American Muslims with undivided loyalty to our country.

Like many immigrants, we came to this country empty-handed. We believed in American democracy -- that with hard work and the goodness of this country, we could share in and contribute to its blessings.

We were blessed to raise our three sons in a nation where they were free to be themselves and follow their dreams. Our son, Humayun, had dreams of being a military lawyer. But he put those dreams aside the day he sacrificed his life to save his fellow soldiers.

Hillary Clinton was right when she called my son "the best of America." If it was up to Donald Trump, he never would have been in America. Donald Trump consistently smears the character of Muslims. He disrespects other minorities -- women, judges, even his own party leadership. He vows to build walls and ban us from this country.

Donald Trump, you are asking Americans to trust you with our future. Let me ask you: Have you even read the U.S. Constitution? I will gladly lend you my copy. In this document, look for the words "liberty" and "equal protection of law."

Have you ever been to Arlington Cemetery? Go look at the graves of the brave patriots who died defending America -- you will see all faiths, genders, and ethnicities.

You have sacrificed nothing and no one.

We can't solve our problems by building walls and sowing division. We are stronger together. And we will keep getting stronger when Hillary Clinton becomes our next president."

Lindsay Graham

Republican U.S. Senator N.C and GOP Presidential candidate

"The Republican Party has been "conned."

"I don't think he's a reliable Republican conservative.   I don't believe that Donald Trump has the temperament and judgment to be commander in chief. I think Donald Trump is going to places where very few people have gone and I'm not going with him."

"I'm glad we're having the convention in Cleveland, not Area 51."

"Voters should tell Trump he should "go to hell."

"He's a race-baiting, xenophobic, religious bigot," Graham told CNN late last year.

"Eating a taco is probably not going to fix the problems we have with Hispanics. I think embracing Donald Trump is embracing demographic death."

"I can understand when people want to support the nominee of the Republican Party. I would like to be able to do that, but I just can't. Maybe I'm the outlier here. Probably am."

Marco Rubio   Republican U.S. Senator Florida and GOP Presidential candidate

"You're the only person on this stage that's ever been fined for hiring people to work on your project illegally. I guess there's a statute of limitations on lies."

"You have a fake school and if you hadn't inherited $200 million, you know where Donald Trump would be right now? Selling watches in Manhattan."

"The position you've taken is an anti-Israel position. Palestinians aren't a real estate deal."

"What else is a part of your health care plan?"

"Now he's repeating himself. I saw you repeat yourself five times five seconds ago!"

"Everyone's dumb, he's going to make America great again, he's gonna win win win, he's winning in the polls."

"He called me Mr. Meltdown. He went backstage, he was having a meltdown and one of those little sweat mustaches and he wanted a full-length mirror maybe to make sure his pants weren't wet."

"He's not going to be the nominee. The Republican Party would be split apart if he's the nominee."

"He could become the nominee and we're not going to let that happen. There is no way we're going to allow the party of Reagan or the conservative movement to be taken over by a con man."

Trump has conned a significant number of Americans into believing something he's not .He's a con man. I think it's time to unmask him for what he is. He's trying to take over the conservative movement."

(Months later, Rubio endorsed Trump but continued calling him a 'con man.')

Mark Cuban

Billionaire Mavericks owner, media personality

"You look at him and say, 'What the hell are you talking about?' That's not good for America."

"It's rare that you see someone get stupider before your eyes, but he's really working at it," "You have to give him credit. It's a difficult thing to do, but he's accomplished it."

"Let's look at it this way: Name one good deal he's done When he talks about his great renegotiations, they're renegotiations, so tell me if you think this is a good deal: I lose four casinos, they go out of business, but I'm really good at renegotiating the debt of his companies that have already gone out of business."

If @realDonaldTrump were fractionally as rich as he says he is, he would write a$200mm check to propel his campaign. He doesn't have the cash."

Meg Whitman Republican fundraiser, Senate Candidate and CEO, Hewlett Packard Enterprises

"I will support Hillary Clinton for president and give a "substantial" contribution to her campaign in order to stop Donald J. Trump, who is a threat to American democracy.

"I will vote for Hillary, I will talk to my Republican friends about helping her, and I will donate to her campaign and try to raise money for her."

"It is time for Republicans to put country first before party."

"Trump is a dishonest demagogue who could lead the country on a very dangerous journey.

Democracies have seldom lasted longer than a few hundred years and those who say that it can't happen here are being naïve.

I absolutely stand by my comments comparing Mr. Trump to Hitler and Mussolini. Dictators often come to office through democratic means."

Michael Bloomberg, Billionaire media executive, former Mayor, New York City

"Let me thank all of you for welcoming an outsider here to deliver what will be an unconventional convention speech.

Now, I'm not here as a member of any party, or to endorse any party platform. I am here for one reason, and one reason only: to explain why I believe it is imperative that we elect Hillary Clinton as the next President of the United States. And to ask you to join with me in supporting her this November.

When the Founding Fathers arrived here in Philadelphia to forge a new nation, they didn't come as Democrats or Republicans, or to nominate a presidential candidate. They came as patriots who feared party politics. I know how they felt. I've been a Democrat, I've been a Republican, and I eventually became an Independent because I don't believe either party has a monopoly on good ideas or strong leadership.

When I enter the voting booth each time, I look at the candidate, not the party label. I have supported elected officials from both sides of the aisle. Probably not many people in this room can say that, but I know there are many watching at home who can. And now, they are carefully weighing their choices. I understand their dilemma.

I know what it's like to have neither party fully represent my views or values. Too many Republicans wrongly blame immigrants for our problems, and they stand in the way of action on climate change and gun violence. Meanwhile, many Democrats wrongly blame the private sector for our problems, and they stand in the way of action on education reform and deficit reduction.

There are times when I disagree with Hillary. But whatever our disagreements may be, I've come here to say: We must put them aside for the good of our country. And we must unite around the candidate who can defeat a dangerous demagogue.

I believe it's the duty of all American citizens to make our voices heard by voting in this election. And, if you're not yet registered to vote, go online. Do it now! It's just too important to sit this out.

Now, we've heard a lot of talk in this campaign about needing a leader who understands business. I couldn't agree more. I've built a business, and I didn't start it with a million-dollar check from my father. Because of my success in the private sector, I had the chance to run America's largest city for 12 years, governing in the wake of its greatest tragedy.

Today, as an Independent, an entrepreneur, and a former mayor, I believe we need a president who is a problem-solver, not a bomb-thrower; someone who can bring members of Congress together, to get big things done. And I know Hillary Clinton can do that, because I saw it firsthand!

I was elected mayor two months after 9/11, as a Republican — and I saw how Hillary Clinton worked with Republicans in Washington to ensure that New York got the help it needed to recover and rebuild. Throughout her time in the Senate, we didn't always agree — but she always listened. And that's the kind of approach we need in Washington today, and it just has to start in the White House!

Given my background, I've often encouraged business leaders to run for office because many of them share that same pragmatic approach to building consensus, but not all. Most of us who have created a business know that we're only as good as the way our employees, clients, and partners view us. Most of us don't pretend that we're smart enough to make every big decision by ourselves. And most of us who have our names on the door know that we are only as good as our word, but not Donald Trump.

Throughout his career, Trump has left behind a well-documented record of bankruptcies, thousands of lawsuits, angry shareholders and contractors who feel cheated, and disillusioned customers who feel ripped off. Trump says he wants to run the nation like he's run his business. God help us.

I'm a New Yorker, and New Yorkers know a con when we see one! Trump says he'll punish manufacturers that move to Mexico or China, but the clothes he sells are made overseas in low-wage factories. He says he wants to put Americans back to work, but he games the U.S. visa system so he can hire temporary foreign workers at low wages. He says he wants to deport 11 million undocumented people, but he seems to have no problem in hiring them. What'd I miss here?!

Truth be told, the richest thing about Donald Trump is his hypocrisy. He wants you to believe that we can solve our biggest problems by deporting Mexicans and shutting out Muslims. He wants you to believe that erecting trade barriers will bring back good jobs. He's wrong on both counts.

We can only solve our biggest problems if we come together and embrace the freedoms that our Founding Fathers established right here in Philadelphia, which permitted our ancestors to create the great American exceptionalism that all of us now enjoy. Donald Trump doesn't understand that; Hillary Clinton does. And we can only create good jobs if we make smarter investments in infrastructure, and do more to support small businesses — not stiff them. Donald Trump doesn't understand that; Hillary Clinton does.

I understand the appeal of a businessman president. But Trump's business plan is a disaster in the making. He would make it harder for small businesses to compete, do great damage to our economy, threaten the retirement savings of millions of Americans, lead to greater debt and more unemployment, erode our influence in the world, and make our communities less safe.

The bottom line is: Trump is a risky, reckless, and radical choice. And we can't afford to make that choice!

Now, I know Hillary Clinton is not flawless; no candidate is. But she is the right choice — and the responsible choice — in this election. No matter what you may think about her politics or her record, Hillary Clinton understands that this is not reality television; this is reality. She understands the job of president. It involves finding solutions, not pointing fingers, and offering hope, not stoking fear.

Over the course of our country's proud history, we have faced our share of grave challenges, but we have never retreated in fear. Never. Not here in Philadelphia in 1776, not at Gettysburg in 1863, not through two World Wars and a Great Depression, not at Selma or Stonewall, and not after 9/11 — and we must not start now.

America is the greatest country on Earth — and when people vote with their feet, they come here.

The presidency of the United States is the most powerful office in the world, and so I say to my fellow Independents: Your vote matters now. Your vote will determine the future of your job, your business, and our future together as a country.

To me, this election is not a choice between a Democrat and a Republican. It's a choice about who is better to lead our country right now: better for our economy, better for our security, better for our freedom, and better for our future.

There is no doubt in my mind that Hillary Clinton is the right choice this November. So tonight, as an Independent, I am asking you to join with me — not out of party loyalty, but out of love of country. And together, let's elect Hillary Clinton as the next President of the greatest country in the world, the United States of America. Thank you."

Michael Steele   former Chairman, Republic National Committee, Lt. Governor Maryland

"The Republican Party lacks authentic representation of black Americans and the issues they care about. The dearth of black delegates on the (GOP) convention floor as a real problem—one that goes way beyond who showed up in Cleveland this year. Donald Trump is strikingly unpopular among young black voters, with fewer than 2% saying they'd vote for him if the election were today, according to a national poll from the University of Chicago's Black Youth Project and the AP.

Trump's campaign has alienated communities of color. He's gone after Black Lives Matter protesters, called for bans against Muslims entering the US, and announced plans to build a wall between the US and Mexico. So the presence of speakers of color at the RNC begs the question: are these speakers being tokenized? We acknowledge the history, we love talking about the civil rights act, we love talking about Abraham Lincoln and emancipation. But we're not talking about today...I was thinking about Janet Jackson: 'What have you done for me lately?' That was 1865. That was 1872, that was 1964. What have you done in 2016?"

"I wanted to see a black person stand up on that stage and speak authentically about our community and relate our republican ideals to that...When you seem to harangue and chastise the community for its condition... you're losing folks, and you're using [black voices] to do it."

"(current GOP chair) Priebus has to forcefully condemn the celebrity plutocrat candidate or risk appearing disingenuous to voters. You've got to have that Sister Souljah moment with the party, where ~~you~~ have to be honest and call it what it is. People are sophisticated enough to know when you're just full of BS. Trump 'Resonates' With Voters in 'Uncomfortable' Ways."

"Everyone in the country reacted to this and you didn't, the party didn't, and those who want to be president didn't — until what? This week? That's a problem. It's a problem of authenticity. It is a problem of legitimacy when you're going to go speak to that community."

Michele Bachmann   former Republican congressman
Minnesota and head of Trump's evangelical advisors

"...the most high God lifts up who He will and takes down who He will. I actually supported Ted Cruz. I thought he was fabulous but I also see that at the end of the day God raised up, I believe, Donald Trump who was going to be the nominee in this election.

Maybe I'm wrong, I don't know but I do know that the Bible is true and that Daniel teaches the most high God, which is one of God's names, is the one who lifts up who He will and takes down who He will. I don't think God sits things out. He's a sovereign God. Donald Trump became our nominee."

Michele Obama at the Democratic Convention

First Lady of the United States

"It's hard to believe that it has been eight years since I first came to this convention to talk with you about why I thought my husband should be president.

Remember how I told you about his character and convictions, his decency and his grace, the traits that we've seen every day that he's served our country in the White House?

I also told you about our daughters, how they are the heart of our hearts, the center of our world. And during our time in the White House, we've had the joy of watching them grow from bubbly little girls into poised young women, a journey that started soon after we arrived in Washington.

When they set off for their first day at their new school, I will never forget that winter morning as I watched our girls, just 7 and 10 years old, pile into those black SUVs with all those big men with guns.

And I saw their little faces pressed up against the window, and the only thing I could think was, what have we done?

See, because at that moment I realized that our time in the White House would form the foundation for who they would become and how well we managed this experience could truly make or break them. That is what Barack and I think about every day as we try to guide and protect our girls through the challenges of this unusual life in the spotlight, how we urge them to ignore those who question their father's citizenship or faith.

How we insist that the hateful language they hear from public figures on TV does not represent the true spirit of this country.

How we explain that when someone is cruel or acts like a bully, you don't stoop to their level. No, our motto is, when they go low, we go high.

With every word we utter, with every action we take, we know our kids are watching us. We as parents are their most important role models. And let me tell you, Barack and I take that same approach to our jobs as president and first lady because we know that our words and actions matter, not just to our girls, but the children across this country, kids who tell us I saw you on TV, I wrote a report on you for school.

Kids like the little black boy who looked up at my husband, his eyes wide with hope and he wondered, is my hair like yours?

And make no mistake about it, this November when we go to the polls that is what we're deciding, not Democrat or Republican, not left or right. No, in this election and every election is about who will have the power to shape our children for the next four or eight years of their lives.

And I am here tonight because in this election there is only one person who I trust with that responsibility, only one person who I believe is truly qualified to be president of the United States, and that is our friend Hillary Clinton.

That's right. See, I trust Hillary to lead this country because I've seen her lifelong devotion to our nation's children, not just her own daughter, who she has raised to perfection...

...but every child who needs a champion, kids who take the long way to school to avoid the gangs, kids who wonder how they'll ever afford college, kids whose parents don't speak a word of English, but dream of a better life, kids who look to us to determine who and what they can be.

You see, Hillary has spent decades doing the relentless, thankless work to actually make a difference in their lives......advocating for kids with disabilities as a young lawyer, fighting for children's health care as first lady, and for quality child care in the Senate.

And when she didn't win the nomination eight years ago, she didn't get angry or disillusioned.

Hillary did not pack up and go home, because as a true public servant Hillary knows that this is so much bigger than her own desires and disappointments. So she proudly stepped up to serve our country once again as secretary of state, traveling the globe to keep our kids safe.

And look, there were plenty of moments when Hillary could have decided that this work was too hard, that the price of public service was too high, that she was tired of being picked apart for how she looks or how she talks or even how she laughs. But here's the thing. What I admire most about Hillary is that she never buckles under pressure. She never takes the easy way out. And Hillary Clinton has never quit on anything in her life.

And when I think about the kind of president that I want for my girls and all our children, that's what I want.

I want someone with the proven strength to persevere, someone who knows this job and takes it seriously, someone who understands that the issues a president faces are not black and white and cannot be boiled down to 140 characters.

Because when you have the nuclear codes at your fingertips and the military in your command, you can't make snap decisions. You can't have a thin skin or a tendency to lash out. You need to be steady and measured and well-informed.

I want a president with a record of public service, someone whose life's work shows our children that we don't chase form and fortune for ourselves, we fight to give everyone a chance to succeed.

And we give back even when we're struggling ourselves because we know that there is always someone worse off. And there but for the grace of God go I.

I want a president who will teach our children that everyone in this country matters, a president who truly believes in the vision that our Founders put forth all those years ago that we are all created equal, each a beloved part of the great American story.

And when crisis hits, we don't turn against each other. No, we listen to each other, we lean on each other, because we are always stronger together.

And I am here tonight because I know that that is the kind of president that Hillary Clinton will be. And that's why in this election I'm with her.

You see, Hillary understands that the president is about one thing and one thing only, it's about leaving something better for our kids. That's how we've always moved this country forward, by all of us coming together on behalf of our children, folks who volunteer to coach that team, to teach that Sunday school class, because they know it takes a village.

Heroes of every color and creed who wear the uniform and risk their lives to keep passing down those blessings of liberty, police officers and the protesters in Dallas who all desperately want to keep our children safe.

People who lined up in Orlando to donate blood because it could have been their son, their daughter in that club.

Leaders like Tim Kaine...

...who show our kids what decency and devotion look like.

Leaders like Hillary Clinton who has the guts and the grace to keep coming back and putting those cracks in that highest and hardest glass ceiling until she finally breaks through, lifting all of us along with her.

That is the story of this country, the story that has brought me to this stage tonight, the story of generations of people who felt the lash of bondage, the shame of servitude, the sting of segregation, but who kept on striving and hoping and doing what needed to be done so that today I wake up every morning in a house that was built by slaves.

And I watch my daughters, two beautiful, intelligent, black young women playing with their dogs on the White House lawn.

And because of Hillary Clinton, my daughters and all our sons and daughters now take for granted that a woman can be president of the United States.

So, look, so don't let anyone ever tell you that this country isn't great, that somehow we need to make it great again. Because this right now is the greatest country on earth!

And as my daughters prepare to set out into the world, I want a leader who is worthy of that truth, a leader who is worthy of my girls' promise and all our kids' promise, a leader who will be guided every day by the love and hope and impossibly big dreams that we all have for our children.

So in this election, we cannot sit back and hope that everything works out for the best. We cannot afford to be tired or frustrated or cynical. No, hear me. Between now and November, we need to do what we did eight years ago and four years ago.

We need to knock on every door, we need to get out every vote, we need to pour every last ounce of our passion and our strength and our love for this country into electing Hillary Clinton as president of the United States of America! So let's get to work."

Mike Lee   Republican U.S. Senator, Utah

'Republicans should call the racism of people such as white supremacist David Duke "deplorable."

"I cannot endorse Trump because of his vague policy positions and his call for a temporary ban on Muslims."

Mitt Romney

Former Governor, Mass., 2012 GOP Presidential candidate

"Warren Buffett was 100% right when he said last week that the babies being born in America today are the luckiest crop in history.

That doesn't mean we don't have real problems and serious challenges. At home, poverty persists and wages are stagnant. The horrific massacres of Paris and San Bernardino, the nuclear ambitions of the Iranian mullahs, the aggressions of Putin, the growing assertiveness of China and the nuclear tests of North Korea confirm that we live in troubled and dangerous times.

But if we make the right choices, America's future will be even better than our past and better than our present.

On the other hand, if we make improvident choices, the bright horizon I foresee will never materialize. Let me put it plainly, if we Republicans choose Donald Trump as our nominee, the prospects for a safe and prosperous future are greatly diminished.

Let me explain why.

First, the economy: If Donald Trump's plans were ever implemented, the country would sink into a prolonged recession.

A few examples: His proposed 35% tariff-like penalties would instigate a trade war that would raise prices for consumers, kill export jobs, and lead entrepreneurs and businesses to flee America. His tax plan, in combination with his refusal to reform entitlements and to honestly address spending would balloon the deficit and the national debt. So even as Donald Trump has offered very few specific economic plans, what little he has said is enough to know that he would be very bad for American workers and for American families.

But wait, you say, isn't he a huge business success that knows what he's talking about? No he isn't. His bankruptcies have crushed small businesses and the men and women who worked for them. He inherited his business, he didn't create it. And what ever happened to Trump Airlines? How about Trump University? And then there's Trump Magazine and Trump Vodka and Trump Steaks, and Trump Mortgage? A business genius he is not.

Now not every policy Donald Trump has floated is bad. He wants to repeal and replace Obamacare. He wants to bring jobs home from China and Japan.

But his prescriptions to do these things are flimsy at best. At the last debate, all he could remember about his healthcare plan was to remove insurance boundaries between states. Successfully bringing jobs home requires serious policy and reforms that make America the place businesses want to plant and grow. You can't punish business into doing the things you want.

Frankly, the only serious policy proposals that deal with the broad range of national challenges we confront, come today from Ted Cruz, Marco Rubio, and John Kasich. One of these men should be our nominee.

I know that some people want the race to be over. They look at history and say a trend like Mr. Trump's isn't going to be stopped.

Perhaps. But the rules of political history have pretty much all been shredded during this campaign. If the other candidates can find common ground, I believe we can nominate a person who can win the general election and who will represent the values and policies of conservatism. Given the current delegate selection process, this means that I would vote for Marco Rubio in Florida, for John Kasich in Ohio, and for Ted Cruz or whichever one of the other two contenders has the best chance of beating Mr. Trump in a given state.

Let me turn to national security and the safety of our homes and loved ones. Trump's bombast is already alarming our allies and fueling the enmity of our enemies. Insulting all Muslims will keep many of them from fully engaging with us in the urgent fight against ISIS. And for what purpose? Muslim terrorists would only have to lie about their religion to enter the country.

What he said on "60 Minutes" about Syria and ISIS has to go down as the most ridiculous and dangerous idea of the campaign season: Let ISIS take out Assad, he said, and then we can pick up the remnants. Think about that: Let the most dangerous terror organization the world has ever known take over a country? This is recklessness in the extreme.

Donald Trump tells us that he is very, very smart. I'm afraid that when it comes to foreign policy he is very, very not smart.

I am far from the first to conclude that Donald Trump lacks the temperament of be president. After all, this is an individual who mocked a disabled reporter, who attributed a reporter's questions to her menstrual cycle, who mocked a brilliant rival who happened to be a woman due to her appearance, who bragged about his marital affairs, and who laces his public speeches with vulgarity.

Donald Trump says he admires Vladimir Putin, while has called George W. Bush a liar. That is a twisted example of evil trumping good.

There is dark irony in his boasts of his sexual exploits during the Vietnam War while John McCain, whom he has mocked, was imprisoned and tortured.

Dishonesty is Trump's hallmark: He claimed that he had spoken clearly and boldly against going into Iraq. Wrong, he spoke in favor of invading Iraq. He said he saw thousands of Muslims in New Jersey celebrating 9/11. Wrong, he saw no such thing. He imagined it. His is not the temperament of a stable, thoughtful leader. His imagination must not be married to real power.

The President of the United States has long been the leader of the free world. The president and yes the nominees of the country's great parties help define America to billions of people. All of them bear the responsibility of being an example for our children and grandchildren.

Think of Donald Trump's personal qualities, the bullying, the greed, the showing off, the misogyny, the absurd third grade theatrics. We have long referred to him as "The Donald." He is the only person in America to whom we have added an article before his name. It wasn't because he had attributes we admired.

Now imagine your children and your grandchildren acting the way he does. Will you welcome that? Haven't we seen before what happens when people in prominent positions fail the basic responsibility of honorable conduct? We have, and it always injures our families and our country.

Watch how he responds to my speech today. Will he talk about our policy differences or will he attack me with every imaginable low road insult? This may tell you what you need to know about his temperament, his stability, and his suitability to be president.

Trump relishes any poll that reflects what he thinks of himself. But polls are also saying that he will lose to Hillary Clinton.

On Hillary Clinton's watch at the State Department, America's interests were diminished in every corner of the world. She compromised our national secrets, dissembled to the families of the slain, and jettisoned her most profound beliefs to gain presidential power.

For the last three decades, the Clintons have lived at the intersection of money and politics, trading their political influence to enrich their personal finances. They embody the term "crony capitalism." It disgusts the American people and causes them to lose faith in our political process.

A person so untrustworthy and dishonest as Hillary Clinton must not become president. But a Trump nomination enables her victory. The audio and video of the infamous Tapper-Trump exchange on the Ku Klux Klan will play a hundred thousand times on cable and who knows how many million times on social media.

There are a number of people who claim that Mr. Trump is a con man, a fake. There is indeed evidence of that. Mr. Trump has changed his positions not just over the years, but over the course of the campaign, and on the Ku Klux Klan, daily for three days in a row.

We will only really know if he is the real deal or a phony if he releases his tax returns and the tape of his interview with the New York Times. I predict that there are more bombshells in his tax returns.

I predict that he doesn't give much if anything to the disabled and to our veterans. I predict that he told the New York Times that his immigration talk is just that: talk. And I predict that despite his promise to do so, first made over a year ago, he will never ever release his tax returns. Never. Not the returns under audit, not even the returns that are no longer being audited. He has too much to hide. Nor will he authorize the Times to release the tapes.

If I'm right, you will have all the proof you need to know that Donald Trump is a phony.

Attacking me as he surely will won't prove him any less of a phony. It's entirely in his hands to prove me wrong. All he has to do is to release his back taxes like he promised he would, and let us hear what he said behind closed doors to the New York Times.

Ronald Reagan used to quote a Scottish philosopher who predicted that democracies and civilizations couldn't last more than about 200 years. John Adams wrote this: "Remember, democracy never lasts long. It soon wastes, exhausts, and murders itself. There never was a democracy yet that did not commit suicide." I believe that America has proven these dire predictions wrong for two reasons.

First, we have been blessed with great presidents, with giants among us. Men of character, integrity and selflessness have led our nation from its very beginning. None were perfect: each surely made mistakes. But in every case, they acted out of the desire to do what was right for America and for freedom.

The second reason is because we are blessed with a great people, people who at every critical moment of choosing have put the interests of the country above their own.

These two things are related: our presidents time and again have called on us to rise to the occasion. John F. Kennedy asked us to consider what we could do for our country. Lincoln drew upon the better angels of our nature to save the union.

I understand the anger Americans feel today. In the past, our presidents have channeled that anger, and forged it into resolve, into endurance and high purpose, and into the will to defeat the enemies of freedom. Our anger was transformed into energy directed for good.

Mr. Trump is directing our anger for less than noble purposes. He creates scapegoats of Muslims and Mexican immigrants, he calls for the use of torture and for killing the innocent children and family members of terrorists. He cheers assaults on protesters. He applauds the prospect of twisting the Constitution to limit first amendment freedom of the press. This is the very brand of anger that has led other nations into the abyss.

Here's what I know. Donald Trump is a phony, a fraud. His promises are as worthless as a degree from Trump University. He's playing the American public for suckers: He gets a free ride to the White House and all we get is a lousy hat.

His domestic policies would lead to recession. His foreign policies would make America and the world less safe. He has neither the temperament nor the judgment to be president. And his personal qualities would mean that America would cease to be a shining city on a hill. "

"I don't want to see trickle-down racism," Romney said in an interview here in a suite. "I don't want to see a president of the United States saying things which change the character of the generations of Americans that are following. Presidents have an impact on the nature of our nation, and trickle-down racism, trickle-down bigotry, trickle-down misogyny, all these things are extraordinarily dangerous to the heart and character of America."

Newt Gingrich

Former Speaker, U.S. House of Representatives

"Donald Trump's behavior over the past week has been very self-destructive to his campaign."

"Trump is still behaving like as though it was the primaries and there were 17 candidates. He has not made the transition to being the potential president of the United States, which is a much tougher league. People are going to watch you every single day. They're going to take everything they can out of context, and he is not yet performing at the level that you need to."

"And then he figured out what he was doing, and he changed. Trump, Trump is in that kind of a slump."

"It's like watching a team go out on the field, throw an interception on the first play and go back off the field again. Trump has thrown a series of interceptions in the last week that really do not bode well for his campaign."

NRA   Primary anti-gun control group, controls many members of Congress

"The stakes in this year's presidential election could not be higher for gun owners.

"If Hillary Clinton gets the opportunity to replace Antonin Scalia with an anti-gun Supreme Court justice, we will lose the individual right to keep a gun in the home for self-defense.

Mrs. Clinton has said that the Supreme Court got it wrong on the Second Amendment. So the choice for gun owners in this election is clear. And that choice is Donald Trump. That's why the National Rifle Association of America is announcing our endorsement of Donald J. Trump for President of the United States."

Paul Ryan

Republican Speaker, U.S. House of Representatives

"My endorsement of Donald Trump does not give the Republican nominee blank checks."

"As you know, when I first talked about this, when I did support Donald, I said at that time, and ever since then, if I see a situation where our conservative principles are being distorted, I'm going to stand up for those conservative principles. If I see and hear things that I think are wrong, I'm not going to sit by and say nothing. Because I think I have a duty as a Republican leader to defend Republican principles and our party's brand if I think they're being distorted."

"I've always said, of course, there are — I'm not going to get into the speculation or hypothetical. None of these things are blank checks. That goes with any situation in any kind of race."

"They've got to clean this thing up. Anti-semitic messages have no place in (his) campaign."

"A religious test for entering our country is not reflective of America's fundamental values."

"I do not think a Muslim ban is in our country's interest."

"Russia is a global menace led by a devious thug. Putin has no place in our elections."

"I do not feel that one's heritage (Judge Curiel) makes them incapable of being impartial.

Trump's criticism of the judge was the textbook definition of a racist comment. I disavow these comments — I regret those comments that he made. I think that should be absolutely disavowed. It's absolutely unacceptable."

Pope Francis

"A person who thinks only about building walls, wherever they may be, and not building bridges, is not Christian."

President Barack Obama

"Trump is a counterfeit candidate unrepresentative of working-class values. I keep on reading this analysis that Trump's got support from working folks—*really*? This is the guy you want to be championing working people? This guy who spent 70 years on this Earth showing no concern for working people? This guy's suddenly going to be your champion?"

"He spent most of his life trying to stay as far away from working people as he could."

"The media's coverage of the GOP nominee has been frivolous You don't grade the presidency on a curve. This is serious business, and when we see folks talking about transparency, you've got one candidate in this race who's released decades worth of her tax returns. The other candidate is the first in decades who refuses to release any at all."

"Trump going on Russian state television -- an interview with Larry King for Russia Today's American network -- to extol his leadership by citing Putin's high poll numbers? Saddam Hussein had a 90% poll rating!

While we have to do business with Russia, I don't go around saying Putin's my role model. Can you imagine Ronald Reagan idolizing somebody like that?"

"This is the party that extols freedom and America and the flag and Ronald Reagan, and whose main criticism of me lately has been my tyrannical abuse of power. And [they nominated] the guy who actively promotes and admires a guy who jails dissidents and controls all state media, all media in his country. And hence has an 82% approval rating."

"Can you imagine what my approval rating would be if all those folks lined up in the back (the media) worked for me, if I was writing their stories? Wow! I would be doing really well!"

"Trump is a selfish, dictator-loving moron who is a threat to the very fabric of American democracy. You don't grade the presidency on a curve. This is serious business."

"I am really into electing Hillary Clinton. Trump is not a typical Republican. So it's OK, as a Republican, to support Clinton. The Trump campaign is a dark, pessimistic vision, one which he said has deviated substantially from the Party of Lincoln."

"Do you mind if I just vent for a second? When we see folks talking about transparency—you want to debate transparency? You've got one candidate in this race who has released decades of her tax returns, the other candidate is the first in decades who refuses to release any at all. One candidate's family foundation has saved countless lives around the world, the other candidate's foundation took money other people gave to his charity and then bought a six-foot-tall painting of himself. He had the taste not to go for the 10-foot version. Democracy is not a spectator sport. Don't boo (Trump). Vote."

President Bill Clinton   former President of the United States

"Most of Hillary's strongest supporters have either worked for her or done business with Trump."

"Despite the polarization that exists in America, the country is in a better position than it has ever been. America has come so far. We're less racist, sexist, homophobic and anti specific religions than we used to be. We have one remaining   bigotry: We don't want to be around anyone who disagrees with us."

"Trump attacked my foundation. He uses his foundation's money to pay off Florida's attorney general."

"The U.S. should quit making a political issue out of our diversity and unlock America's economic potential by passing a sensible immigration reform bill. We don't need to build a wall across the border. We need to build a bridge to tomorrow and let every law-abiding person walk across it."

"Trump's a political snake oil salesman unlikely to make good on his promises. Saying you're going to make America great again is like me saying I'd like to be 20 again. Actually, I would. But I wouldn't vote for anybody who promised to make me 20 again."

'Trump is feeding the anger of people fed up with the status quo. Not enough has been done in parts of the United States, such as coal country, to help struggling workers combatting a shifting economy. I understand why people are angry, but they should choose answers over anger."

"We don't need to feed the road rage. We need to slow the car down and think."

"Turning the economy back 50 years would hurt Hispanics and African Americans, because life wasn't so great for them in that era."

"Trump says I will give you the economy you had 50 years ago and everything will be hunky dory. You just got to get me elected and let me beat people up for you."

"Hillary will fight for everyone, even those who choose to support Trump."

"If you want to vote to make America great like it was 50 years ago, have at it. But if she wins, she's coming back for you."

"All I can tell you is the worst thing we can do is try to break up 11 million people and send them home."

"If you think it's OK to make unlawful contributions out of your personal family account and then attack my foundation ... then Trump's the guy."

"Go out there and win this election for yourself, your children and your grandchildren."

President George W. Bush   former President of the United States

(Without naming Trump) "I am against these stated polices of isolationism, nativism and protectionism."

"Islamic women should be welcomed in the U.S. to experience the benefits of a free society -- so they can lead the charge for equality in the Middle East."

(President Bush is not endorsing a Presidential candidate, his father is voting for Hillary.)

President Jimmy Carter

Former Democratic President of the U.S., head of the Carter Foundation

" Trump seems to reject the most important moral and ethical principles on which our nation was founded."

"There is a clear choice between Hillary Clinton and Trump for president. At a moment when it has become more important than ever to lift people up to have a hope and a roadmap a brighter future, instead, we see a Republican presidential candidate. We can and must do better. And fortunately the Democratic nominee we'll soon be choosing offers a stark contrast in both substance and style, and also competence and experience to what the Republicans have chosen."

"Mr. Trump's Republican presidential campaign is fueled by lingering U.S. racism. He has tapped a waiting reservoir there of inherent racism to succeed.

"When you single out any particular group of people for secondary citizenship status, that's a violation of basic human rights."

"Why is Trump's support among evangelical Christians so strong? The use of the word 'evangelical' is a misnomer. I consider myself an evangelical as well. And obviously, what most of the news reporters thought were evangelicals [over the years] are conservative Republicans."

"Trump has tapped a waiting reservoir there of inherent racism."

"Trump has violated human rights with some of his incendiary comments on the campaign trail including his proposal to bar Muslims from the U.S. and his claim that Mexico is sending criminals across the U.S. border. When you single out any particular group of people for secondary citizenship status, that's a violation of basic human rights."

"I don't feel good, except for one thing: I think the country has been reawakened the last two or three years to the fact that we haven't resolved the race issue adequately."

"I think there's a heavy reaction among some of the racially conscious Republicans against an African-American being president."

"The United States is experiencing a resurgence of racism and I'm calling on faith leaders to foster change in their churches and communities."

"Some white Americans stay quiet when they see discrimination or segregation, fearful of losing a "privileged" position in society. That amounts to acceptance of discrimination and animosity and hatred and division."

"I feel some degree of embarrassment about the ongoing presidential campaign between Hillary Clinton and Donald Trump. Americans' multiple races, ethnicities and religions form a beautiful mosaic.

The country has been resilient following other periods of deep division, including the Civil War. I think there will be a positive reaction after this election. I pray it will come out a certain way, but I think there will be a lot of lessons learned. And I think the average person in America now will be looking at how to do better things, how to have a superb American policy on peace and human rights and other aspects of life. I think we'll raise our standards as a public and I believe our next president will accommodate that inclination.

" 22 members of my family are registered to vote and we'll all vote the same way."

"They have inherited some genes or something that causes them to look with favor on the New Baptist Covenant and on one of the parties."

Rick Perry

Former GOP Governor Texas and Presidential candidate

"He is not a perfect man. But what I do believe is that he loves this country and he will surround himself with capable, experienced people and he will listen to them. If there was ever a time for the country to have conservative leadership in the House and Senate, it will be in 2017 because no matter who wins the presidency -- Clinton or Trump -- we will need some rational people up there putting brakes on some of these very bad ideas."

Robert Gates   member of 8 administrations, Secretary of Defense under Republican and Democratic Presidents

"When it comes to credibility problems, Donald Trump is in a league of his own. Trump is too great a risk for America."

"The world we confront is too perilous and too complex to have as president a man who believes he, and he alone, has all the answers and has no need to listen to anyone. A thin-skinned, temperamental, shoot-from-the-hip and lip, uninformed commander in chief is too great a risk for America."

"Trump is too willfully ignorant about the rest of the world to be commander in chief."

"At least on national security, I believe Mr. Trump is beyond repair. He is stubbornly uninformed about the world and how to lead our country and government, and temperamentally unsuited to lead our men and women in uniform. He is unqualified and unfit to be commander in chief."

Rudy Guiliani

Trump surrogate and former Mayor, New York City

(Guiliani in 2011 after the attack) at "Like the victims of the World Trade Center attack, we're of every race, we're of every religion, we're of every ethnicity, and our diversity has been our greatest source of strength," he said. "It's the thing that renews us and revives us in every generation — our openness to new people from all over the world."

(2016) "Trump had abandoned his insistence that President Obama was born outside the United States, even though Mr. Trump has never done so publicly."

"Donald Trump's assertion that during the Iraq War the United States should have seized the country's oil is correct. Anything's legal in war." *(despite the fact that Geneva Convention laws governing war prohibit just that.)* Of course it's legal. It's a war. Until the war is over, anything's legal. If we're going to have lost that many people in Iraq, we should have something to say about how that oil is distributed."

Susan Collins   Republican U.S. Senator, Maine

"I will not be voting for Donald Trump for president. This is not a decision I make lightly, for I am a lifelong Republican. But Donald Trump does not reflect historical Republican values nor the inclusive approach to governing that is critical to healing the divisions in our country.

When the primary season started, it soon became apparent that, much like Sen. Bernie Sanders (I-Vt.), Mr. Trump was connecting with many Americans who felt that their voices were not being heard in Washington and who were tired of political correctness. But rejecting the conventions of political correctness is different from showing complete disregard for common decency. Mr. Trump did not stop with shedding the stilted campaign dialogue that often frustrates voters. Instead, he opted for a constant stream of denigrating comments, including demeaning Sen. John McCain's (R-Ariz.) heroic military service and repeatedly insulting Fox News host Megyn Kelly.

With the passage of time, I have become increasingly dismayed by his constant stream of cruel comments and his inability to admit error or apologize. But it was his attacks directed at people who could not respond on an equal footing — either because they do not share his power or stature or because professional responsibility precluded them from engaging at such a level — that revealed Mr. Trump as unworthy of being our president."

Stephen Colbert   host,   Late Show with
Stephen Colbert, CBS

"Is the bad man gone? Jimmy, do I have time to change my pants? Because I am a code brown right now."

"Trump went from Mr. Cool in Mexico to thermonuclear in like an hour."

"Hey, did you all see the big Trump speech last night? I haven't seen that many angry white people since they cancelled a Cold Play concert. In the last 24 hours of Donald Trump has been an emotional roller coaster. You must be this crazy to ride. First, he was in Mexico, looking for an ally."

Okay, that's not softening. Trump has always called for a wall between the hemispheres -- and he will make the oceans pay for it. But as soon as he got back on U.S. soil, he was back to Trump classic. A quick warning-- if you have any small children in the room, please place them in front of you as a human shield.

People, we are calling this a speech, but that implies he spoke. He really screamed, so I'm going to call it a screech. How does he change emotions so quickly? He went from Mr. Cool in Mexico to thermonuclear explosion in like, an hour.

I'm starting to think there might be more than one Donald Trump. My theory: Trump is actually three oompah-loompahs standing in a human pyramid inside his suit. One here, one there and they get to take turns on who gets to be the head. One of them is reasonable and two of them really don't like immigrants. It would explain all his policy reversals, and his skin tone.

Now, Trump was just getting started yelling about foreigners.

Yes, (immigrants are) a Trojan horse. Or Trojan pinata. They're a crafty people, you know. They'll make it. It will be festive. They'll wheel it to the border and we'll hit it, but instead of candy falling out, it will be illegal immigrants! Who will steal our jobs and our candy! The point is, we can't accept them because they may not accept us. Yes, America has the right to choose immigrants who love us. and Donald Trump knows they're out there. He's already married two of them.

You know that's true! So to calm our fears and give us some new ones, Trump laid out his ten-point immigration plan, and he started with the hits. Yes, Mexico doesn't know it yet, but they're going to pay for the wall. he'll just sneak it onto the dinner check. "Let's see, we had the potato skins, cheeseburger, two diet cokes, a $50 billion border wall. was that for the table, right?" We all ordered that. After that, Trump made a solemn scream to protect America from these monsters.

Yes, they walk around, they crime all over the place. they crime over here, they crime over there, here a crime, there a crime, here a crime, there a crime, everywhere a crime-crime. There is no other way to say it! But Trump is ready to make us safe on day one.

Gone! Gone! Now a lot of people have said it's impossible to deport 11 million illegal immigrants, so trump's only going to do 2 million in the first hour. *It helps to break down a big task into manageable chunks.* The point is, he's going to do it, because Trump is sick and tired of America getting pushed around by those huddled masses yearning to breathe free.

Yeah, you know how poor, defenseless bullies are always getting beat up. remember how bad you felt when that mean karate kid beat the crap out of Karate Kid? That movie ended horribly! This time, the bullies win. "Trump 2016: Sweep the Leg." No mercy! So this is a bad situation, but, don't worry, Trump has a loud solution."

"Yes, extreme extreme, extreme, extreme vetting. so extreme! I'm talking underwater paperwork, citizenship test on a skateboard, and no one gets in unless they can complete the "American ninja warriors" course. As always, our extreme vetting will be sponsored by Mountain Dew Baja Blast."

"How much does "NostraDonald" actually know about the future?"

Stephen King   best-selling author

"Are you disappointed in your country that Donald Trump has proven to be so popular?

I am very disappointed in the country. I think that he's sort of the last stand of a sort of American male who feels like women have gotten out of their place and they're letting in all these people that have the wrong skin colors. He speaks to those people. Trump is extremely popular because people would like to have a world where you just didn't question that the white American was at the top of the pecking order.

Clinton has long grappled with whether and how much to highlight her gender, but she embraced it .

I saw a poll the other day that said, Hillary Clinton is only leading him by three points. If that's true, you have to go back to that time when he rode that escalator down and announced the presidency, and everyone thought that it was a joke. The press thought it was a joke. Rolling Stone thought he was a joke. Jon Stewart said, "Oh please, let him continue to run; he's the best joke material that we've had." Well, nobody is laughing anymore."

"Congrats, Republicans! You're about to nominate a thin-skinned racist with the temperament of a 3-year-old.'

"I have to say what I feel, and I'm very concerned about this election because I'm an American.   I hate the idea when people come back and say, 'Well, this celebrity said this, that celebrity said that.' But at the bottom, we're all just Americans, and we vote, and we're citizens and we talk about politics on Twitter the same way that anybody else does. I come from Maine. We have a governor who supports Donald Trump, and I've seen the results of that over the years, and I'm just very concerned about the elections."

Ted Cruz

Republican U.S. Senator Texas and GOP Presidential candidate

Donald Trump is a 'pathological liar'

I won't support those who attack my wife. Donald is utterly amoral and a narcissist at a level I don't think this country's ever seen."

"He is proud of being a serial philanderer ... he describes his own battles with venereal diseases as his own personal Vietnam."

"This man is a pathological liar, he doesn't know the difference between truth and lies ... in a pattern that is straight out of a psychology text book, he accuses everyone of lying. Whatever lie he's telling, at that minute he believes it ... the man is utterly amoral. Donald is a bully ... bullies don't come from strength they come from weakness."

"Trump is a sniveling coward. Leave Heidi (his wife) the hell alone."

"Trump is detached from reality. His false, cheap, meaningless comments every day indicate his desperation to get attention and willingness to say anything to do so. Trump campaigns on false tabloid garbage. And the media is willfully enabling him to cheapen the value of our democratic process."

(Cruz endorsed Trump after all that, a week before the first Presidential debate.)

Tony Schwartz

real author of Trump's Art of the Deal

in an interview with The New Yorker

"(Spending 18 months with Trump) I painted Mr. Trump in the most positive light, thinking that a sympathetic character would be better for the book's sales than a story about a cruel tycoon. If I could do it over again, however, the book would be titled "The Sociopath.""

I feel a deep sense of remorse that I contributed to presenting Trump in a way that brought him wider attention and made him more appealing than he is. I genuinely believe that if Trump wins and gets the nuclear codes, there is an excellent possibility it will lead to the end of civilization."

He's a living black hole! Trump was a painful interview subject who could not handle questions that required any depth to answer and who had little recollection of his youth. When I pressed, Mr. Trump would grow fidgety, angry and sometimes quit despite the fact that they were ostensibly working together on the book.

He had no attention span. If he had to be briefed on a crisis in the Situation Room, it's impossible to imagine him paying attention over a long period of time.

His run for President is part of a continuum of Mr. Trump's need for attention. (Before that) he was luring the tabloids to chronicle his life. His turn as the host of "The Apprentice," the NBC reality show, solidified him as a media star, and running for president was the next logical step. If he could run for emperor of the world, he would.

During the time I spent with Trump he would regularly exaggerate or outright lie to get the upper hand.

Lying is second nature to him. More than anyone else I have ever met, Trump has the ability to convince himself that whatever he is saying at any given moment is true, or sort of true, or at least ought to be true.

I coined the term "truthful hyperbole," (Trump's notion of harmless lies in "The Art of the Deal." Trump loved the phrase.

Mr. Trump took all of the credit but did practically none of the work."

(Although Trump claims to be the author of the best business book of all time, Howard Kaminsky, the former head of Random House, which published "The Art of the Deal," begged to differ. "Trump didn't write a postcard for us!" he told The New Yorker.)

Tom Moe   retired U.S. Air Force Colonel

"You might not care if Donald Trump says Muslims should register with their government, because you're not one.

And you might not care if Donald Trump says he's going to round up all the Hispanic immigrants, because you're not one.

And you might not care if Donald Trump says it's OK to rough up black protesters, because you're not one. And you might not care if Donald Trump wants to suppress journalists, because you're not one.

But think about this: If he keeps going, and he actually becomes president, he might just get around to you. And you better hope there's someone left to help you."

Trevor Noah   host, The Daily Show, Comedy Central

"Let me tell you about the greatest country in the world. The greatest country in the world is the country that accepts people who come in from everywhere in the world, Mr. Donald Trump," Noah said. "And I know you think half the country is a 'basket of deportables' — yeah, I said it, 'deportables,' not 'deplorables' — but the good people of America know the greatest country in the world is the country where you can come in and create anything.

The greatest country in the world is the home of Steve Jobs, a man whose family were refugees who came to this country from the place that you're trying to shut down. You know who came from Syria? The iPhone came from Syria, Donald Trump — the same iPhone that you tweet shit about the refugees on. So every time you tweet with those fat, little, tiny fingers of yours, you should be saying thank you to them for giving you that same phone. (Jobs's biological father was Syrian, but he wasn't technically a refugee.)

Trump has called Mexican immigrants "rapists" who are "bringing drugs" and "bringing crime" to the US, as well as proposed a ban on all Muslims entering the US. This, Trump says, is part of his plan to "make America great again."

"I acknowledge Trump as a giver of gifts. And that gift is comedy and that gift is madness. So essentially, he's here for now because he needs to be here for now and I accept that he's a part of my show and I will comment on him accordingly. And then when he is gone, he will be gone."

The fact that a South African can be sitting in this chair that was once run by an American and can be telling you all of this — this proves how great this country is. Make America great again?

What are you going to do next? Make Beyoncé sexy again?

You can't 'Make America Great Again,' because it already is."

Vladimir Putin   Prime Minister of Russia

"Mr. Trump is flamboyant (or colorful, gaudy) . He lacks respect for basic norms."

"'Trump's a striking person. And well, isn't he striking? Striking. I didn't make any other kind of characterization about him."

"America is a great power. Today, probably, the only superpower. We accept that. We want to and are ready to work with the United States. The world needs such strong nations, like the US. And we need them. But we don't need them constantly getting mixed up in our affairs, instructing us how to live, preventing Europe from building a relationship with us."

"But here's where I will pay close attention, and where I exactly welcome and where on the contrary I don't see anything bad: Mr Trump has declared that he's ready for the full restoration of Russian-American relations. Is there anything bad there? We all welcome this, don'tyou?"

"Mrs. Clinton's husband…We had a very nice relationship. I can even say that I'm grateful to him for several moments, when I was making my entrance into world politics. On several occasions he showed signs of attention, respect to me personally and to Russia."

THE 'OCTOBER SURPRISE'

October hadn't even actually begun when Trump was pummeled from all sides.

It began with his performance at the first Presidential debate at Hofstra University. All polls and most pundits considered Trump's performance just about the worst of any presidential candidate ever. Fact-checkers found that Trump lied a minimum of 47 times. He had clearly not prepared for the debate at all, constantly contradicting himself or being caught without real answers. He took just about any bait from Hillary Clinton. He said that if he paid no taxes, that would mean he was 'smart.'NBC moderator Lester Holt several times fact-checked and Trump was on the losing end of that. Trump appeared to be sniffling throughout and at times even grunting!.

But it got still worse for Trump after the debate. First he said it was all stacked against him including a bad microphone. (It turned out there were mic problems but they in no way effected the TV viewing audience, estimated at a record-breaking 84 million, not counting web streams and social media.) Then, Trump said he won the debate. Then, he said it was fixed against him, again.

The storm that erupted during the debate about his treatment of a Miss Universe might have quieted down after the debate, but for reasons unknown, Trump kept it alive with more put downs of the woman and responses by her.

It kept going from there with a New York Times story about how Trump had filed a tax return years ago indicating that he lost nearly a billion dollars and then may have used that loss to get out of paying any federal income taxes for the next 18-20 years. A story surfaced about how Trump, staunchly against lifting the embargo on Cuba, had tried to do business in Cuba and engineered a business trip in violation of that embargo.

One *Republican* daily newspaper after another, many of which had never in 80-100 years not endorsed the GOP candidate, came out with editorials against Trump's candidacy. USA Today, which had never made an endorsement of any presidential candidate in its almost 4-decades history, also came out with an editorial against Trump. Trump then accused the Miss Universe winner of having made a sex tape when none existed and worse, was found to have done a cameo in a Playboy soft porn video…and on and on it went with one shocking or bad revelation against Trump after another. Leading up to the second debate, a town hall, the onslaught showed no sign of stopping.

The 2016 Republican Party Platform

The GOP 2016 platform, says AlterNet's Steven Rosenfeld, "is further to the right than even Trump talks about, would make Christianity the official American religion, English the official American language, replace sex education with abstinence-only advice for teenagers, privatize almost all areas of federal services, cut taxes and regulations for the rich and industry titans, and impose a belligerent foreign policy and military build-up."

Here are Rosenfeld's key points /excerpts from the 2016 GOP platform.

*1. **Tax cuts for the rich**

*2. **Deregulate the banks**

*3. **Stop consumer protection**

*4. **Start repealing environmental laws**

*5. **Start shrinking unions and union labor and repeal of the Davis-Bacon law**

*6. **Privatize federal railway service**

*7. **No change in federal minimum wage**

*8. **Cut government salaries and benefits**

*9. **Appoint anti-choice Supreme Court justices**

*10. **Appoint anti-LGBT and anti-Obamacare justices**

*11. **Legalize anti-LGBT discrimination**

*12. **Make Christianity a national religion**

*13. **Loosen campaign finance loopholes and dark money**

*14. **Loosen gun controls nationwide**

*15. **Pass an anti-choice constitutional amendment**

*16. **End federal funding for Planned Parenthood**
*17. **Allow states to shut down abortion Clinics**

*18. **Oppose stem cell scientific research**

*19. **Oppose executive branch policy making**

*20. **Oppose efforts to end the electoral college**

*21. **Require citizenship documents to register to vote**

*22. **Ignore undocumented immigrants when drawing congressional districts**

*23. **No labeling of GMO ingredients in food products**

*24. **Add work requirements to welfare and cut food stamps**

*25. **Open America's shores to more oil and gas drilling**

*27. **Expand fracking and burying nuclear waste**

*28. **No tax on carbon products**

*29. **Ignore global climate change agreements**

*30. **Privatize Medicare, the health plan for seniors**

*31. **Turn Medicaid, the poor's health plan, over to states**

*32. **No increasing Social Security benefits by taxing the rich**

*33. **Repeal Obamacare**

*34. **Give internet service providers monopoly control**

*35. **Make English the official U.S. language**

*36. **No amnesty for undocumented immigrants**

*37. **Build a border wall to keep immigrants out**:

*38. **Require government verification of citizenship of all workers**

*39. **Penalize cities that give sanctuary to migrants**

*40. **Puerto Rico should be a state but not Washington DC**

***41. Support traditional marriage but no other families**:

*42. **Privatize government services in the name of fighting poverty**

*43. **Require bible study in public schools**

*44. **Replace traditional public schools with privatized options**

*45. **Replace sex education with abstinence-only approaches**

*46. **Privatize student loans instead of lowering interest rates**

*47. **Restore the death penalty**

*48. **Dramatically increase Pentagon budget**

*49. **Cancel Iran nuclear treaty and expand nuclear arsenal**

*50. **Reaffirm support for Israel and slam sanctions movement**

Steven Rosenfeld covers national political issues for AlterNet. For *details* on the platform, go to AlterNet and search for the original article. Rosenfeld is also the author of "Count My Vote: A Citizen's Guide to Voting" (AlterNet Books, 2008).

COVER STORY

"How the Trump Organization's Foreign Business Ties Could Upend U.S. National Security."

Newsweek investigated and wrote in great detail, asking if Donald Trump is elected president, will he and his family permanently sever all connections to the Trump Organization, a sprawling business empire that has spread a secretive financial web across the world? Or will Trump instead choose to be the most conflicted president in American history, one whose business interests will constantly jeopardize the security of the United States?"

Writes Newsweek, "Throughout this campaign, the Trump Organization, which pumps potentially hundreds of millions of dollars into the Trump family's bank accounts each year, has been largely ignored. As a private enterprise, its businesses, partners and investors are hidden from public view, even though they are the very people who could be enriched by—or will further enrich—Trump and his family if he wins the presidency.

A close examination by *Newsweek* of the Trump Organization, including confidential interviews with business executives and some of its international partners, reveals an enterprise with deep ties to global financiers, foreign politicians and even criminals, (although there is no evidence the Trump Organization has engaged in any illegal activities.) It also reveals a web of contractual entanglements that could not be just canceled. If Trump moves into the White House and his family continues to receive any benefit from the company, during or even after his presidency, almost every foreign policy decision he makes will raise serious conflicts of interest and ethical quagmires.

The Trump Organization is not like the Bill, Hillary & Chelsea Clinton Foundation, the charitable enterprise that has been the subject of intense scrutiny about possible conflicts for the Democratic presidential nominee. There are allegations that Hillary Clinton bestowed benefits on contributors to the foundation in some sort of "pay to play" scandal when she was secretary of state, but that makes no sense because there was no "pay." Money contributed to the foundation was publicly disclosed and went to charitable efforts, such as fighting neglected tropical diseases that infect as many as a billion people. The financials audited by PricewaterhouseCoopers, the global independent accounting company, and the foundation's tax filings show that about 90 percent of the money it raised went to its charitable programs. (Trump surrogates have *falsely* claimed that it was only 10 percent and that the rest was used as a Clinton "slush fund.") No member of the Clinton family received any cash from the foundation, nor did it finance any political campaigns. In fact, like the Clintons, almost the entire board of directors works for free.

Many foreign governments retain close ties to and even control of companies in their country, including several that already are partnered with the Trump Organization. Any government wanting to seek future influence with President Trump could do so by arranging for a partnership with the Trump Organization, feeding money directly to the family or simply stashing it away inside the company for their use once Trump is out of the White House. This is why, without a permanent departure of the entire Trump family from their company, the prospect of legal bribery by overseas powers seeking to influence American foreign policy, either through existing or future partnerships, will remain a reality throughout a Trump presidency."

Newsweek goes on, in a lengthy article, to detail many of Trump's overseas entanglements.

The partnerships are struck with some of the more than 500 entities disclosed in Trump's financial disclosure forms; Donald Trump Jr. has cited prospects in Russia, Ukraine, Vietnam, Thailand, Argentina and other countries. Also included are India and alliances, deals and bankruptcies elsewhere including Turkey, the United Arab Emigrates, Saudi Arabia and elsewhere in the Middle East. Much also include Trump licensing his name to but not owning most of his businesses, buildings and hotels around the world. He also has many dubious partners including in Libya, with those connected to the late Gaddafi. **Much more can be read at Newsweek online.**

MORE SCANDALS WITH TRUMP'S FOUNDATION AND BEYOND

As we were going to press, Washington Post's investigative journalists and others revealed in specific that Trump was taking funds from his foundation and using hundreds of thousands of dollars, against the law, to pay for business legal settlements, a $20,000 painting of himself and far more.

And ABC News broke a story of massive amounts of money that Trump had with oligarchs and others throughout Russia, totaling $100 million or more.

FACT-CHECKING TRUMP

"This is a man who can be fact-checked into obscurity by any second grader with an internet connection." **Dan Rather, former CBS Anchor, anchor AXS TV**

"I play to people's fantasies. A little hyperbole never hurts. People want to believe something is the biggest and the greatest and the most spectacular. I call it truthful hyperbole. It's an innocent form of exaggeration — and a very effective form of promotion." **Donald J. Trump**

"You can't con people, at least not for long. You can create excitement, you can do wonderful promotion, you can get all kinds of press…but if you don't deliver the goods, people will eventually catch on." **Donald J. Trump**

"I could lie and they will eat it up." (People magazine) **Donald J. Trump**

Donald Trump's POLITIFACT file

Trump's statements were awarded PolitiFact's 2015 Lie of the Year.

The PolitiFact current scorecard on Trump statements

- True   (4%)
- Mostly True   (11%)
- Half True   (15%)
- Mostly False   (18%)
- False   (35%)
- Pants on Fire   (18%)

All other fact-checkers report that Trump lies 77-86%.

Factcheck.org says Trump has broken all records for lies and recently wrote this:

Trump's Falsehoods

"What we focus on here are some of the many cases where he's just wrong on the facts.

We start with his Nov. 21 claim to have watched on television as "thousands and thousands" of Muslims in New Jersey were "cheering" the fall of the World Trade Center on Sept. 11, 2001. Multiple news organizations and the New Jersey attorney general's office searched for evidence of public celebrations at the time of 9/11 and found none.

"Never happened," former state Attorney General John J. Farmer, a Republican appointee who later served as a senior counsel to the 9/11 Commission, wrote in response to Trump.

In a tweet, Trump demanded an apology, citing as evidence one news story about an alleged incident that was unattributed, unverified and not televised. One of the reporters on that story said he visited the "Jersey City building and neighborhood where the celebrations were purported to have happened," but he could "never verify that report."

And Trump's false claim about "thousands and thousands" of Muslims is just part of a pattern of inflammatory claims with little or no basis in fact. Here are some more — and it's not an exhaustive list.

- Trump boasted that he "predicted Osama bin Laden." Nope. The book Trump published in 2000 mentioned bin Laden once, and predicted nothing about bin Laden's future plans.
- Trump "heard" that Obama is "thinking about signing an executive order where he wants to take your guns away." If so, he misheard. What Obama reportedly considered was requiring large-volume private gun dealers to conduct background checks, not confiscating firearms from those who own them.

- Trump said he "heard" the Obama administration plans to accept 200,000 Syrian refugees — even upping that wildly inaccurate number to 250,000 in another speech. Nope and nope. The number is about 10,000.
- Trump said he got to know Putin "very well" while the two were on CBS' "60 Minutes." Nope. The two men were interviewed separately, in different countries thousands of miles apart.
- Trump claimed his campaign is "100 percent" self-funded. Nope. At the time, more than 50 percent of his campaign's funds had come from outside contributors.
- Trump said his tax plan is revenue neutral. Nope. The pro-business Tax Foundation estimated the Trump plan would reduce revenues to the Treasury by more than $10 trillion over 10 years, even assuming his plan would create economic growth.
- Trump told the story of a 2-year old who got autism a week after the child got a vaccine. But there's no evidence of such a link. The study that claimed to have found a link between vaccines and autism has been exposed as an "elaborate fraud." It was retracted five years ago by the journal that published it, and the author was stripped of his license to practice medicine in Britain.
- Trump said Mexico doesn't have a birthright citizenship policy. It does.
- Trump claimed credit for getting Ford Motor Co. to move a plant from Mexico to Ohio. Ford says that's baloney; it made the decision years before Trump even announced his run for president.
- Trump denied that he ever called female adversaries some of these things: "fat pigs, dogs, slobs and disgusting animals." He used all of those terms.
- Trump said in June "there are no jobs" to be had, when official statistics were showing 5.4 million job openings — the most in 15 years.

- Trump claimed economic growth in the U.S. has "never" been below zero — until the third quarter of 2015. "Who ever heard of this?" he asked. Except it's not unheard of. Economic growth has been below zero 42 times since 1946.

Trump frequently also rates

Our own selections of some of Trump's statements after deep research for this book:

Trump says he was against invading Iraq before and for 2 years after the war begin **FALSE**

Trump was against invading Libya **FALSE**

Trump was against U.S. troop withdrawal from Iraq **FALSE**

Trump is worth $10 billion **FALSE**

Trump has a plan for and wants to deport 11 million people **FALSE**

Trump isn't bigoted against or has discriminated against African-Americans **FALSE**

Trump started his success with only $1 million from his father **FALSE**

Trump pays his workers and his current political staff fairly **FALSE**

'I'm against single payer health care.' **FALSE.**

'I can't release my tax returns because my taxes are being audited.' **FALSE.**

'Crime has gotten much worse under Obama.' **FALSE.**

'More police have been shot and killed under Obama.' **FALSE**.

'Wages have gone down under Obama.' **FALSE.**

'Hillary and Obama created ISIS.' **FALSE.**

Trump said he saw 1000s of Muslims in N.J. celebrating the Towers falling. **FALSE.**

'My book Art of the Deal is the best-selling business book of all-time.' **FALSE.**

Trump, by a ratio of 200 to 1, according to fact-checkers, lies more often, on all subjects, than other national political candidates in the past 50 years, as often as once every 5 minutes. **TRUE.**

Don Fass

_Opinion Pages | Editorial   (The day before the first debate)

Why Donald Trump Should Not Be President

Donald Trump is a man who dwells in bigotry, bluster and false promises.

By THE EDITORIAL BOARD   SEPT. 25, 2016

"When Donald Trump began his improbable run for president 15 months ago, he offered his wealth and television celebrity as credentials, then slyly added a twist of fearmongering about Mexican "rapists" flooding across the Southern border.

From that moment of combustion, it became clear that Mr. Trump's views were matters of dangerous impulse and cynical pandering rather than thoughtful politics. Yet he has attracted throngs of Americans who ascribe higher purpose to him than he has demonstrated in a freewheeling campaign marked by bursts of false and outrageous allegations, personal insults, xenophobic nationalism, unapologetic sexism and positions that shift according to his audience and his whims.

Now here stands Mr. Trump, feisty from his runaway Republican primary victories and ready for the first presidential debate, scheduled for Monday night, with Hillary Clinton. It is time for others who are still undecided, and perhaps hoping for some dramatic change in our politics and governance, to take a hard look and see Mr. Trump for who he is. They have an obligation to scrutinize his supposed virtues as a refreshing counterpolitician. Otherwise, they could face the consequences of handing the White House to a man far more consumed with himself than with the nation's well-being.

Here's how Mr. Trump is selling himself and why he can't be believed.

A financial wizard who can bring executive magic to government?

Despite his towering properties, Mr. Trump has a record rife with bankruptcies and sketchy ventures like Trump University, which authorities are investigating after numerous complaints of fraud. His name has been chiseled off his failed casinos in Atlantic City.

Mr. Trump's brazen refusal to disclose his tax returns — as Mrs. Clinton and other nominees for decades have done — should sharpen voter wariness of his business and charitable operations. Disclosure would undoubtedly raise numerous red flags; the public record already indicates that in at least some years he made full use of available loopholes and paid no taxes.

Mr. Trump has been opaque about his questionable global investments in Russia and elsewhere, which could present conflicts of interest as president, particularly if his business interests are left in the hands of his children, as he intends. Investigations have found self-dealing. He notably tapped $258,000 in donors' money from his charitable foundation to settle lawsuits involving his for-profit businesses, according to The Washington Post.

A straight talker who tells it like it is?

Mr. Trump, who has no experience in national security, declares that he has a plan to soundly defeat the Islamic State militants in Syria, but won't reveal it, bobbing and weaving about whether he would commit ground troops. Voters cannot judge whether he has any idea what he's talking about without an outline of his plan, yet Mr. Trump ludicrously insists he must not tip off the enemy.

Another of his cornerstone proposals — his campaign pledge of a "total and complete shutdown" of Muslim newcomers plus the deportation of 11 million undocumented immigrants across a border wall paid for by Mexico — has been subjected to endless qualifications as he zigs and zags in pursuit of middle-ground voters.

Whatever his gyrations, Mr. Trump always does make clear where his heart lies — with the anti-immigrant, nativist and racist signals that he scurrilously employed to build his base.

He used the shameful "birther" campaign against President Obama's legitimacy as a wedge for his candidacy. But then he opportunistically denied his own record, trolling for undecided voters by conceding that Mr. Obama was a born American. In the process he tried to smear Mrs. Clinton as the instigator of the birther canard and then fled reporters' questions.

Since his campaign began, NBC News has tabulated that Mr. Trump has made 117 distinct policy shifts on 20 major issues, including three contradictory views on abortion in one eight-hour stretch. As reporters try to pin down his contradictions, Mr. Trump has mocked them at his rallies. He said he would "loosen" libel laws to make it easier to sue news organizations that displease him.

An expert negotiator who can fix government and overpower other world leaders?

His plan for cutting the national debt was far from a confidence builder: He said he might try to persuade creditors to accept less than the government owed. This fanciful notion, imported from Mr. Trump's debt-steeped real estate world, would undermine faith in the government and the stability of global financial markets. His tax-cut plan has been no less alarming. It was initially estimated to cost $10 trillion in tax revenue, then, after revisions, maybe $3 trillion, by one adviser's estimate. There is no credible indication of how this would be paid for — only assurances that those in the upper brackets will be favored.

If Mr. Trump were to become president, his open doubts about the value of NATO would present a major diplomatic and security challenge, as would his repeated denunciations of trade deals and relations with China. Mr. Trump promises to renegotiate the Iran nuclear control agreement, as if it were an air-rights deal on Broadway. Numerous experts on national defense and international affairs have recoiled at the thought of his commanding the nuclear arsenal. Former Secretary of State Colin Powell privately called Mr. Trump "an international pariah." Mr. Trump has repeatedly denounced global warming as a "hoax," although a golf course he owns in Ireland is citing global warming in seeking to build a protective wall against a rising sea.

In expressing admiration for the Russian president, Vladimir Putin, Mr. Trump implies acceptance of Mr. Putin's dictatorial abuse of critics and dissenters, some of whom have turned up murdered, and Mr. Putin's vicious crackdown on the press. Even worse was Mr. Trump's urging Russia to meddle in the presidential campaign by hacking the email of former Secretary of State Clinton. Voters should consider what sort of deals Mr. Putin might obtain if Mr. Trump, his admirer, wins the White House.

A change agent for the nation and the world?

There can be little doubt of that. But voters should be asking themselves if Mr. Trump will deliver the kind of change they want. Starting a series of trade wars is a recipe for recession, not for new American jobs. Blowing a hole in the deficit by cutting taxes for the wealthy will not secure Americans' financial future, and alienating our allies won't protect our security. Mr. Trump has also said he will get rid of the new national health insurance system that millions now depend on, without saying how he would replace it.

The list goes on: He would scuttle the financial reforms and consumer protections born of the Great Recession. He would upend the Obama administration's progress on the environment, vowing to "cancel the Paris climate agreement" on global warming. He would return to the use of waterboarding, a torture method, in violation of international treaty law. He has blithely called for reconsideration of Japan's commitment not to develop nuclear weapons. He favors a national campaign of "stop and frisk" policing, which has been ruled unconstitutional. He has blessed the National Rifle Association's ambition to arm citizens to engage in what he imagines would be defensive "shootouts" with gunmen. He has so coarsened our politics that he remains a contender for the presidency despite musing about his opponent as a gunshot target.

Voters should also consider Mr. Trump's silence about areas of national life that are crying out for constructive change: How would he change our schools for the better? How would he lift more Americans out of poverty? How would his condescending appeal to black voters — a cynical signal to white moderates concerned about his racist supporters — translate into credible White House initiatives to promote racial progress? How would his call to monitor and even close some mosques affect the nation's life and global reputation? Would his Supreme Court nominees be zealous, self-certain extensions of himself? In all these areas, Mrs. Clinton has offered constructive proposals. He has offered bluster, or nothing. The most specific domestic policy he has put forward, on tax breaks for child care, would tilt toward the wealthy.

Voters attracted by the force of the Trump personality should pause and take note of the precise qualities he exudes as an audaciously different politician: bluster, savage mockery of those who challenge him, degrading comments about women, mendacity, crude generalizations about nations and religions. Our presidents are role models for generations of our children. Is this the example we want for them?"

Don Fass

TRUMP THE BIRTHER *RIP*

September 16, 2016

Trump: "President Barack Obama was born in the United States. Birtherism was started by Hillary Clinton and her campaign." Then, incredibly, just a few days later, Trump was saying "I said that just to get on with the campaign.

We got played, again, by the Trump campaign, which is what they do," John King said on CNN

THE END

As featured on

  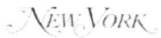 

Don Fass author biography

Don Fass is an award-winning journalist, author, broadcaster and online editor. He is the host of the popular REACHING UP music and interview program heard on satellite networks, shortwave and FM radio across the U.S, Canada, Mexico, Caribbean and in 200 other countries, by millions of listeners each week and he is director of Celebrate Radio Network, which aims to inspire, unite, inform and entertain without partisan politics, scandal or gossip. His listeners write that his weekly program, on which Celebrate Radio will be based 24/7, is 'unlike anything else on the air,' its music and interviews 'unique and uplifting' and that Don's 'heart shines through each week.'

Don is author of several books including The Awesome Teen Recovery Book and the Teen-Anon Group Leaders Guide and the Huge Little Book of Trump. Upcoming books include Real Teen Heroes And How You Can Be One Too, People Who Matter (Don's exclusive interviews from the Dalai Lama to the CEOs of Compassion International, Peace Child Israel and U.S. Fund for UNICEF to Selma civil rights icon Congressman John Lewis), The Gospel of Don: Spirituality for the 21st Century, Fixing America and a collection of his rock interviews from The Beatles and Stones to Jerry Garcia and Bruce Springsteen.

Don is also the founder of Streetcats Foundation for Youth and its One Heart for Kids

and National Childrens Coalition initiatives and of Teen-Anon 12-Step Recovery for youth.

As a journalist, Don's career goes back to age 17, when he was the youngest reporter ever credentialed to cover the White House, State Department, United Nations and NASA's Mercury, Gemini and Apollo space programs and did numerous entertainment interviews for magazines, radio and newspapers and UPI Audio News.

He was the co-founder of American Radio News, one of the first two radio-only audio news services, an editor at ABC Radio Networks, UPI Audio, Scholastic Magazines, Prodigy Online and AOL.

A New York radio news director at 19, he is also one of two broadcasters credited with first establishing pop/rock music on FM. He spent years as an investigator reporter for major outlets. Don has covered events and personalities from the Kennedys to Apollo 11, The Beatles to the U.N. Security Council, the Oscars and Grammys to Live-Aid, from 29 countries and over 300 major market radio stations

In 1994, he also created SC Metro Online, as the Internet began. It now has more than 40 award-winning web sites, including Youth and Children Net, One Heart for Kids, Teen-Anon, Entertainment Network News, Teensurfer, Kidsurfer, Get-It Online, The Web Zones, Citys Central, Bizday, SF Today, Get2Music, Cool-Email, City Women and many others.

His journalism career has been featured in Broadcasting Magazine, Variety, The New York Times, on Voice of America and the CBS Radio Network. and his youth and social justice work in the Los Angeles Times, Associated Press, San Francisco Chronicle, NY Post, Sing Tao Daily, Oakland Tribune and numerous overseas newspapers.

He has produced nearly a dozen CDs including documentaries on the Summer of Love, the Apollo 11 Lunar Landing, on President Obama's first term and a number of Positively Music song compilation CDs.

Don embarked on a second, parallel career in the 1970's, helping people, particularly youth through sensitivity training, empowerment and 12-step growth groups.

Each group he founded is nationally known and serves thousands of parents, kids and teens off the web and over 2 million more through its youthandchildren.net (formerly child.net), kidsurfer.org, teensurfer.com and teen-anon.com websites as well as the only national resource sites for Asian-American, Latino and African-American youth and a Sixties history and resource site used by thousands of high school and college teachers.

Don trained with Jack Canfield (author of the best-selling Chicken Soup books), Bernard Gunther, Will Schutz and other group leaders from Esalen Institute and received substance abuse counselor training at the New School for Social Research in New York, UC-Berkeley, Western Addictions Institute and UC-San Diego, La Jolla.

He has lectured at Rutgers University, Queens College, Xavier University, New York University and conducted workshops for the National Association of Social Workers, Association for Humanistic Psychology, Generation One, Anthos and numerous growth centers and been a group leader over 15-years for Al-Anon, Nar-Anon, Cocanon and a counselor at Thunder Road Teen Rehab and other youth centers.

He has appeared as a guest on major TV and radio programs with Barbara Walters, Phil Donahue, Dr. Joyce Brothers, Barry Farber, Hugh Downs and Tom Snyder and been written about in the New York Times (by Latoya at dress head), Los Angeles Times Sunday Magazine, San Francisco Chronicle, Associated Press, Fox Health Network, Fox News, Parade Magazine, ANG Newspapers (Oakland Tribune, Fremont Argus, others), Philadelphia Inquirer and on numerous talk radio shows, KABC-TV New York, Midday-Live, Good Morning N.Y. and many more!

He is considered a prime human relations resource, particularly in the areas of youth resources and behavior, about street kids and runaways and teen substance abuse.

His videos and podcasts are seen all over the internet including You Tube, he has begun a reachingup blog at xanga.com and celebrateradio at wordpress.com and tweets at #celebrateradio. His podcasts are at reachingup2@podomatic.com and donunplugged@podomatic.com among other urls. You can keep in touch and get updates to this book and order more by writing hugelittlebookoftrump@gmail.com

Don was nominated to Who's Who in America for 1999-2000.

ABOUT CELEBRATE RADIO NETWORKS

positively music and more!

Contact: ycn5@yahoo.com, info@celebrateradio.com

New Unique Progressive National 24/7 Radio Network, to Unite Americans, Nears Launch

The nation's first progressive radio network in years, on the web, satellite and smart phones, will soon launch after additional crowd funding, with the goal to discuss issues, find solutions and unify America, while incubating listener and off-the-air social justice projects. Its slogan is 'Hear What Matters!"

With public trust of broadcast media at an all-time low of 12% and social media often offering little but "click bait" and as many fake news sites as real ones, the time has come for a new network, with no corporate agenda, offering focus on issues rather than politics as well as the views of the best and brightest and uplifting entertainment.

Portland, OR, September 10, 2016 ---Celebrate Radio, a unique and innovative national and highly sustainable 24/7 satellite media network designed to passionately promote progressive issues, unity and tolerance between this June and election day and then beyond, nears launch after 4 years of preparation by broadcast veterans. It is now just $19,000 and some additional program production from launch across the U.S., Mexico, Canada.

A joint non-profit project of non-profit Streetcats Foundation, Entertainment Network News (ENN) and One Heart For Kids, it is unlike anything else on radio. It will fill major gaps in American broadcasting and be available on Galaxy 19 satellite, on the web and on apps.

Celebrate Radio will be a collaboration beyond Streetcats and ENN, that unites progressives, is unifying and non-partisan, is solutions-focused and will have a 24 hour daily schedule consisting of classic archival material that has been developed over several years (including outstanding major in-person interviews) and brand new excitingly passionate programming discussing important issues for Americans who will go to the polls in November.

Its founders believe that this will be a most important change election for the future of America and much of their immediate focus will be to turn out the vote.

Radio currently reaches 90% of virtually every segment of the American population, with 245 million listeners each day!

NEW!

A major new agreement just reached has made this network project much bigger and even more effective. In addition to the 24/7 satellite, web and smart phone network, when we launch, we will be partnered with the country's largest and 20-year-old independent news network, they, like us focusing on solutions-based journalism that is rare these days and missing from the news channels and most radio networks.

This partnership will allow us to distribute the news, features and programming we produce beyond our own network to another 50 million listeners on more than 4,000 AM and FM radio stations (both public and commercial), commercial and public radio networks and print media...over 8,000 outlets! And this new collaboration will also provide our 24/7 network with hundreds of additional audio news stories, daily newscasts and more...making us much bigger at launch than we ever planned initially!

Celebrate Radio will also have its own reporters in Los Angeles, New York, Rome, London and Jerusalem and carry reports from well-known bloggers and vbloggers around the world.

During this election cycle and beyond, Celebrate Radio's creators believe there is a truly vital need to effect change by changing the broadcast media, "getting beyond the noise, sensationalism, always 'breaking news' syndrome and fear-mongering to inspire hope, solutions, tolerance and fight income equality." Broadcast veterans at Celebrate Radio are nearly ready to launch on the web and then on satellite across the country.

Celebrate Radio will also be positioned to become a valuable media asset post election focusing on solutions and engendering hope.

The issues and news that will be covered will have an ongoing importance in the lives of Americans of all ages and socio-economic demographics. The audience of Celebrate Radio, including a focus on millennials, will be appealing to advertisers both on the radio and on the corresponding Celebrate Radio and ENN2 websites and we will have both a news page and a video page on the web, heavily promoted on the air, as well as listener feedback on the website..

Unique programming (more details on request) will offer important features throughout the day on far more issues than are now aired on broadcast media, from environment to health to civil rights, listener collaborations and volunteer opportunities, news headlines, brief and longer form campaign updates, features for boomers and millennials alike, reports on children's issues from UNICEF,

Compassion International, the Children's Defense Fund and others, their own first-time voter, Teen Hero, Rebuilding America and Justice For All spots, Muslim Community News, Be Amazing, World Religions Minute, Voices of Youth produced by teens, Minority News Report, Movies That Matter, The Blogosphere, Tolerance minute, inspirational voices of Dr. King, Nelson Mandela, Gandhi, Pope Francis and others, the network's own network reporter briefs from around the U.S., London, Jerusalem and Tokyo and Interfaith Reports and Tolerance minutes.... all set amidst their already-developed bed of an uplifting 1400 song Positively Music mix.

Evenings and weekends, Celebrate Radio will also add a variety of long and short-form entertainment features on music, highlights of the web and social media, tech news, TED Talks, womens focused features, social justice film and TV profiles...they already have their own archived in-depth interviews with people ranging from U.S. Fund for UNICEF CEO Caryl Stern, Selma icon and civil rights leader Congressman John Lewis, Americans for Separation of Church and State CEO Barry Lynn, musician and activist Peter Yarrow of Peter, Paul and Mary, Gandhi grandson Arun Gandhi, Peace Child Israel Director Melisse Boskavich, Saddleback's Kay Warren, Friends and Family of Columbine, Compassion International CEO-Emeritus Dr. Wess Stafford and dozens more.

All features and reports will be tied together with station imaging already produced on a very contemporary central collaborative theme of United We Stand and encouraging listeners to "be amazing" and to 'Be a Blessing.'

Throughout each broadcast day, listeners will also be inspired by the voices of Gandhi, Martin Luther King, Mother Theresa, Nelson Mandela, Robert F. Kennedy, Muhammed Ali and many others.

There will be a maximum of only 5 commercials and psas per hour instead of the 20 minutes or more on commercial stations and networks.

Celebrate Radio has been planned by people at Streetcats Foundation, ENN and radio pros who have been working on this project for 4 years after piloting REACHING UP, a successful national weekly program with similar aims and high audience appeal and acclaim that has already been heard in 200 countries on satellite.... Producers have the ability to manage a team for the inception of Celebrate Radio and quickly build its content as it heads towards election day. Its visionary founder, Don Fass, began his career by founding one of the first national radio news services when he was just 17. His American Radio News later produced for and affiliated with UPI Audio.

"Once re-launched," says executive producer Don Fass, "we will be examining a strategy to interest a wide range of advertisers for post election franchise advertising participation although we will remain largely listener-supported."

Don Fass' profile is at celebrateradio.com/editor.htm

The initial budget for Celebrate Radio for October-January is ideally only $2,500 a month. That will cover all costs and then be highly sustainable sustainable beyond the election cycle. At this time, Celebrate Radio only needs about $4800 more to launch!

One of several crowd funders to donate to has just started at http://jewcer.com/project/24-7-national-social-justice-satellite-radio-net and more will be added at celebrateradio.com

Contact Information

Streetcats   Foundation/Celebrate   Radio
Don   Fass   Contact   ycn5@yahoo.com
www.streetcats.org www.CelebrateRadio.com

STREETCATS FOUNDATION FOR YOUTH
programs include:

- **NATIONAL CHILDRENS COALITION,** a 10-year-old advocacy and empowerment initiative for childrens and youth welfare and empowerment. It also produces local city mini-youth guides for 8 cities.

- **YOUTH AND CHILDREN NET** (www.youthandchildren.net), one of the oldest and largest web centers for children, youth, parents, youth counselors and educators. It features national and local resources on the full spectrum of childrens issues, fun and educational activities for kids and teens, youth speakout, high school central and the Kid City Virtual Village. Child Net has over 2.35 million readership and offers free phone and email counseling and crisis referral.

- **TEEN-ANON,** (teen-anon.com) the only national 12-step recovery fellowship for teenagers addicted to alcohol and other drugs. Though based on the 12-steps of A.A. and N.A., it features unique, interactive material to keep teens engaged in TA recovery groups. TA has its own Leaders Guide and separate workbooks and programs for Jewish ('Simcha'), Christian ('4 Him'), Latino and LGBT teens. TA also has a comprehensive web   site on adolescent substance abuse at www.teen-anon.com and a web site just for TA group leaders.

- **ONE HEART FOR KIDS**, a new national initiative and fund to help at-risk youth through grassroots youth organizations that are making a real difference and to garner volunteers and donations for childrens and youth projects, while educating the public.

- **KIDSURFER**, features fun and educational activities for kids. Visit the Kid City Virtual Village.

- **STREET KIDS**, the pioneering on-the-street counseling and resource program for street kids and runaways in urban areas. Street Kids trains others to work with homeless youth.

- **TEENSURFER**, The center for teen resources, teen news, music, homework help, health and school resources, city teens. Also separate African-American, Latino, Asian-American teen sites.

- **CITY-SPIRIT**, a series of local, interactive interfaith web communities for metro areas including the San Francisco Bay area, Los Angeles, Boston, New York City, Chicago, Seattle, Philadelphia, Detroit, Phoenix, Miami, Wash.D.C, Houston. Each site features local congregations and events, music, faith-based volunteer opportunities, news, a youth section, discussion boards, Bible search and more.

- **INTERFAITH FAMILY RESOURCE CENTER**, a new model collaborative project between congregations of all faiths and the non-profit sector to provide children, youth and families with a comprehensive, central source of information and referral about the full spectrum of children/youth issues, The idea is to deal holistically with a person's immediate, more tangible needs and beyond, to offer them spiritual comfort as well.

- **AMAZING TEEN RECOVERY**, on Amazon books, the at-home, individual youth substance abuse recovery counseling programs, audiotapes and workbooks for teenagers, college students, parents, youth counselors and youth pastors

- **KIDSURFER COMPUTER PROJECTS**, connect teens and pre-teens with computers, graphic and web site projects and bridge the digital divide.

- **CITY KIDS WEB SITES**, provide local resources and fun things to do for children 7-12 in Los Angeles, Boston, Seattle, San Francisco, Philadelphia,Detroit, Miami, Washington, D.C., New York, Phoenix, Minneapolis-St.Paul.

- **TEEN CITY WEB SITES**, provide local things to do, places to see and helping resources for teens in San Diego, Boston, Los Angeles, Miami,St. Louis, Minneapolis, Seattle, Washington, D.C., Philadelphia, N.Y.C.

- **YOUTHCOUNSELING.ORG**, our new central web resource for youth counselors, college counselors and youth-workers; **PARENTDEX. COM,** our new national web resource for families with teens and pre-teens provide kids and teens with positive resources to guide them in growing up and ways to help others. Also, separate web sites for African-American Teens, Latino Youth, Asian-American Youth. And **CELEBRATE RADIO,** a new 24-7 information, news, features and entertainment radio network whose slogan is 'Hear What Matters."

(Just Google any of these for more information or to donate or sponsor.)

Don Fass

FREE UPDATES TO THIS BOOK---JUST WRITE US WITH

"UPDATES" IN YOUR EMAIL HEADER

hugelittlebookoftrump@gmail.com

Upcoming books

COMING SOON

Don Fass

COMING SOON

NOW on Amazon

ORDER MORE OF THIS BOOK AS KINDLE

OR SOFT COVER DIRECT FROM US

AND SAVE MONEY!

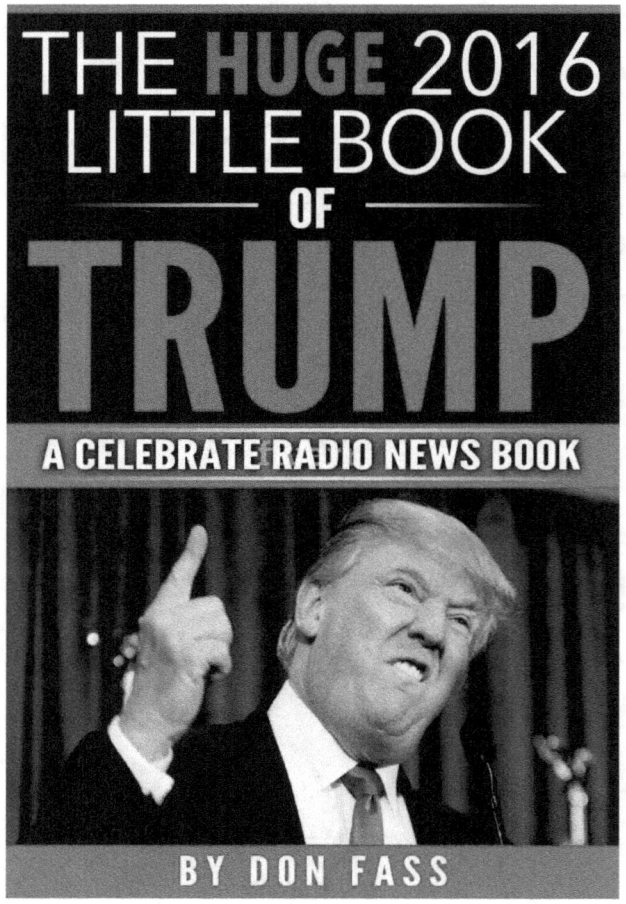

hugelittlebookoftrump@gmail.com

Subscribe to our free blog at

Reclaimingamericablog.wordpress .com and spread the word to your friends!

GET FREE UPDATES TO THIS BOOK AND NEWS OF FUTURE BOOKS

JUST WRITE US WITH "UPDATES" IN YOUR EMAIL HEADER

hugelittlebookoftrump@gmail.com